On the Mystery

On the Mystery

DISCERNING DIVINITY IN PROCESS

Catherine Keller

Fortress Press
Minneapolis

ON THE MYSTERY
Discerning Divinity in Process

Biblical passages, unless otherwise noted, are from the New Revised Standard Version of the Bible, ©1989 National Council of the Churches of Christ in the USA. Used by permission. All rights reserved. Biblical passages from the New King James Version are ©1979, 1980, 1982 Thomas Nelson, Inc. Used by permission. All rights reserved.

Excerpts from "Ha Shem" from *Dancing with God* by Karen Baker-Fletcher, ©2006 Karen Baker-Fletcher, and from "Tongues-Talk" by Jim Perkinson, are reprinted by permission of the authors.

Cover image: *Cruciform* by Elliot R. Wolfson. Photo © James Kelly. Used by permission.
Cover design: Laurie Ingram
Book design: PerfecType, Nashville, Tenn.

Library of Congress Cataloging-in-Publication Data
Keller, Catherine
On the mystery : discerning divinity in process / Catherine Keller.
  p. cm.
Includes bibliographical references and index.
ISBN 978-0-8006-6276-9 (alk. paper)
1. Process theology. I. Title.
BT83.6.K45 2008
230'.046—dc22   2007032772

The paper used in this publication meets the minimum requirements of American National Standard for Information Sciences—Permanence of Paper for Printed Library Materials, ANSI Z329.48-1984.

Manufactured in the U.S.A.

For all my seminary students, ever mysterious

CONTENTS

PROLOGUE

When she was barely five, my niece Jennifer took me for a walk in her neighborhood. "Come this way, Catherine," she said, with a dramatic air of hushed excitement. Wielding a stick like a magnifying glass, poking and probing beneath the shrubs along the sidewalk, she handed me a pebble, then a petal, to examine for myself—as though for clues. "What are we looking for, Jennifer?" "We're on the mystery!" she exclaimed.

I don't know where she had picked up this precocious imitation of Sherlock Holmes—perhaps from her father, a policeman. She grew into a geologist, so her fascination with the puzzling detail of the world stayed with her. That peculiar phrase stayed with me. With a child's spontaneity it combines the adventure of a mystery with an intense purposefulness, echoing "We're on the job" or "We're on the way." And yet there wasn't any crime she was trying to solve. Here was mystery for its own sake!

The way of this mystery, the wonder of its process, is not justified by its endpoint. It wanders ahead in time and in space by no terribly linear path. Yet each step matters. The mystery draws us onward. We are always trying to figure it out; to discern our way; to gather clues, hints, and signs. (So a little event with a child, itself satisfying, becomes a parable for something more.) Along the way we solve one problem after the next. But the content that concerns us here may pose a real enigma: When we think we've finally *got* it, have we already lost it?

> But we speak God's wisdom in a mystery.
>
> —1 COR. 2:7

Is the mystery "God"? This is a work of theology, *theos/logos*, "God-talk" after all. So the answer must be yes. Divinity is surely a mystery. But notice what already happens? Isn't it as though the mystery has already gotten solved? Oh, God, sure. *Him.* If you believe in God, you know where we are going. If you don't, you are out of here. Even to say "God is a mystery" seems to give away the mystery. Like skipping to the end of a book. We bring so much baggage to the concept of "God" that we can hardly move, let alone undertake a journey. Whether we "believe in God" or not—most of us are already loaded down with presumptions about divinity. Theists and atheists more often than not share the same smug concept of God. For example, they presume that what we call God is omnipotent and good, that He proved his love by sending His only Son to die for us . . .

Can we stop right there?

Do you see how loaded with presuppositions just that little sentence is: it presumes that love and dominance work smoothly together, and that nothing that happens to us, however horrible, happens apart from the will of God. It presumes that divinity should be addressed as "He." It presumes a Christian monopoly on the truth. Moreover, most folk will assume that these presuppositions are simply "biblical." Yet there is, for example, no biblical term for "omnipotence." The closest notion, "the Almighty," is actually a mistranslation of *El Shaddai*, "God of the Mountain"—literally in Hebrew "the Breasted One"!

I am just making a point about the heavy cargo of presumptions that "God" carries for most of us. I am not at this moment disputing any particular presumptions—except for the presumption that such truisms about "God" add up to a meaningful theology, let alone to a living faith. I am wondering whether it is still possible—theologically—to "speak God's wisdom in a mystery."

What an attractive definition of theology Paul's phrase delivers. Yet even in the New Revised Standard Version, the translation I most rely upon, a telling shift happens (no doubt in the interest of clarity). It reads: "But we speak God's wisdom, secret and hidden." That sounds as if *now* we are able to speak God's wisdom directly and transparently, whereas it had been hidden *before*. Yet the point of the text in Greek is that *if* we are speaking this wisdom, we *are now* speaking "in a mystery"—*en mysterio*. The mystery got lost in translation!

What might Paul have in mind? He is reflecting on what "God has revealed to us through the Spirit." Apparently this spirited "wisdom" (his Greek word is the feminine *sophia*) is not a set of recitable propositions. He is here opposing this enigmatic *sophia* to the wisdom "of this age or of the rulers of this age" (1 Cor. 2:6). In other words, revelation is not the dictation of some unquestionable piece of knowledge. Rather, it resists knowledge in that sense, the top-down knowledge that masters its objects, that confers power on those who possess it: what the cultural critic Michel Foucault calls "knowledge/power." How ironic that Christian theology would become the ideology of the rulers. Even now.

This book is an exploration of the wisdom and the way of a theology that can only be spoken—when it can be spoken—in the spirit of mystery: in attunement to that which exceeds our knowing. Such knowing of the limits of our knowledge comes not, however, from the stifling of critical questions and the obstructing of open quests—but from their adventurous pursuit. Theology as the language of faith partakes of historical analysis and critical reason, as do the other -ologies. But it is older. And it has always pushed beyond academic boundaries into the language of communities of faith and into the enquiries of individuals alienated from any church, temple, synagogue, or mosque. It has a massively Christian history. But as a term *theology* originates in ancient Greece; it branches into the development of all three "peoples of the book" (the prophet Mohammad's term for the biblical legacy); it travels beyond monotheism, as in current discussions of "comparative theology." Theology is not better or truer than other disciplines of thought. Indeed, it has over its complex and conflictual history legitimated more violence than any other -ology.

Those who involve themselves in theological questions seek wisdom only as we relinquish any pretense of innocence. Wisdom has always already outgrown innocence. The biblical prototype—the divine Sophia—precedes all creation, after all (Prov. 8:22-23). She has seen it all. This mystery does not warrant ignorance of our history and our institutions, of our hugely varying effects on the planetary contexts of theology. Often what is called "mystery" (as in "Don't ask questions, it is a holy mystery") is mere mystification, used to camouflage the power drives of those who don't want to be questioned.

The church began in a mysterious transcultural event of questioning: "All were amazed and perplexed, saying to one another, 'What does this mean?'" That is the collective vision-experience depicted in Acts 2, when the spirit drove the little secluded community out into the public square. Over their ecstatic heads were glimpsed shimmering fiery tongues; from their mouths, in the author's amazing pun on *tongues*, were heard the multiple *tongues* of several foreign languages. My classrooms in theology are more sedate. But they are rich with international students, not to mention students of all kinds of U.S. backgrounds—so this "speaking in tongues" speaks to the concrete perplexities of understanding one another across all of our difficult, strangely accented, differences. All of our different religious and irreligious backgrounds. Our raced, sexed, cultured, and truly spirited complexities. Our burning disappointments and our unspeakable desires. Yet moments of fiery discernment do take place.

Open-Ended Interactivity

An ancient theological tradition captures the paradox of speech about the unspeakable in a beautiful metaphor: that of "the luminous dark."[1] This book proposes a way for theology to avoid the garish neon light of absolute truth-claims, which wash out our vital differences. Yet this way will just as firmly elude the opaque darkness of the casual nihilism that pervades our culture—the "whatever" of indifference. That indifference takes cover behind a secularism that, as we shall see, sometimes mimics the fundamentalist absolutism it reacts against. This book shares the worry of Jim Wallis about "both religious and secular fundamentalists." The first group, he writes in *God's Politics*, "would impose the doctrines of a political theocracy on their fellow citizens, while the other would deprive the public square of needed moral and spiritual values often shaped by faith."[2]

In the interest both of our widest social values and our innermost spiritual yearning, this theology has much to speak—even about the unspeakable! But its proposals will never boil down to theological truth-propositions with which you must finally agree or disagree—though hopefully you will do much of both. It pursues instead the way of a theology in process: which is to say, a way of *open-ended interactivity*.

Faith is not settled belief but living process. It is the very edge and opening of life in process. To live is to step with trust into the next moment: into the unpredictable. I hope this book will unsettle some presumptions that you had begun to doubt anyway. I hope it will help you think, feel, and imagine the next step of your own spiritual path. For this theology the spirit (which I do not capitalize outside of citations, because it is ambiguously both within and beyond us, and because the ancient languages didn't either) is gift and breath and flow and flame.

The spirit in which we journey is a spirit in process. And so divinity itself— that which we can name or conceive as "God"—will be discerned in process. "Discerning divinity in process" carries a double meaning: our theological images shift, diversify, and evolve; and that which we imagine *in* those images is discerned to be a living process. *Process* in this book means *becoming*: it signifies the intuition that the universe itself is not most fundamentally a static being or the product of a static Being—but an immeasurable becoming. Indeed the word *genesis* in Greek means "becoming." The God of a universe in process may in powerful ways turn out to be a God in process: that is, in open-ended interactivity with each of the gazillions of us creatures. For the divine process, if we can imagine it at all, is infinite and therefore inexhaustible. The traditional unchangeables of God may prove to be points of theological fixation rather than fixities of a divine nature. They may be the false fronts of our cultural immobilities: "God as Unchangeable Absolute" functions as "Sanctioner of the Status Quo"—even if that status quo is unjust and unsustainable.[3]

Human power thus reciprocally projects itself into unquestionable images of a changeless divine power. But theology is not as stuck as many presume (dismissively or approvingly). As an example, feminist theology, an undercurrent of the present text but not its primary concern, has over a few decades begun to demystify the changeless masculinity of the unchangeable absolute. Such highly charged challenges to traditional images may seem to threaten the transcendent otherness of God with new projections. But they may also deepen it. "The mystery of God transcends all images," writes a leading theologian, Elizabeth Johnson, "but can be spoken about equally well and poorly in concepts taken from male or female reality."[4] Mystery is not a stagnant pool but a flowing infinity. A theology of becoming discerns its divinity in and as a living process.

In the interest of this process this book draws on the wisdom of a particular twentieth-century ecumenical tradition, with roots in philosophy and natural science as well as religion, called process theology. This book can be read as an introduction to process theology. But compared to much of the process tradition, which I continue to value and teach, I am using the metaphor of "process" in a multivalent and fluid sense, more tinged with mysticism, more freighted with scriptural narrative.

Seven Signs

The process of this book unfurls through the seven thematic phases encoded in the seven chapters. Reminiscent of the seven seals of the Apocalypse? If so, the opening of each of these will, I pray, unleash not doom but hope! Each involves a familiar doctrinal and scriptural symbolism, unfolded in perhaps unfamiliar ways. Different themes could have been chosen, another number would have been possible. But these are the themes that called to me, sometimes gently, sometimes urgently. Writing a book is a mysterious process, too.

We open with the question of theology itself. Putting theology in process means freeing it from a deadly mirror game I will call the binary of the *absolute* and the *dissolute*. In this polarization, the desire for absolute certainty reacts against the fear of a nihilistic dissolution, a relativism indifferent to meaning and morality: "At the end of another lost highway / signs misleading to nowhere," go the popular Green Day lyrics of "Jesus of Suburbia," "No one really seems to care."[5] So the first chapter asks, must the alternative to the lost highway be a rigid "my way"? Do we need unquestionable beliefs in an immutable transcendence—to save us from signs misleading to nowhere? Other signs become legible.

What if truth itself is a way, not an endpoint? What if the way and its truth deliver no totalizing absolute—nor deliver us to the indifferent dissolute? What if we have here to find a third way? In the second chapter, under the sign of truth, certain biblical figures begin to accompany this theological process, such as that of Pontius Pilate, signifying a dissolute relativism; and that of the vulnerable one offering testimony before him. Of a changeless omnipotence? Or of a becoming relationship?

On this nonlinear journey of becoming, the third chapter sends us back to the beginning—where under the sign of creation, the universe emerges out of some mysterious and long-forgotten waters. An exegesis of the first chapter of the Bible yields fishy results, suggestive of an open-ended process of creativity, of a creation that didn't happen way back when, once and for all and once upon a time, but is happening even now.

The fourth chapter explores the sign of divine power. So many lose faith over the dogmatic assumption of God's all-controlling power. What did they do to deserve this disease, this war, this natural catastrophe, they ask? Here the third way surrenders neither to the Calvinist doctrine of omnipotent providence—nor to a mere presumption of holy impotence. What would happen if power begins to redefine itself in terms of the gospel of love?

Yet love has been rendered such a dissolute notion, sexed up or sappy, selfish or self-demeaning, that the potency and passion of the ancient scriptural symbols of love, in both Testaments, have drained out of our collective consciousness. But can we afford to abandon the wisdom of love? So under the sign of passion, we explore the process theological idea of the divine Eros, the lure, that dares us to become. To become more than we are. We surface the desire hidden in our doubts. And then in the sixth chapter we look at the other side of the model, the reception of us in the divine. In the interaction of this passionate creativity and this responsive compassion, another model of justice, alien to vengeance, suggests itself.

The seventh sign unfolds a few familiar parables of the *basileia*, "the kingdom of God." Here a more explicit reflection on the meaning of the figure of Jesus as the Christ becomes possible. The messianic process that he at once actualizes and shifts reveals his *priority*—over and against the standard focus on his *identity*. Yet it is precisely the interplay of revelation and concealment in the parables that will keep Christology on the mystery.

In a theology that emphasizes the open-ended, an ending poses a problem. So we consider the ultimate story of end things, the Apocalypse, as a way of coming not to closure but to dis/closure. That slash will remind us to keep disclosure *open*: to let revelation reveal something we don't already know! Here, in the sign of the spirit, a hot-tongued "Pentecost in the head" counters our end-of-the-world scripts. Deadlines may become lifelines. The last days may turn into the first, the least may turn out to be the most. A way may open where there wasn't one.

CHAPTER 1

Come, My Way
Theology as Process

Come, my Way, my Truth, my Life:
Such a Way, as gives us breath:
Such a Truth, as ends all strife:
Such a Life, as killeth death.

—GEORGE HERBERT[1]

Boarding Call

Looked like I was going to miss my connection.

I was delayed in St. Louis based on bad weather in the east. I needed to get north, in order to fly south. . . . So there was nothing to do but go gather some comfort food. I asked an older gentleman, who seemed gracious and also stranded, if I could leave my bag next to him. Thanking him when I returned, I mentioned that if I did miss the flight, I'd arrive late to my own lecture in Texas. He sympathized, saying he'd miss the class he was scheduled to teach that evening. I politely asked what he teaches; and did a double-take when he said "theology." I don't believe I've ever bumped into another "theologian" outside of a religious or educational gathering. This spurred real curiosity. I couldn't help but notice, however, the wariness that began to shadow his respectful manner. No warmth of airport connection could conceal the operative codes: we inhabited opposite ends of a split Protestant spectrum. I didn't need to wave any feminist banner for his pleasant drawl to harden, his eyes to shift downward. He mentioned his admiration for my most conservative former colleague.

I affirmed that colleague's hard work on the early church fathers. And I mentioned that his theology asserts a more absolute sense of orthodoxy than the early Christian traditions warrant.

He then put with great care the proposition that haunts this book. "I suppose there're two camps on this. There are those who think that the truth-claim of the tradition is just relative, and those who think that truth is absolute and unchanging."

"Yes, we sure get trapped in that either/or," I replied, willing my tone to convey respect. I glanced down to collect my thought. "But those aren't the only alternatives. There is a third way!" As I looked up, ready to share this friendly revelation—to my shock he had simply vanished. Without any gesture of farewell, he had spun and rushed to get in line. Boarding had just been announced. I spotted him already camouflaged among the passengers, gaze pointedly forward. He *really* wanted out of this conversation. He really did not want to hear of any third way.

But I'd like to share it with *you*.

The Absolute and the Dissolute

Most of us do not want to stay trapped in the binary alternatives, in these camps, these predictable polarities of right vs. left, red vs. blue, us vs. you. But conservative Christians are with good reason worried that loss of absolute truth leads to loss of God, which leads to loss of the meaning and purpose of life, which leads to emptiness and chaos for individuals and their societies. But any vocal secularist will, also with good reason, point out all the undeniable violence, delusion, and repression produced by religious absolutes. There doesn't seem to be a firm middle ground in this argument, or at least none that has much appeal: theological moderates, liberals, or progressives (who may look alike from the absolutist viewpoint) have absorbed much of the secular worldview. They want the best of both faith tradition and secular liberalism. Yet their public voices, and often their private ones as well, often lack the force and timbre of conviction.

The third way I want to explore with you under the sign of "theology" is not a middle ground. That would just leave the two poles in place. It is not a compromise, an Aristotelian mean between two extremes, a laid-back moderation, or a strategy to swing votes. It really is something else, something emerging. Something *on the way*. On this way we can afford to sympathize with the concerns of absolutists and of relativists. Indeed, we cannot afford *not* to. We are always already in *relation* to them. Relation does not entail relativism, which dissolves difference. Relationality implies the practice of *discernment,* which means to distinguish, to attend to difference, and to exercise good judgment. Despite the binary either/ors that back us into corners, there are always *more than two* differences.

On the way of this book the dispiriting polarization will often appear in the guise of religious absolutism and secular relativism. The fact that this antagonism is terribly familiar in Western culture, indeed in much of the global metropolis, doesn't lessen its polarizing grip. Sometimes it breaks into debate; usually it operates subliminally, like a bipolar condition, between us—and also within us.

To make this condition more conscious, let us stage a dialogue between its voices. One party is saying: "There is only one Truth; it is timeless and beyond doubt. We are blessed to possess it. But we are willing to share it for free."

The other is retorting—"Truth? Your belief is just one perspective among many."

"Then it isn't the truth!"

"Let's not talk about 'truth'; let's talk about truth-*claims*; and who has the power to *make* them."

"You are saying that truth is just socially constructed."

"Of course, like any perspective."

"That is just relativism."

"You don't think *your* views are relative to your experiences? You just happen to have the absolute truth?"

"God is the truth, and God is not relative."

"And you own the truth about God?"

"This will offend you: but God gave us His Word!"

"And those who don't 'get' it will go to hell? What kind of God is that?"

"One who holds us accountable!"

"To what—to your parochial patriarchal projections?"

Of course such a dialogue is just a cartoon. We'd better interrupt our conversationalists before they resort to "BANG POW !!#?!"

The camps circle their wagons. Timeless truth vs. a truth-free time! The absolute vs. the dissolute! The more the one trumpets a single and exclusive Truth, the more the other dissolves it—leaving us with a void to be filled by some hollow Reason and its "value-free" science. And the more the latter reduces truth to a modern *nothing-but* (nothing but sex, nothing but power, nothing but profit, nothing but language, nothing but social construction, nothing but natural law, nothing but genes in a pool or atoms in a void), the harder the former clings to its God-given truth.

Of course, secular thought itself is hardly reducible to this stereotype. It rightly supports its claims not by appeal to the revelation of a timeless Truth but to a critical assessment of shifting empirical and historical evidence. These claims are necessarily relative to—not therefore *reducible* to—the perspective of the observer who makes them. Relativity, which we must strictly distinguish from relativism, just describes the reality of a relational universe. The human observer belongs to that universe. Therefore all human truth-claims are relative to context and perspective. But why would it follow that truth, or value, is *nothing but* that perspective?

Similarly, religious thought within and beyond Christianity cannot be reduced to the delusion of an absolute perspective—which is no perspective at all. As we will see throughout this book, there have been theologians from the start resisting the temptation to identify their best human perspective with divine revelation. There are numerous theological perspectives sensitive to their own relativity, without sliding toward relativism. But articulating this third way within theology remains a lively challenge, and the primary motive of this book.

In the present exploration we are particularly concerned with how (our) God-talk ups the ante on truth. But what is the link between the truth question and the God question? There are, of course, truths about anything and everything. But in the vicinity of religion, and in particular of Christianity, truth has also served as code for "God" and whatever God reveals. But even if we understand God to be "absolute"—nonbiblical but conventional language—that understanding does not make, or need not make, any human language (however inspired, however truthful, however revealed) itself absolute.

> The best lack all conviction, while the worst Are full of passionate intensity.
> Surely some revelation is at hand . . .
>
> —WILLIAM BUTLER YEATS[2]

I am arguing that when people of faith step out of the mystery and make totalizing claims for our truth and our beliefs, we perpetuate an antagonistic polarity that actually paralyzes faith rather than fostering its living process. Relativity dissolves into the indifferent relativism, and truth freezes into a deified absolute. But we shall see that the antagonism actually turns into a bizarre two-way mirror-game. When the secular, thus cast as the dissolute, turns reductive in its hostility toward religious absolutes, it slides strangely toward an absolutism of its own.

Is God the Problem?

The camps seem to divide neatly between faith, tending toward absolute and exclusive truth-claims, and secularism, tending toward atheism by way of religious toleration. In the United States, those who are committed to democratic freedom of (and from) religion of course traditionally include the whole range of moderate and liberal Christians. But a secular fear of religion has intensified under pressure from the politically well-mobilized Christian right wing on the one hand and Islamic extremism on the other. This double whammy of fundamentalisms has put some irate atheists on the best-seller list. They help to expose the proclivity of all religious absolutism and exclusivism to violence and repression. With in-your-face titles like *The God Delusion, God is Not Great, The End of Faith*, and *Letter to a Christian Nation*, such authors predictably preach Reason as the great virtue of democracy.

Intriguingly, these authors show little tolerance for religious moderates—precisely, as *The End of Faith* author Sam Harris explains, because they are tolerant! "By failing to live by the letter of the texts while tolerating the irrationality of those who do, religious moderates betray faith and reason equally."[3] He is right that the religious middle does indeed often fail to scrutinize critically certain key presumptions of their own religious faith as well as of their own secular legacy of tolerance. But he presses dauntlessly forward: "Religious tolerance—born of the notion that every human being should be free to believe whatever he wants about God—is one of the principal forces driving us toward the abyss."[4]

Just when one expects a reinforcement of the Jeffersonian wall between church and state, this new anti-tolerance would dismantle it—from the other side! Jefferson had based his hope for democracy—and it was a hope he knew to be far-fetched—precisely on the tolerance of any *beliefs*: "It does me no injury for my neighbor to say there are twenty gods, or no god. It neither picks my pocket nor breaks my leg."[5] Harris, however, leaves Jefferson in the dust: "Some propositions are so dangerous that it may even be *ethical to kill people for believing them*."[6]

Could there be a more dangerous proposition than *that*? Harris then comes out as an enthusiast of Buddhism. Since it doesn't worship a God, it doesn't count as a "religion." I agree that we should all learn from Buddhism's enlightened compassion. Noting that it attends skillfully to the fact that all will die, Harris asks: "Why would one want to be anything but *kind* to them in the meantime?"[7] One must reply, "Well, Sam, because like you said, some of them believe the wrong things and should be killed."

It is heartening to hear voices of the secular left designate such generalizations "secular fundamentalism."[8] But I hope this little debate exposes the way secular relativism mirrors and mimics religious absolutism. That mimicry of opposites makes treacherously difficult the work of a third space—as though theology must find its way through a carnival hall of mirrors. Both atheism and theism can play the game of absolute truth.

Sure, "God" is our problem—when we think that our particular version of God is the only solution. Theological absolutes, especially when deployed against "evil," may themselves turn evil—as surely as the secular absolutisms that seem to mirror and mimic them in reverse. But "God" is not a convincing "Root of All Evil" (despite a BBC documentary of that title and thesis). There is plenty of historical repression and imperial terror before monotheism—not to mention Stalin, Mao, and Pol Pot, *after*.

Christian Right, Planetary Wrong

We have considered how even an ethically minded secularism can turn absolute. Now let us note that the inverse is also the case: the religious absolute can also turn dissolute—and not in a sexy way! When theology portrays our life in this world as a mere pilgrimage to heaven, a mere means to a supernatural end, it tends to dissolve our responsibility for our corner of the material creation. The gross effect is that of an amoral relativism regarding the creation itself. For the earth itself is regarded as "fallen," and almost all—humans and nonhumans—stand outside the clique of the "saved." Thus the Christian absolutist melts the creation down into a *nothing-but* (nothing but matter, nothing but this passing world, fallen nature, and so forth) as surely as does the scientific reductionism.

The tragic indifference of most Christians to date toward the ecological devastation of the earth is the major case in point. When Christianity, such as the evangelical Creation Care movement, does begin to raise ecological consciousness, it is met by well-funded Christian repudiations. A supposed scriptural literalism shares a modernist appeal to "just the facts." But a sophisticated alliance of corporate interests with the religious right has produced an aggressive new anti-environmentalism.[9] For instance, in an "Open Letter," the Cornwall Alliance declares that "the harm caused by mandated reductions in energy consumption in a quixotic quest to reduce global warming will far exceed its benefits."[10] This right-wing politico-religio-economic alliance bases a theology of "forceful rule" of the earth on the "dominion" passage of Genesis 1:28.[11] As we shall see in chapter 3, this supposedly scriptural sense of "dominion" supports the formidable coalition between a materialist, profit-driven reductionism and a religious absolutism. We might say that the most reductionist tendencies of secularism have supported unconstrained, greed-driven economic growth in the name of reason and progress: this is the global face of the dissolute. And it is the dissolute turned absolute. But what is theologically so disturbing is how the laissez-faire capitalism—globalized in the late twentieth century in what the confessed former "eonomic hit man" John Perkins calls the "corporatocracy"— formed such an effective political alliance with the new religious right.[12] "We believe it is far wiser," continues the Open Letter, "to promote economic growth, partly through keeping energy inexpensive, than to fight against potential global warming and thus slow economic growth."[13]

Thus an absolute Christian moralism spins like a dog chasing its tail after an aggressively *amoral* secular economics. Authoritarian Christianity and secular relativism thus mimic and mirror each other's indifference to the fecund differences of earth's human and nonhuman populations. The absolute and the dissolute together act like a solvent on the meaningfulness of this world in its irreducible mystery. And between them we begin to witness the quite literal dissolution of the carrying capacity of the earth: creation being forced to "grow" cancerously toward a man-made [sic] apocalypse.

Honest to God

The dizzying mirror dance of the absolute and the dissolute has become self-destructive for soul and earth. Yet most of us aren't actually at home as relativists or absolutists. Those are caricatures, types, cultural moods, more than positions that thinking people usually espouse. We may identify more with one, yet we can recognize some truth on the other side. But does that mean just creeping off into the muddling middle, into a bland moderation?

Okay, then. Say you are open to self-criticism and exploration; you know that at best you "have this treasure in clay jars," as Paul put it in a letter to the Corinthians (2 Cor. 4:7). As the Christian movement became more public, Paul himself was worrying about the danger of arrogance that comes with "the open statement of the truth."[14] For instance, consider the ancient creeds. Such documents were first forged under the pressure of the Christian emperors from Constantine on to come up with a faith that would help to unify the young Church Triumphant. Creeds are a meaningful mode of theological compression. They certainly make "open statements of the truth."

The problem comes when that truth becomes absolutized as "the faith": as, for example, in "whoever desires to be saved must above all things hold the catholic faith. Unless one keeps it in its entirety inviolate, one will assuredly perish eternally." Faith here means a set of metaphysical *beliefs* about one God in three persons, "without either confusing the persons or dividing the substance."[15] Such conciliar statements often waxed uninhibited in their threats and curses, or "anathemas."[16] For instance, "If anyone will not confess that the Father, Son, and Holy Spirit have one nature or substance . . . let him be anathema." A whole series of anathemas follows, all demanding "confession" of a theology processed with Hellenistic substance metaphysics.[17] Institutional unity was achieved at the cost of massive divisions and expulsions, with repercussions to this day.

Truth was turned into a belief to which you must assent—or be cursed, denounced, excluded. The clay jar was thrown on the trash heap, replaced by an elegant vessel of imperial alabaster. But did it then contain the truth? Or had the truth-flow of an earlier generation been abstracted into transferable, timeless beliefs, convenient to the Christian empires? Tradition of course needs distilled, compressed codes that it can deliver to the next generation. "Tradition" means "to deliver, to hand over"—and without receiving and making its historic deliveries, theology has nothing to offer. Ironically the word *tradition* is etymologically a doublet of "treason." Theology can "hand over" its teaching in either sense.

The claim of absolute truth is the greatest single obstruction to theological *honesty*. It seems that Paul already glimpsed this danger, at a point when a Christian theocracy was almost unimaginable.

So then, say you recognize the mysteriousness of the "treasure." Whether or not you recite some ancient creed comfortably, you don't mistake faith for absolute knowledge. But despite clay jars and clay feet, you don't want to hem and haw your way through life, to compromise and qualify every claim, to relativize every revelation. You may relinquish certainty, but you need *confidence*. You want to be able to live *purposefully*, to communicate the force of those values and insights that burst through the haze of business-as-usual. You want to speak openly and *honestly*.

Ever notice, though, that those who already *have* the truth have little patience with honesty? With honest questions, doubts, observations, differences? They don't have to *learn* anything important anymore. Of course, honesty may lead us again down the road of debunking and doubt—to a dead end where no "open statement of truth" remains possible. What if we don't want to join either camp? What if we want neither a truthless honesty nor a dishonest truth? How do we break out of this circle? Can theology—if it gets out of stasis and into process—really help?

Trails and Trials

"Many black women," according to womanist theologian Delores Williams, "have testified that 'God helped them make a way out of no way.'"[18] For there is no way there already, prepaved. This is all too evident to anyone in a crisis, where prior assurances seem to flee; where we feel abandoned even by the God we thought we knew. And for peoples living in the perpetual crisis inflicted on them by collective injustice, consciousness of this desert wandering is acute. For Moses, responsible for a huge and frightened population in the wilderness: no way! For Hagar, expelled from her fickle surrogate family and lost in the desert with her son: no way. Indeed, "like Hagar and Ishmael when they were finally freed from the house of bondage, African American ex-slaves were faced with making a way out of no way."[19]

Those who know suffering come closer to a truth about the creation: the future is open, alarmingly or promisingly. The way is not laid out in advance. Creation itself is in process. Our own way forward has not yet been charted. There may be no trail before us at all. Sometimes one can only move forward in faith: that is, in courage and confidence, not in a delusional certainty.

Process is ongoing. Amidst trials and tribulations, life is going on. Exoduses happen. But, like Moses, you may not make it to the promised land. That possibility didn't paralyze him.

"Hope," says the theologian Karl Barth, laying to rest any facile faith in end-times or immortality, comes "in the act of taking the next step."[20] His theology was born amidst the catastrophic struggles of Europe during the period of the World Wars. Barth witnessed the failure of German Christianity, liberal and conservative, to avert the horrors of Nazism, or even, but for the small Confessing Movement, to protest it. He denounced "religion" for its compromises with secular modernity and the death machines. For Barth "faith" is opposed to the theological arrogance—a form of the mirror-dance discussed above—that underlies this unholy alliance.

He insisted instead that all theology is "on the way": *theologia viatorum*. Any theology on the mystery will resonate. The way is not straight nor the utterance smooth. Theology does not seize—the German for "grasp"—God as its object and the truth as its property. And the different angles of our varied contexts infinitely complicate our inescapably finite and fragmented capacities.

In the many decades since Barth, theology has been winding through radically altered spiritual landscapes. Feminist and liberation theologies have made more explicit the complex ways context forms and deforms faith. (Indeed, they would note Barth's own systematic blindness to his patriarchal context.)

Context signifies the interplay within a historical geography of all the social, ethnic-racial, sexual patterns that shape our perspective but are often masked by the more conscious beliefs. And in theology *context* is truly *with* text: the way, for instance, Christians, Jews, or Muslims interpret their scriptures will be influenced by the complex interplay of contextual factors—rendered ever more confusing if the interpretative input is ignored.

> All theology is *theologia viatorum*. . . . It is broken thought and utterance to the extent that it can progress only in isolated thoughts and statements directed from different angles to the one object. It can never form a system, comprehending and as it were 'seizing' the object.
>
> —KARL BARTH[21]

The clay of our merely human perspectives is mixed of these contextual elements. The context touches content, and content reciprocally affects context. For good *and* ill. From the interaction comes change. Because we are beings in relation we are always becoming. Change is inevitable but not necessarily for the better: process in interpretation, as in life, may or may not mean *progress.*

And so we embark on the path of a *theology in process*, a process whose ends are many and open, a way no less purposeful than that which moves toward some fixed goal. The ends of this way do not yet exist: it is truly *viatorum.* The ends are more open than Barth could have recognized. They signify possibilities, not actualities. Theology is not ever identical with faith or with belief—but, rather, motivated by faith, it takes all our beliefs into the evolving perspective of its interactive process.

Theology as Truth-Process

Theology as process remains—like every living, breathing organism—open-ended. And as such it is no less carefully contoured than a closed system. Such theology is on the go. But this does not mean "anything goes," as absolutists fear. *Many* things go, and some better than others. Discernment between ways better and worse, between the promising directions and the dead ends, never ceases. Theology cannot escape its own edge of judgment, not in the sense of an ultimate retribution but of a critical and self-critical truth-process.

In the very notion of "process" echoes the old meaning of a formal procedure, as in a "legal process." The French *procès* preserves the dual meaning of both an *ongoing activity* and a *trial*. The term gains a new resonance through the "truth and reconciliation process" of South Africa. This was a model developed after the stunning, unpredictable end of apartheid: a way opened where there was no way. The truth and reconciliation process evolved in order to facilitate a nation-healing justice. It invented an alternative to a formal trial, a procedure for seeking accountability without vengeance. Reconciliation rather than retribution was the goal, and truth-telling rather than punishment the means. In South Africa it was "a public process of disclosure by perpetrators and public hearings for victims . . . with the intent of moving a country from its repressive past to a peaceful future, where former opponents could work side by side."[22] The success of such truth-processes remains controversial, in contexts in which there can be no quick fix for a hell of history.[23] But the political metaphor of the "truth process" contributes new meaning to the concept of process as ongoing interactivity.

"*Such a Truth, as ends all strife*"?[24] Only temporarily, as far as history goes. But amidst the trials of history we are beginning to see the slow coalescence of traditions of nonviolent struggle, in which truth cannot be extracted or imposed by force. Theology as process becomes a resource—one among many resources—for nonviolent conflict resolution at all levels. Because we are who we are only in our open-ended processes of interaction, we require a radically relational theology. This relationalism moves always toward what Martin Luther King Jr. called "the beloved community." A *theologia viatorum* opens vistas of peace without abandoning the struggle for justice. To forge democratic paths of spiritual well-being and public honesty, Christian theology, as we saw in the civil rights movement as well as in the struggle against apartheid, must be mobilized *against* the Christian legitimations of any unjust status quo. But the *against* is the negation of a negation. On the mystery and in hope: we take another step. Love, however, is full of pitfalls.

Touch of Truth

Along with the public witness of a theology in process are also enfolded difficult intimate truths. Take, for instance, the riveting moment in Rita Nakashima Brock and Rebecca Parker's *Proverbs of Ashes* when the young pastor Rebecca is confronted in her study by a walk-in, Lucia. Lucia's husband is an abuser. "I went to my priest twenty years ago. I've been trying to follow his advice. The priest said I should rejoice in my sufferings because they bring me closer to Jesus. He said, 'Jesus suffered because he loved us.' He said, 'If you love Jesus, accept the beatings and bear them gladly, as Jesus bore the cross.'" She has tried, but now her husband is turning on the kids. "Tell me, is what the priest told me true?"[26]

The truth question: it *matters*. It takes material form in our embodied, terribly touchable, existence—and demands a theological response. Rebecca pauses. Her own relational faith that, in Paul's words, "love bears all things," is reeling. "If I answered Lucia's question truthfully, I would have to rethink my theology."

She does. "'It isn't true,' I said to her. 'God does not want you to accept being beaten by your husband. God wants you to have your life, not to give it up. God wants you to protect your life and your children's life.' Lucia's eyes danced."

Rebecca has answered theology

> You say love is a temple,
> love a higher law
> Love is a temple, love the
> higher law.
> You ask me to enter, but
> then you make me crawl
> And I can't be holding on
> to what you got, when
> all you got is hurt.
> —U2[25]

with theology. And Christian love suddenly ceases to mean: tolerate abuse. Love may bear, for instance, the spouse's illness, irritating habits, or occasional ill temper. But love does not mean: enable abusers to continue in their abuse. Even the problematic metaphor of "turning the other cheek" means, read *in context*, the very opposite of enabling more enmity: it is a strategy for interrupting it. The patience of love is not placation of injustice. In the wake of the women's movement, the context for all future theology shifted. If "the personal is the political," neither domestic abuse nor global violence can be pacified. As our chapters on passion and com/passion will probe more deeply, we make peace and we make love only inasmuch as we make justice. The authors of *Proverbs of Ashes* narrate many such events of religiously sanctioned violence—not to put the kabash on Christian theology but to call it to account.

Notice that right in the episode, Rebecca used strong truth-talk: no relativism here! But we hear not a truth imposed, but *in touch*: it takes place in reciprocity. And it unfolds as a *process*. First in the form of a dialogue, in which Lucia could tell her truth, could witness to it, and be heard. Without such validation by Rebecca, the truth of Lucia's life would not be happening. She was not on her way. Lucia "had been heard to her own speech," in the classic phrase of feminist theologian Nelle Morton.[27] Lucia soon moved out, got new job training, a new job, a new life. Formal legal processes were involved. Her husband eventually got help, and she permitted visitation with the children.

One sort of truth had been scripted by the priest, with very material, devastating effects. The proposition "Jesus suffered because he loved us," like "democracy is the best form of government," is in itself a plausible claim. But I am suggesting that its *truth* depends on the context of the spirit: is it in *touch* with the very *love* it names? Abstracted from its living relationships, even a proposition about divine love can be cited "in bad faith." It can be turned into a terrorizing absolute. Such abstraction from text and context, whereby a proposition can then be reinserted unilaterally into any life situation, is the temptation of all forms of truth-language, but above all of theology. It is the fertilizer of every atheism.

The apostle Paul warned of those who "exchanged the truth about God for a lie" (Rom. 1:25). But such a lie is so good because it looks and sounds like the truth. The exchange can happen under cover of theology itself! Such spiritual dishonesty will not be answered by a wimp-out relativism (as in "The priest had his opinion, I have another, what is yours?"). It was answered in this case by a spontaneous and confident *counter-truth*. The capacity to speak truth— sometimes to power, sometimes to the disempowered—is what in the religious traditions we mean by "witness" or "testimony." We will discuss this biblical sense of truth in the next chapter.

Rebecca was not just expressing a truth that she already "possessed." She didn't. Rather, the truth she heard herself articulate had the character of an event, a happening: it surprised her as well. She makes no claim, like the prior clergyperson, to tell The Truth. Nonetheless she finds herself speaking honestly, truth*fully*. She offers a *touch of truth*: a humble, fleeting, and healing gesture. Yet the theological truth-claim she made only arose in response to Lucia's courage to come in and tell the truth of her life.

A touch, a connection, takes place—and a fullness flows into our waste and void spaces. It begins to wash out the dysfunctional absolutes that have kept us trapped. Such truth of flow replaces fixed truisms with living relationship. But then we must not confuse relationalism with relativism, in which every relationship is equally good.

It is the process and the caress of this truth-fullness in which the present book is interested. Theology that matters, a theology in touch, can help open a way where there had been none. But it is likely to stir up our own uncertainties in the process. It may confront us with the chaos in our lives. For instance, the chaos of an abusive family system may remain hidden under the socially sanctioned order of marriage. At another scale, the chaos produced by war may result from the attempt of one power to inflict its order—whether under the name of "democracy" or "God"—on others. And in terms of theology itself, thoughtful people who had been subjected to an unquestionable set of beliefs cannot begin to question those absolutes without undergoing some sense of dissolution, some crisis of belief. The truth-process does not eliminate uncertainty or its chaos. It makes it visible, in order to release a livelier, more redemptive, *order*. But such order, like the truth it supports, cannot be imposed: it must *emerge*. It resembles what scientists now refer to as "self-organizing complexity," the nonlinear order of an open system. The chaos of dissolution can become the very stuff of creation, as chapter 3 on the creation will propose. Exposing the dissolute ethics legitimated by abusive theological absolutes, we break out of the mirror game. We approach not a *relativism* of anything goes—but a *relationalism* of: everything flows.

Calling "God"

What would it mean to do theology as an *open system*? Theology as an academic and church discipline is usually referred to as "systematic," suggestive of a majestic architecture of doctrines, a medieval cathedral of the mind. Without losing the gothic brilliance of the discipline, let us recognize the dilemma. The very word *theology* seems to yank our gaze upward, away from the pain of abused persons, away from our intimate or public passions, away from the adventures and misadventures of our embodied lives, here, now.

Theology: bits of an old creed echo through our brain: I believe in God the Father Almighty, Maker of Heaven and Earth, and in Jesus Christ his only begotten son . . . born of the Virgin Mary. . . . All vivid images, snatched from the biblical story. Their familial resonances may strike us as meaningful and indispensable, as beautiful in their antiquity, as patriarchal pontifications, or as childish nostalgia, kitschy among adults. But whatever emotional coloration they may have for us, they condense wide systems of thought and lively biblical narratives into compact abstraction.

Theological language is an odd mix: of vivid story-characters extracted from scripture and the most cosmically stretched ideas from ancient Greek philosophy onward. I love this mix. But it is complex—and dangerous, when we neglect its complexity. From the rich and messy set of narratives comprising the Bible, certain metaphoric themes were lifted up, repeated, generalized—a process of abstraction beginning to happen within the Bible itself, at least in Paul's writing, touched by Greek Stoic philosophy. Abstraction is a necessary part of any reflective process. But by means of these abstractions, stories have been often dogmatically pounded into simple propositions of belief. These abstractions are convenient. But they too easily mask the complex mix of metaphor, history, and philosophy. Indeed, they may disguise the metaphors as pseudo-facts.

When we forget that these metaphors are metaphors, when we think, for instance, that the metaphor of "God the Father Almighty" refers in a direct and factual way to an entity up there, we are committing what the philosopher of process, Alfred North Whitehead, called "the fallacy of misplaced concreteness."[28] Those concrete attributes of fatherhood refer to the particular experiences of biological fathers within the context of a monotheistic patriarchy, in which an "almighty" deity could of course only be imagined as masculine. The fallacy lies in confusing the concreteness of metaphors derived from a particular, finite historical context with the infinity we may call—for want of a better word—"God." *Literalism* is the simple word for this fallacy. It freezes theology into single meanings. Instead of flowing from an inexhaustible truth-*process*, meaning gets trapped in a truth-*stasis*.

Yet mystery is itself not absolute. Otherwise we would have nothing to say. And that is why we use metaphors of all sorts in theology: to realize our relationship to the mystery.

> Words strain,
> Crack and sometimes
>   break, under the bur-
>   den,
> Under the tension, slip,
>   slide, perish,
> Decay with imprecision,
>   will not stay in place,
> Will not stay still.
>   —T. S. ELIOT[29]

To realize it in language: to *speak* God's *sophia* in a mystery. But in such speech, words, as Eliot says, "strain/Crack and sometimes break under the burden . . ." Scripture is littered with broken words, words breaking open new meanings, breaking open closed systems. The Bible brims with metaphor, trope, figure of speech, parable, psalm, prayer, story. When abstract propositions of belief (like "Jesus Christ is our Lord and Savior" or " I believe in the triune God") that are rare in scripture become fixed in a closed system, the fallacious factualism kicks in. The propositions then draw our concern *away* from the concrete processes of our shared creaturely life, rather than spiritually illumining them. Metaphors (like the Christ, Lord, Savior, Trinity, and so forth) then lose their metaphoric valency, their open-ended interactivity: for metaphors are language in process, not in stasis.

The metaphors are ground down into changeless truths when the *abs*traction makes itself *abs*olute: those terms mean almost the same thing in their Latin root: both signify a "drawing away from," a separation. When that separation is absolute it becomes irreversible; the abstraction frees itself of reciprocity with the bodily world. Thus an absolute truth is deemed nonrelative to anything else, *abs*olved of all interdependence, all conditions, all vulnerability, all passion, all change. Those with some theological training will recognize the abstract (and surprisingly nonbiblical) features of the God of classical theism.

But what if that sort of changeless stasis is not even what God—let alone the creation—*means?* What if "God" did not first and need not now mean some super-entity up there in an abstract heaven, invulnerably transcendent of time and its trials? Scripture has no such notion. Its metaphors suggest a transcendence of qualitative difference but not of dispassionate immutability. But, of course, the Bible virtually never gives any abstract definition of God. One of the (two) times it seems to, it announces: "God is love" (1 John 4:16). Does this suggest some changeless and dispassionate paternal entity? Or rather a mystery of infinite relationship?

And yet the metaphors of this love, in its inexhaustible interactivity, got frozen twice over: in the abstractions of a changeless omnipotence on the one hand, and the stereotypes of a literal and literally masculine Person on the other. "He" appears (and for this book the masculine article will be used strictly in historical citation or in present irony) at once chillingly distant and intrusively present: an absolute masculine infinity can combine with the violently loving interventions. Of course, some can catch subtler meanings behind the popular clichés of a God-man who "comes down," presumably from Heaven Up There, dons a birthday suit, and after gamely sacrificing himself "for our sins" soon gets beamed up again. . . . But far too many thoughtful people, through too much early exposure to the Big Guy in the Sky, develop life-long God allergies.

Allergic reactions, I hear, can only be treated with a bit of the original allergen. In other words, the literalisms of God-talk can be cured not by atheism but by an alternative theology. What, however, would such a therapy for secularists have to do with the needs of people of faith? For communities of faith will naturally and necessarily speak in their own traditional codes; they will play what Wittgenstein called "language games," with their own peculiar grammars and rules of communication nowhere more apparent than in the liturgy. But I have come to trust that members of these communities must not be insulated from their own doubts. Their doubts will only deepen if they are protected from the solvents of secular relativism. Particularly when it comes to the leaders and the thinkers among communities of faith, they will find that they share something of the allergic reaction; they are inevitably, for good and for ill, immersed in a secular culture. Both its habitual nihilism and its healthy skepticism are part of us all. For the sake of our own honesty and therefore our own confidence, indeed the confidence of our testimony, we need the breathing room of a theology in process. We need its adventure and its guidance. This is not a way of what is Sunday-schoolishly called "learning about God." But it is a way of discerning divinity in process. In the process of our open-ended, on-the-ground interactions, a theology of process, itself open-ended and interactive, discerns a process and an interactivity that it may also call "God."

Anselm classically defined theology as *fides quaerens intellectum*—"faith seeking understanding." Not faith that already understands and so no longer needs to seek. That would by definition no longer be theology. Theology is not itself the faith but its quest. If we stop seeking, we are no longer *on the way*. Faith seeking understanding has then turned into "belief that understands." It then closes down the very root of *quaerens*, from which come both *question* and *quest*. Speaking the divine wisdom in a mystery, theology remains a work of human speech. Theology is not the same as faith or belief, but a disciplined and relational reflection upon them. God calls, but we are responsible for what we call "God." And God may be calling us to that very responsibility!

Can an open-systems theology, operating as it must in the third space beyond the absolutes of rigidified metaphors and the dissolutes of mere repudiation, set theology itself back on the mystery? Or does any *theology as such* presume too much? What does the faith that seeks already presume? As a theological process, faith is of course somehow *in* God.

"God"! As *theos-logos*, God-talk, theology cannot take its first step without a leap of faith: if not into an entire apparatus of dogmatic answers, into a discourse in which the *name* of God already shapes our questions. So after all does God-talk always solve the mystery before it even starts?

Speaking of the Mystery

Is it possible that the very name *God* endangers the mystery that it names? The practice of not pronouncing the name of GXD, yet writing it as the tetragrammaton YHWH[31] answered over two millennia ago to this paradox. In more casual speech, Jewish tradition began early to use a delightful nickname for the mystery: the unnameable One is addressed as *Ha Shem*—"The Name"![32] Sixteen centuries ago, Augustine put it perfectly: *Si comprehendis, non est Deus*—"If you have understood, then what you have understood is not God."[33] And eight centuries ago, another monk, the great mystic Meister Eckhart, tried to still the knowing "chatter" of religious folk: "And do not try to understand God, for God is beyond all understanding."[34] He was carrying on the tradition of "negative theology": a strategy within theology, indeed within classical theology itself, that negates any presumption or pretense of knowledge of God. For it reminds us that, like us, all our concepts and names are finite, creaturely language spoken by creatures, based strictly on creaturely experience—and so radically different from the mystery "God" names. Indeed sometimes the term *absolute* is used not to amplify beliefs about God but to protect God's radical difference from all creatures—as ab-solved from all "positive attributes." And just a bit later, Nicholas of Cusa, an early Renaissance cardinal who loved Augustine and Eckhart, characterized this tradition in its radicality: "Therefore the theology of negation is so necessary to the theology of affirmation that without it God would not be worshiped as the infinite God but as creature; and such worship is idolatry, for it gives to an image that which belongs only to truth itself."[35]

> So be silent and do not chatter about God; for when you chatter about him, you are telling lies and sinning. . . .
>
> —MEISTER ECKHART[30]

What we call "God" is literally—*not*. The only proper name for God, from the perspective of negative theology, is the infinite: a purely negative term. Theology, however, whether in scholastic sophistication or in popular religion, is perpetually tempted to mistake the infinite for the finite names and images in which we clothe it. And this is idolatry. Idolatry of a most deceptive kind, the truth made lie: we might call it *theolatry*.

Mysticism means, as the word itself hints, not primarily special experiences or esoteric gifts, but a persistent attunement to the mystery. Every religion has its mystical tradition, its language of mystery, where words point toward the silence. These are very verbal disciplines, by which theology itself learns to check its own theolatries—not to inhibit its metaphors, its narratives, but their reification, their absolutization. These traditions cultivate discernment of the unknowable God—or of what in other traditions does not bear the name *God*. As Lao Tzu, the great Chinese mystic of the "Dao," the name for "way," put it over 2,500 years ago, the Dao that can be spoken is not the true Dao. All language is finite and creaturely, however inspired. Mystics groove on inspiration. But they rigorously negate, or as we say now, deconstruct, the absolutism that presumes to name the infinite like some person or entity over there; that knows God with any certainty, abstract or literal. They keep theology on its way. In her richly traditional theology of the divine Wisdom/Sophia, Elizabeth Johnson, for instance, shows how the classical way of negation is now crucial for challenges to exclusively masculine God-images: "no name or image or concept that human beings use to speak of the divine mystery ever arrives at its goal: God is essentially incomprehensible."[36]

Nonetheless the negative theologians of Judaism, Christianity, and Islam did not stop naming God. As Franz Rosenzweig put it: "Of God we know nothing. But this ignorance is ignorance of God."[37] To the contrary, the challenge of naming the unnameable, seems to clear the space for fresh metaphors of the mystery. Cusa called this ignorance, an ignorance not innocent of its own ignorance, the knowing ignorance: *docta ignorantia.* The mystics never tire of speaking of the unspeakable. The infinity of the divine generates an endless multiplicity of possible names. So the mystical traditions, with their iconoclastic edge, may help us all to discern the mystery of the infinite within the finite. It is like a depth, bottomless and eerie, that now and then boils up at the shadowy edges of our experience. *Bullitio,* "bubbling over," was Eckhart's word for the overflow of the divine into the world. At this effervescent edge theology itself is bubbling over, speaking—in burning tongues and modest metaphors—"God's *sophia* in a mystery." Or we really should just shut up.

Yet in the mystical traditions, orthodox or countercultural, God-talk is not forbidden or forbidding. Its mystery attracts. The caress of that mystery is like the touch of truth—delicate rather than abusive. But mystery becomes mystification if it inhibits the struggle to understand, if it blocks the quest. Mysticism becomes repressive if it restricts truth to the exotic experiences of an elite. Eckhart, when he tells us to stop chattering, is not telling anyone to remain silent. Nor is Karl Barth, not at all a mystic but a booming proclaimer of the Word of God, when he whimsically likens theology—properly broken speech—to "the 'old wife's' stammering."[38]

The calls to be quiet, to listen, to meditate, or to pay attention are not orders of silence or censorship. Theology needs breathing room between its words— the better to speak them! "Silence," writes Elliot Wolfson on Jewish mysticism, "is not to be set in binary opposition to language, but is rather the margin that demarcates its center."[39] Silence folds in and out of speech as breath folds in and out, inspiration and expiration, of the body. *Spirit* in Hebrew, Greek, and Latin literally means "breath."

Yet Protestantism especially has been afraid of silence, even in a worship service—as though it would swallow the Word. Odd that we in the West must turn to yoga or Zen to recover the incarnate moment-to-moment attention to our breathing. This attention was implicit in the occidental contemplative pathways. Contemplative prayer breathes beneath and beyond our theologies of misplaced concreteness.

"Such a way as gives us breath."

Attractive Propositions

Nonetheless theology routinely gets called "knowledge of God." I am suggesting that this definition smacks of the dreary theolatry. But all the *-ologies* are disciplines of knowledge, with their scholarly traditions and historical texts. Am I making theology an exception?

On the contrary, it is an arrogant exceptionalism that I am questioning. Theology as an academic discipline comprises a vast compendium of knowledge—none vaster. But this is *knowledge of its myriad texts and contexts, not of God,* their supreme symbol. This history will be important to any student of theology, especially if he or she is studying for the ministry in a historic Christian tradition. The historically anti-intellectualist, fundamentalist, or "Bible-believing" ministries have no patience with theology, and often consider it all more or less heretical. But their identification of faith with propositional beliefs—"fundamentals"—then becomes all the more absolute.

All that has been revealed, thought, understood, and rethought is the basis and background for a faith that is still, always, seeking; but none of it adds up to the truth. Truth, like the manna, cannot be hoarded, refrigerated, or dried. It is a gift of the present and a grace of relation.

Theological truth, in other words, cannot be captured in propositions, no matter how correct. But neither does it happen *without* propositions. Theology is one hulking body of truth-*claims,* including that made by the present sentence. Theology—not the truth it seeks—comprises a shifting set of propositions, frayed and porous at the edges. Some of its propositions will *propose* more attractive, more healing and redeeming possibilities than others. To propose is not to impose—but to invite. A proposition may be more like an erotic appeal than a *compelling* argument: we get propositioned! In chapter 5 we will consider the process theological idea of the divine lure as God's invitation to each of us, at every moment, to become. Indeed, we are putting some key propositions to the test in this volume—propositions encoded in such ancient doctrinal loci of the tradition as the creation, the power, and the love of God. These will be *doctrines in process*: on trial and in movement. If these symbols do not help you think differently about what most *matters* in your life *now*—not looking back in a haze of nostalgia for the lost Plan A, nor forward to some Plan B afterlife, but *now*—they fail the test.

Theology then is a truth-process, not a set of truths. It speaks "God's *sophia* in a mystery" but *is* not that wisdom. If theology is not for you a bubbling process that helps your life *materialize* differently and gladly, its propositions have lost their life. Its metaphors have become frozen and brittle. Toss your theology on the waters.

It may come back—manifold.

Process Theology

Nothing more surely characterizes our era, which we might as well call postmodern, than awareness of multiplicity. High-speed global travel and communication confront us with an endless array of cultural and religious differences. This plurality sends some running back to the security of some absolute: *nulla salvus extra ecclesiam*—"No salvation outside of the church." And it dissipates others in a global marketplace of options: in my city you can buy dreamcatchers, hand-painted Guadalupes, plump plastic Buddhas, and a neon flashing Jesus all in one shop, on your way to do yoga after work on Wall Street. But when the many become the manifold, folded together, held in relationship, the third way is unfolding. To put this propositionally: relationality saves pluralism from relativism. Indeed, that proposition proposes something about how all propositions propose to us: they make new relationships possible, amidst the clutter of options.

For a relational theology, the multiplicity of the universe and of our own lives within it exercises profound spiritual attraction. Getting to know other religions, participating in secular movements for social justice—these count as positive theo-

> God-relatedness is constitutive of every occasion of experience. This does not restrict the freedom of the occasion. . . . It is God who, by confronting the world with unrealized opportunities, opens up a space for freedom and self-creativity.
>
> —JOHN B. COBB JR. AND DAVID RAY GRIFFIN[40]

logical activities, not threatening to one's own faith but clarifying and enriching. Again, only an absolutist Christianity views other inviting ways as competitors rather than conversation partners. A robust and living faith does not feel threatened by dissolution in the face of multiple possibilities. But pluralism represents a steep learning curve for the monotheistic traditions. What theologian Laurel Schneider calls "the logic of the One" has operated to abstract the divine from the manifold of metaphors and manifestations evident in each of the scriptural traditions.[41] In this book we cannot explore the intersections and differences of various religions. But we distinguish carefully between the relativism that slides toward the dissolute, offering a smorgasbord of ideas for sale—and a *discerning pluralism*.

Pluralism, if bound together with a robust relationalism, lets us build on and beyond Jeffersonian tolerance. It lets us *engage*, recognizing that we influence one another already anyway. We are willy-nilly interconnected. This has always been true, but in this century it has become obvious. For good and for ill, no creature, not even a hermit in the Himalayas or a molecule of oxygen a mile over her head, is untouched by the whole life-process of the planet.

No theology has earlier or better embraced the truth of our radically relational interdependence than has the movement called process theology. Rather than sensing in the impinging multiplicities of the world a growing threat for the Christian faith, it has recognized a bottomless gift. As Cobb and Griffin write, process thought "gives primacy to interdependence over independence as an ideal. Of course it portrays interdependence not simply as an ideal but as an ontologically given characteristic." It is the source of our mutual vulnerability as well as our fondest community. "We cannot escape it. However, we can either exult in this fact or bemoan it."[42] And it is precisely the dynamism of our interdependence, by which we constantly influence each other—flow into each other—that keeps us in process. "We influence each other by entering into each other."[43] If the world is an open-ended process of interactions, it is because we may exercise choice in the way we influence each other's becomings and the way we shape our own becoming out of the manifold of influences. We are indelibly marked by our past. We cannot escape the process of being influenced and of influencing. But we may exercise creative freedom within it.

For a growing number in this millennium, theology is of renewed interest, but only as a living and relational process, sensitive to difference. To say that theology is a process is to say that theology itself unfolds in relationship and in touch. It has always been multiple. It is unfinished, always, and on the way. But the metaphor of process only takes on this intensity because of the many decades of the tradition called "process theology."

Process theology is grounded in the cosmology of Whitehead, the early-twentieth-century mathematician who became a philosopher in order to connect the radical new insights of Einstein's relativity theory and quantum indeterminacy to our living sense of value. He announced that the primary task of philosophy must be the reconciliation of religion and science. His elaborate rethinking of the universe as one immense, living, and open-ended network of spontaneous interactions inspired the movement called process theology. It was developed early by Henry Nelson Wieman and Charles Hartshorne; John Cobb made it a systematic theology and a practical movement, with the collaboration of David Ray Griffin, Marjorie Suchocki, and the Claremont Center for Process Studies. This ecological and pluralist vision comprises a vast community of authors, teachers, clergy, and activists collectively rethinking the core values and symbols of the West. It is finding ever more spokespeople throughout Asia as well. The present book does not seek converts to process theology. But it takes part in the richly theological, political, and ecological vision of a process-relational universe.

It is perhaps becoming apparent that *theology as process* proposes something not just about the process of God-talk, but about what we mean by the name *God*. It does not negate theological absolutes *absolutely;* indeed, it is not often developed in relation to negative theology at all.[44] For it affirms an open system of theological metaphors. For process theologians, *God,* at once eternal and becoming, is a living process of interaction. In other words, the mystery may be addressed with metaphors of eros, of flow, of illimitable interactivity, of open ends and unknowable origins, of immeasurable materialization. But for process theology God does not lose the personal aspect. The infinite creativity of the universe is limited, contoured, drawn into relationship by what Whitehead called "the divine element in the universe." The impersonal infinity can be appropriately addressed with the interpersonal metaphors of the biblical God.

The language of prayer, the metaphors of mysticism, the scriptures of the world, provide various strategies for intimacy with the infinite. Theology is another such strategy of relationship, which process theologians have sought to revive within and beyond the churches. Such theology seeks to understand without abstracting ourselves from the process we seek to understand. Like quantum theory, it recognizes that the observer participates in that which s/he observes. Any theological standpoint outside of the process of the universe would be a fallacy of misplaced concreteness. To discern God in process means to discern at the same time our own participation in that process: our participation as social individuals, that is, as individuals who participate in one another and in God.

Amidst the uncertainties of our own history, we matter to this divinity whose *sophia* we utter. The interrelationships that bind all creatures together produce both risk and stability, change and conservation. The God of process theology resists stasis but also fragmentation. For the open, self-organizing complexity of the world can only develop through bonds that hold firm, that channel life and support meaning. Those who wish to protect elements of religious orthodoxy without rigidification, for example, or those who wish to protect the global environment without denying human need and natural shifts, will appreciate the refusal of predictable polarizations. A third way proposes both theory and practice for theology. Its discerning pluralism thrives in the conjunctions of spirited change with living traditions. The God of process theology, whose incarnate context is what William James called "the pluralistic universe," is the discerning pluralist *par excellence*.

> There are two principles inherent in the nature of things . . . the spirit of change and the spirit of conservation. There can be nothing real without them.
>
> —ALFRED NORTH WHITEHEAD[45]

Such a Way

"We are not alone," in the words of a great twentieth-century hymn: "therefore let us make thanksgiving, and with justice, willing and aware, Give to earth and all things living, 'liturgies of care.'"[46] Theology, if it lives, expresses a liturgical cadence and care. We who are finite moments participating in an infinite process need more than our own individual inventions of meaning—even if we cannot escape the constructive process. Theology, as in Augustine's *Confessions*, is itself a kind of prayer. It breathes a prayer, like his, full of poetry, arguments, quotes, doubts, and discoveries. A text that breathes, that leaves its readers breathing room. A prayer evidently intended for a much wider readership than just God!

Once I was lost, but now I'm found: and still finding my way. "Such a Way as gives us breath"—will also keep us on the mystery. To do theology with honesty and without mystification, to "speak God's *sophia* in a mystery," is a process we will have to undertake together. Theology—if it means God-talk—is not God talking to us or through us. It is not our talk about God, like an object we could know. We talk critically and creatively about the God-talk of scripture and tradition. But theology signifies something more: theology is a way of discerning divinity in process. The process is both that of our faith seeking understanding—and of that which we seek to understand.

Theology is not a truth I already possess and can write out and deliver to you. The argument of this writing is that truth—and above all theological truth—cannot be *had*. But as the next chapter demonstrates, under the sign of truth and in a familiar scene of trial, we can take part in its process. "Willing and aware."

Between the absolute and the dissolute, arises the *resolute*. Like a gift, our confidence flows. And we take that next step. We might even board together.

We have only begun to make our connections.

CHAPTER 2

Pilate's Shrug

Truth as Process

Tell all the Truth but tell it slant—
Success in Circuit lies
Too bright for our infirm Delight
The Truth's superb surprise . . .
—EMILY DICKINSON[1]

Early in the present millennium, *The Colbert Report*, a wildly popular late-night-comedy parody of right-wing news shows, launched the word *truthiness* on its first airing. Truthiness belongs to "those who *know* with their *heart*."[2] "Heart" here signifies not love, but rather a kind of feeling brewed of an unquestion-ing and unquestionable belief. For instance, ". . . what about Iraq? If you 'think' about it, maybe there are a few missing pieces to the rationale for war. But doesn't taking Saddam out 'feel' like the right thing?"

"Truth," as Daniel Boorstin notes more grimly of current U.S. culture, "has been displaced by believability."[3] George W. Bush gained a reputation as "our most postmodern president" for his facility at changing the facts to fit the posi-tion: "Call the estate tax a 'death tax.' Present relaxed environmental regulations as a Clean Air Act. Tout increased logging in national forests as a fire-prevention measure called the Healthy Forest Initiative."[4] Yet absolute truths are emitted from the same sources. We have been bombarded by a shifting, hallucinogenic radiation of over-processed absolutes—concerning economic growth, terror-ism, war, good, evil, and God—by the very media that have made truth a matter of spin. A spin, far from Dickinson's "slant," pretends to be the straight-talking truth. (Indeed the politics of 'straightness' is currently in high dudgeon.) In the first chapter we glimpsed how the polarization of the absolute and the dissolute turns into a mirror game. In the media matrix in which the *real* news is the comedy show news about how serious news shows actually are fake news shows pretending to be real—the mirror game of believability keeps us all dizzy!

> Paganism never gets nearer the truth than Pilate: what is truth? And with that crucifies it.
>
> —SØREN KIERKEGAARD[5]

To speak of truth is to speak of some kind of knowing. But though we are chock-full of information, we seem as a people to be hypnotically out of touch, out of truth. So let us now consider what kind of knowing, what kind of speaking, is theologically at stake when we *tell the truth*. Accompanied by a diverse and disputacious ensemble of biblical icons, we delve now into the question of *truth as open-ended interactivity*. I will argue in this chapter that theology—if it is truth-full—is not a matter of processed truth but of a truth in process.

Torturous Truth

"What is truth?" Thus the Roman legate retorts in his exasperation with the difficult Jew before him (John 18:38). He asks the best of questions—if only he were actually *asking*. It would become possibly the world's most famous rhetorical question, uttered with the world-weary shrug of one accustomed to moral contradictions and religious extremists. The Fourth Gospel's version of Pontius Pilate, the urbane representative of the empire, represents the dissolute in rather pure form.

"After he had said this" (for such a question, the ultimate conversation stopper, is *said*, not asked) "he went out to the Jews again and told them, 'I find no case against him.'" He recognizes Jesus' judicial innocence. As New Testament scholar Stephen Moore paraphrases Pilate's pronouncement to the Jews, "Your accusations notwithstanding, I find this man to be politically innocuous."[6] John's Pilate appears as a reasonable cosmopolitan, not interested in the intensities of local messianism until they threaten the *pax romana*. He is an imperial relativist, accustomed to adjudicating between conflicting cultures, interests, and truths.

The Temple leadership, "the Jews," cleverly refute Pilate's complacency. To continue with Moore's exegetical paraphrase: "On the contrary, he deserves to be executed in the excruciating manner reserved for those who imperil the imperial status quo. He is actually more of an affront to the Emperor, and hence a more serious threat to you, even than that rabidly militant insurgent Barabbas."[7]

So Pilate evades responsibility and passes the guilt for the crucifixion on to "the Jews."[8] But not until, for all his presumed aura of classical dignity, indeed his partial defense of Jesus, he "took Jesus and scourged him" (19:1). Some scholars assume that Pilate must have had others do the dirty work for him.[9] But Moore argues that John has "the inquisitor now become torturer" to enact in person the lash and force of Roman imperial power.[10]

The Bible in its living context can only be understood "in the light of an omnipresent, inescapable and overwhelming sociopolitical reality—the reality of empire, of imperialism and colonialism, as variously constituted and exercised during the long period in question."[11] From Egypt and Babylon, on to Greece and Rome, Israel was engulfed by globalizing cultures based on the involuntary coexistence of multiple ethnicities and their deities. Imperial order demanded a *de facto* pluralism uncharacteristic of prior, more local or tribal, unities. The fierce particularism of the Jews, especially when it irrupted in the anti-imperialist fervor of messianic movements, posed special problems for Roman stability in the region. And it also threatened the local elite, the class of rulers which in that colony, as in all nations subject to colonial rule or neocolonial dependence since, benefits from collusion with the imperial overlords.

So, then, what "truth" could the difficult figure before Pilate signify under such circumstances? He stood there with his own complex and elusive relationship to the politically dissident symbol "Messiah," the Hebrew symbol of the royal "anointed," translated into Greek as *christos*. Lost in translation would be the political substance of those messianic hopes. Only when we recall them do we feel the lashing irony of Pilate's question. It encapsulates the pluralism of indifference. It recognizes the differences of peoples, their gods, and their truths—with a shrug. It tolerates them as long as they remain "politically innocuous." But there was uncertainty about this case. So with a rhetorical shrug he tortures Jesus before handing him over to crucifixion.

The Johannine scourging, argues Jennifer Glancy, represents a case of Roman judicial torture. Torture was due process. The *Digest of Justinian* summarizes succinctly the Roman policy: "By torture we mean the infliction of anguish and agony on the body to elicit the truth."[12] So it seems that beneath the indifference to truth, a different approach to the truth and its confession is operating. This "truth" would be information you could extract from another, a proposition you could abstract from the quivering flesh, from the anguish and the resistance. Indeed, the ability to transcend the pain of your victim in the interest of truth would mark you as superior, rational, civilized.

This truth of torture, with its violent embodiment, mocks the truth of touch, the touch of truth. Might we recognize in the torturous truth an extreme instance of every totalizing absolute? For doesn't every notion of a truth that can be demanded or commanded top-down finally threaten to extract its confession through torture—whether now on earth or later in hell? Such a "truth-regime" (Foucault) brooks no uncertain terms, no slant: a simple yes/no, either/or proposition is exacted. But in the presence of Pilate we are not yet in the realm of the Christian inquisitors, with their combined force of religious and state absolutism. In the dissolute hands of the Roman Empire, the absolute political power oddly anticipates a modern relativism. "Empire," writes Joerg Rieger of both Rome and the present one, "presents its own claims to truth even if, as in the contemporary embodiments of the postcolonial empire, often in hidden fashion."[13]

In our apparently postcolonial context, a new sort of imperial power laid claim to the prerogative of torture for truth. In Abu Ghraib and Guantanamo, we sense Pilate's proximity. But the Christian millennia have shifted the terms. So we have seen during this recent, "truthier" period a morally dissolute "corporatocracy" colluding with the theocratic impulses of a wide Christian fringe. Barely hidden under its down-home, processed "heart," the current truth-regime makes it more difficult, and more imperative, to *take heart* collectively—and discern a more knowing way. That way will prove not straight but risky. As the metaphor and the strategy of the "truth and reconciliation process" suggested, truth is indeed a process, *en procès*, demanding an improbable justice. In this trial of Jesus, it would seem that truth itself, the very idea, is tried.

Johannine Testimonies

What, then, of the tortured figure under interrogation in Pilate's palace? In the messianically supercharged atmosphere of the Gospel of John, we might presume that he utters, indeed that he *is*, the *truly* absolute truth. We might also presume that when Pilate gives the great shrug of relativism, he gives it in response to Jesus' absolute truth-claim. But we are seeking understanding, not presuming it. So let us back up just a couple of verses, to see what elicited the famous rhetorical question in the first place.

"So, you are a king?" demands Pilate. This question is also little more than rhetorical. Let us listen with fresh ears to the too-familiar reply: "*You* say that

I am a king." Thus deflecting the projection of imperial rivalry, Jesus—not the taciturn witness of the other Gospels—continues: "For *this* I was born, and for this I came into the world, *to testify to the truth*" (John 18:37a). Testimony: this metaphor signifies truth as an activity in language, appropriate to a *testament*. *"Everyone who belongs to the truth listens to my voice"* (18:37b). He attests to a truth to which he belongs; others who also belong will listen. This is itself testimony, making a claim at once messianic only in its humility.

We do well to hear what he is *not* claiming. He does not say: those who belong *listen to the truth*; or, they hear that I am telling the truth. This is a more mysterious claim. This truth doesn't seem to be something that could be simply *said*. It does not propose a propositional belief or a correct position. Jesus (unlike many Christians) is not claiming to *have* the truth. Truth is not eternal information processed by God and revealed in timeless sentences. Jesus doesn't seem to think truth belongs to anyone.

One could, however, *belong to the truth*. Indeed, we will shortly explore how we are invited in this Gospel to "worship in spirit and truth" (4:24). Or to abide in the "Spirit of truth" (14:17). Jesus before Pilate does not ask that the other obey, or believe, or even recognize: but only "listen." Give him a hearing. Enter a relationship. Truth seems to be an *interaction*: an inter-activity. It is what he has been *doing* all along. The Johannine truth is an action: "do the truth"—*facere veritatem* (John 3:21). We don't simply *know* it; we have to make it *happen*. Even in the high Christology of John, truth does not signify a timeless or abstract absolute. At the same time—by the same token—this Jesus will not play imperial mirror games with the dissolute: Pilate cannot make him accept the title of "king."

In fact, the Johannine emphasis on "truth" is new to the New Testament. The Jesus portrayed in the other three Gospels hardly mentions "truth," whereas John's Gospel is radiant with it. Testify to it, belong to it, do it, dwell in it, even in Jesus' case to *enflesh* it: John gives truth multiple metaphors. Far from any abstract absolute, each sign of Johannine truth touches off a happening, a revealing interaction, a step on an open-ended way.

Truth Wells

Earlier in the same Testament, along a dry and dusty way, by the side of an ancestral well, this relational space had bubbled open. The parched traveler just wanted water. But the woman resists her own instrumentalization: "How is it that you, a Jew, ask a drink of me, a woman . . . ?" This gets his attention. He liked this sort of chutzpah in women. Yet the truth-process has here, too, the character of a trial, one infinitely more gentle. If she tests Jesus with her first question, he responds with a playful courtesy: "If you knew the gift of God, and who it is that is saying to you, 'Give me a drink,' you would have asked him, and he would have given you living water." "Living water" has the double meaning of running rather than stagnant water and of a more mysterious liveliness. When she points out his lack of a bucket, he releases the water—"gushing up to eternal life" (John 4:14b).

In response to this sudden welling-up of metaphor, the woman displays a disarming honesty about her own life. A reader now may not fathom the unimaginable pain of all those husbands, lost presumably to death, the inevitable sense of curse, social marginality, and finally unmarriageability.[14] She displayed no shame and he wanted none. Later preachers may moralize about her life, but the text does none of it. It is her honesty, not any sin, that interests the thirsty rabbi: what she has said, in risky trust, "is true." Within its patriarchal context, this interaction should not have happened at all ("They were astonished that he was speaking with a woman," [4:27]). Yet it comprises one of the longer dialogues in the Bible.

In its improper reciprocity, Jesus initiates a radically mobile sense of truth.[15] It moves like living water. The way is a truth-flow. It bursts out of the territorialism of religion, of worship fixed here or there, mountain or Jerusalem, my group or yours, my church or your temple, mosque or yoga mat. "God is spirit," announces Jesus by the well (John 4:24). This is one of only two definitional propositions about God in scripture. The other is "God is love." These are not accidentally correlated proposals: they proposition us to and from a bottomless well of compassion. This fresh sense of spirit Jesus offers does not deny divine presence in local sites and practices. Rather, it resists the dispiriting absolutisms that would lock the mystery into a single venue. God the spirit is in all of these places and containable in none. The manna will not keep. Those who would worship this spirit must "worship *in spirit and truth*" (4:24).

That preposition *in* is revelatory. What is this space of spirit—this *truth-space*? Surely not something that we find ourselves in, as in a jar or a house. "You have set my feet in a broad place" (Ps. 31:8). "If God's Spirit," comments Jürgen Moltmann, "is experienced as this broad, open space for living conferred on created beings, then it is easy to understand the spatial designations which declare that people live 'in' God's Spirit, and experience God spatially as 'breadth.'"[16] This is a *way-ward spirit*. Its mobile, animating spatiality is comprised not of territories to be guarded or invaded, but of a process of interactivity. Not just any interactive process, but one characterized by the flow of truth.

Process theology has shown that we do not exist outside of our relationships. We become who we are only in relation: we are network creatures. But how often do our relationships radiate the unexpected honesty of this well-side dialogue? To "worship in spirit and in truth" is to be *in* our world of relationships, but differently. *Worthily.* Our word *worship* comes from the Old English *weorthscipe, weorth* (worthy), and means: "to attribute worth to someone, to esteem another's being." As a leading preacher and liturgical scholar has taught us, "*Weorthscipe* is grounded in the relationships that sustain our lives as worthy."[17] Such worship is not a cringing genuflection before an alien Power but an intimate interaction that endows all participants with worth. A long-shamed woman by a well glows with worth in the exchange, knowing herself valued—and glimpsing the bottomless source of all value. Our often edgy and unsatisfactory relations to each other get touched by a meaning beyond themselves. Our limited networks suddenly seem to open into that which infinitely exceeds them. The touch of truth may not cure our losses. It can, however, redeem them for the open future. For that future, if it's truly open, opens into the God within whom all process happens.

The Johannine narrative betrays traces of a way beyond the mirror-play of absolutism and relativism. It wells up from within, it flows between, it blows from without. But this truth is not to be *had. To own the truth is to lose it.* The flow of truth is in this text the movement of the holy spirit in the world. Spirit and truth together name the fluidity of a process that we cannot possess, neither in propositions nor in practices, neither in creeds nor in prayers. We belong within it. It does not belong to us. This testimonial truth is a relation, not a possession. It is a way, not an end. It is not a processed proposition but a proposal for an endless process. Are you and I not taking part in it even now? Do we begin to go dry when we cease to *realize* it within and among us?

Way or Wall?

Theology is a question-driven quest. But the trails sometimes disappear. Sometimes they turn into trials. In our attempts at honest testimony, we will be tested and tempted by voices within and before us: by the sophisticated mockery, the shrug, of some Pontius Pilate; or by its polar opposite, the pontificating paternalism that always knows best. Pulled by many forces, the search cannot follow a linear trail; if one graphed its process, it would look more like a meander than a highway. It pushes toward the future by way of big spirals into the past (as the encounter at the well pulled up the history of a woman's personal past, with its implicit trauma). In order for the "truth to make us free," we must confront the formative impact of our past, whether painful or just addictive. Otherwise our histories will obstruct our becoming. Thus John places the story of the encounter with the Samaritan woman, like a parable of bottomless becoming, by the well of Jacob. Ancient traditions still live, their truths still moist within us—*inasmuch as* they morph into new transcultural possibilities. The past can either dam or support the new flow of the spirit.

Many Christians, however, think the newness of that spirit was new only then—in the past! They may also believe it blew the Jews right out of the water; or that it can be new *once* again for you, when you are "*bornagain*." That phrase supposedly comes from the Johannine story of the literalist Nicodemus, who was mocking the metaphor of being reborn from the spirit. But if being "born-again" is once and for all, if it means before I didn't have the truth and now I do: Doesn't such a theology obstruct the way of a "wind that [still] blows where it chooses" (John 3:8)? Folk who think they have already got that way and its truth no longer seek the "Spirit of truth" that permeates John's Gospel. They have "the word of God" as a prooftext.

The metaphor of the "way," for instance, has been used by Christian absolutists in a way that neither John nor Pilate could have imagined. "I am the way, and the truth, and the life" (John 14:6). How often is this quoted at us as code for, Why bother to learn about other religions? For instance, in the leading magazine of my own denomination, I read: "Why should we try to imagine other possible ways, truths, and lives? We've got our hands full just trying to keep up with Jesus."[18] True, but what if the way that is Jesus takes us into loving and respectful encounters with the religious other? Shall we shut the way down in the name of this "Jesus"? In the same issue: "We don't even begin to pretend that Jesus' claim is not exclusive. We excitedly share the 'good news' that this exclusive claim is inclusive in its scope."[19]

Such familiar arguments presume that the only alternative to exclusivism is relativism, with no significant distinctions between ways. And however warmly this "good news" is proclaimed, it uses John as a prooftext for its implicit logic: anyone who doesn't convert to this "Christ" is damned—at least to Christian indifference.[20]

Of course, if we Christians hadn't lost our innocence so long ago, through so many crusades, witch burnings, conquests, enslavements, pograms, holocausts in the very name of Christ and of "including" others in our exclusive Way—such excited absolutism would not be bad news. At least until Christianity became the religion of the Roman Empire, it was not hypocritical to cite these scriptures out of context.

Truth becomes not a way but a wall: separating the in group from the out. And it is being erected not just between religions but within each religion, within Christianity, and indeed within each of the denominations. And no scripture has been used more than the Gospel of John to justify this wall. For that reason many Christian scholars quietly give up on John's distinctive Jesus as alien to the testimony of the other three Gospels. For the same reason—I refuse to let him go.

Christian Shibboleths

So many citations of Jesus—not only but usually from the Gospel of John— have been abstracted from their context and turned by convenient repetition into passwords to salvation. There is a biblical story about the original password of exclusion: "Whenever one of the fugitives of Ephraim said, 'Let me go over,'" the men of Gilead would say to him, 'Are you an Ephraimite? When he said, 'No,' they said to him, 'Then say *Shibboleth*,' and he said, '*Sibboleth*,' for he could not pronounce it right. Then they seized him and killed him at the fords of the Jordan. Forty-two thousand of the Ephraimites fell at that time" (Judg. 12:5-6). Here, as routinely still, the expedience of security trumps justice. As before Pilate, there is no due process, but a simple either/or and a death sentence. These are pre-Jewish tribal tales that exemplify all too honestly what we must as humans come to terms with—else the competitive brutality of our collective past will keep playing itself out in the form of sanctioned violence. But it is the metaphor of exclusionary language, of foreign tongues, and of proper pronunciation, that we need from this story. Let it signify the linguistic violence that theology itself can perpetrate: the habitual force of what we can call *Christian shibboleths*.

Usually they take the form of prooftexts from scripture. "I am the way, and the truth, and the life" has been appropriated as a prime Christian shibboleth. Even the literal pronunciation matters: read "*I* am *THE* Way," in the arrogant accents of a divine dictator with a touchy ego. The point would be: "my way or no way." "If you are not one of us, if your theology is foreign, alien, strange, too different—your way is a *dead* end."

The shibboleth and the shrug: making a *no exit* where there *was* a way.

Johannine Vines

Yet in the interest of a truth-process, we might insist on interpreting such an influential verse as John 14:6 with a very different theological accent. In its actual scriptural context that "way" is a beautiful metaphor of reassurance offered to disciples freaked out by Jesus' prediction of his death. And he reassures them that their relationship to him will not end with his death; the truth-space they have shared will open into new and mysterious dimensions: "I go to prepare a place." There's that mysterious spirit-space, again. But this kind of talk naturally terrifies the disciples: "Lord, we do not know where you are going. How can we know the way?" (14:5).

The famous response of the next verse, pronounced differently, is then no exclusivist truth-claim. It is not addressing the problem of other ways, let alone other religions, but the disciples' fear of getting lost. He is saying: because they know him and love him, they will always *know* him—in this relational sense of "knowing." Our word *consciousness* reveals this root meaning: of "with-knowing." Only knowledge that is a knowing-with, a knowing-together, attains to consciousness.

In this Gospel the "I am" embodies the *logos*, the cosmic word of God, the word with which the world (*kosmos*) is created. Knowing-together on the way of this word, they need never get lost. They *will* know their way. The line in context is paraphrasing the "new commandment," just offered a few lines earlier, to "love one another. Just as I have loved you, you also should love one another" (John 13:34). In other words, in loving each other they *will* be testifying. They will not be alone, they will not get lost, they will not get finally separated from him: they will be able to take the next step. This dense relationality of the Gospel is inevitably defeated by the exclusivist shibboleth. Such dead-end deployments of scripture abstract its truthfulness from both the context of the Gospel and the context of our own reading.

The abiding power of this mysterious interactivity, this intertwining inter-dependence—of God and Jesus and of all who follow Christ's way—is signified by a verdant metaphor: "I am the vine, you are the branches" (John 15:5). The vine exceeds and includes every branch and depends on no one of them, as it is the "place" in which the branches dependently dwell; yet the vine is dead without its branches. The interactive truth of this "life" has little to do with the shibboleths of correct belief, and everything to do with a living faith: with the vining process of interactive becoming.

Truth in Relation: The Risk of Trust

Faith in these stories, in these relations of hearing, of risky self-disclosure, of facing fear, lets us step forward in mystery. This step would be "faith" in the New Testament sense of *pistis,* "trust," and precisely not "belief" as a proposition or a prescription. Of course theology, as God-language, makes assertions (as I am doing, piling proposition on proposition). But then theology is not the *same* as faith. It is faith's quest for understanding. But if faith means trust, what does *trust* have to do with truth?

Truth and *trust* are closely related words, as displayed in the archaic form of the word for truth, "troth," as in "to pledge your troth." "Truth" at its root signifies a covenant of trustworthiness, in a marriage contract. To be true to another means to be *trusty!* This root meaning is not peculiar to European etymologies. Indeed, the Hebrew concepts that used to be translated in the Old Testament as "truth"—*emet, emunah*—actually mean "faithfulness" or "trustworthiness." To see the shift, consider, for instance, the King James translation of Psalm 33:4: "For the word of the Lord is right; and all his works are done *in truth.*" The translation is not exactly wrong; but it reinforces a conventional European notion of truth as cognitive correctness. Compare the NRSV version: "For the word of YHWH is *upright,* and all his work is done *in faithfulness.*" The cognitive content of *emet* remains secondary to fidelity. The psalm flows then meaningfully into

> Justice is turned back,
> and righteousness stands
>   at a distance;
> for truth stumbles in the
>   public square,
> and uprightness cannot
>   enter.
> Truth is lacking,
> and whoever turns from
>   evil is despoiled.
>   —ISA. 59:14-15

the next verse: "He loves righteousness and justice; the earth is full of the stead-fast love of YHWH" (33:5). Truth and justice come linked in cosmic love. It is this Semitic semantic cluster, and precisely this phrase *in faithfulness* that the author of the Gospel of John renders as *en aletheian*: in truth.[21]

They are terms with a high threshold of relationality and a low threshold of cognition. When they do have a cognitive sense they mean a faithful use of language: "honesty."[22] We could multiply examples: "Those who walk blamelessly, and do what is right, and speak the *truth* [*emet*] from their heart; who do not slander with their tongue" (Ps. 15:2). This "truth" has little to do with right or wrong belief or dogma; nor is it some eternal verity engraved in our souls; it is a truth of right relation, to be embodied and enacted. This faithfulness cannot be boiled down to propositions; but it will transform our language, and indeed our propositions. Faithfulness in the genre of truth means *trusty language.* The true *is* the trusty.

This truth of faithful relationality in which we are called to walk and talk has everything to do with con/sciousness ("knowing *with*") and nothing to do with certainty. Certainty renders faith redundant. As Paul Tillich insisted half a century ago, faith is not the opposite of doubt: "*If faith is understood as belief that something is true, doubt is incompatible with the act of faith. If faith is understood as being ultimately concerned, doubt is a necessary element in it. It is a consequence of the risk of faith.*"[23] If we do not sometimes doubt, it is certainty we have—not faith. What Tillich called "ultimate concern" refuses the idolatry, indeed the theolatry, of mere beliefs (truthiness about God, about Christ, and so forth). What ultimately concerns us will take many names. Its theology supports a high-risk, high-yield truth, a way and an adventure on a planet saturated, for all its suffering, with "steadfast love."

"Hereticks in the Truth"

If this trusty truth cannot be boiled down to any cognition or confession, it nonetheless offers a *way* of knowing. Like the lampooned truthiness, it makes reference to feeling: but it uses the heart not to authorize fake certainties but to deepen understanding. It requires a holistic thinking that draws deeply on our intuitions, our passions, our bodily experiences, and our relations—even as it tests them, tries them, keeps them in process. A theology that would unfold "in truth" does not confuse itself with "the truth." Thinking its way through the anathemas of premodern absolutes and the nothing-buts of modern secularism, it practices what we may call a *critical fidelity.*

> Truth received begins—it does not end—a journey.
>
> —DANIEL C. MAGUIRE[24]

Yet the more inquisitorial forms of religion continue to demand blind faith in the name of absolute Truth. An accusation of heresy is a quick way to shut down thought—and therefore honesty—and therefore faith. The great seventeenth-century Protestant poet John Milton wrote with delicious irony: "A man may be a heretick in the truth; if he believes things only because his Pastor says so, or the Assembly so determines, without knowing other reasons, though his belief be true, yet the very truth he holds becomes his heresie."[25] The doctrinally correct "heretick" is content with prefabricated truths. A processed truth is a shibboleth for membership in some group.[26] The empirical sense of testing assumptions, of putting presumed truths on trial—a fair trial, not an inquisition—was part of the discipline of giving "other reasons," of practicing critical thinking, that was gaining importance in Milton's early modern England.

The truth-process can get testy. Getting into theology always means getting into an *argument*. Christian theology was formed by the Platonic practice of critical dialogue—which stimulated grand arguments about what is true, real, and good. Greek philosophy was the language by which the Jewish followers of Jesus could spread their scripture-larded teaching through the Empire. Debates between the sophisticated schools of philosophy of the Greco-Roman empire formed the template of Christian theology. This more abstract reasoning is different from the relational confrontations that characterize biblical arguments. But they are not unrelated. Abraham *argued* successfully with God to make exceptions vis-à-vis Sodom and Gomorrah: he gave good *reasons*. Honest arguments presume a certain faith in the relationship—even when they test the boundaries of that trustworthiness.

The drama of Job, for example, is one long argument with his theological counselors—and through them, with God. For three dozen chapters Job, with the agonized fidelity of anger, insists on his right to *honesty*: "As long as my breath is in me and the spirit of God is in my nostrils, my lips will not speak falsehood, and my tongue will not utter deceit" (27:3-4). "You whitewash with lies" (13:4), says Job to God's pious defenders. God, improbably, agrees in the end, saying to them curtly, "you have not spoken of me what is right, as my servant Job has" (42:7). Yet what the counselors were saying sounded perfectly orthodox: "Far be it from God that he should do wickedness . . . for according to their deeds he will repay them," and so forth (34:10b, 11a). But it is to Job's angry uncertainty rather than to the pious shibboleths of his counselors, that YHWH responds. For all his wounded rage, Job is honored with the single longest divine speech in the Bible. God will answer "out of the whirlwind" (38:1). We will return to the creative chaos of the whirlwind in subsequent chapters.

Spirit may inspire windy rhetoric and stormy confrontation. We know how argument can release tempests of difference in our relationships. Yet Jews in the Yeshiva practice debate as a matter of piety: "Jewish learning is carried on in a loud, hectic hall called the *bet midrash* (study house) where students sit in pairs or threesomes, reading and discussing out loud, back and forth."[27] If the interpretation of texts demands testing and disputation, it presumes a high level of fidelity not just to the text but to one another. Christians argue no less, but with greater discomfort and mistrust. The family fights of Christendom have routinely led to violence, permanent schisms, and war. As in many private families, we do not know how to differ faithfully, to argue *trustworthily*. Is this because we began to think the truth was something already received, settled, and single? Did we mistake differences of perspective for the impasse of either/ or? Did we develop a phobia toward the open forcefield of the spirit? The spirit, the one who is according to John "sent" in the ambiguous absence of the aftermath of Jesus' death, is as invisible and elusive as a breeze. When the spirit "guides into all truth," it is a different sort of presence then, say, quotations of Jesus. Amidst our noise, it is "a more muffled presence, an internal guidance," writes the theologian Philip Clayton, "the still small voice which, often as not, does not wear its source on its sleeve."[28] It does not take the place of reasons but inspires us to seek them. It may lead us to question the very propositions that in another context had been truthful utterances. One person's honest testimony becomes another's truthy shibboleth. The mystery requires our critical fidelity, not our mystification. We can suppress the breezes and the whirlwinds of spirit. But then we just lock into our exclusivism or flee into our relativism. It takes courage, private and public, to open a truth-process where we may differ, even passionately, without violence. Often in the interest of avoiding violence, families, communities, churches, governments all routinely shut down challenges to authority and boundary—but then violence becomes inevitable. The challenges may or may not have good reasons, but usually they deserve a hearing. Not a shrug. Otherwise the truth-process becomes a truth-stasis. For "hereticks in the truth" have too often already imposed their orthodoxy.

Truth or Terror

"The true Christian teaching is very simple, clear, and obvious to all, as Jesus said," wrote Leo Tolstoy a century ago. "But it is simple and accessible only when man [sic] is freed from that falsehood in which we were all educated, and which is passed off upon us as God's truth." By falsehood he means the script of a six-thousand-year history from Creation to End, climaxing in the birth of a supernatural Son of God from a virgin: a "gross hash of . . . superstitions and priestly frauds." Of course, Tolstoy is reacting to frozen images, not living metaphors. If faith means "believing" them, it shuts down the gospel. Tolstoy, who began seriously reading scripture only after the age of fifty, defines that gospel simply indeed: *to act to others as we wish them to act to us.*[30] In the context of his writings on nonviolence, the golden rule radiates both personal and political relevance. In its practical—practicable—simplicity, it may be capable of sustaining life in context of increasing complexity. It cuts right through the aggressions of Truth; puts any "belief" to the test; or rather, in the terms of this meditation, it puts its truth in process.

When I started this project, I was thinking that there is at least one biblical definition of truth that could function to deconstruct any totalizing Christian truth. (Deconstruction is always an inside job!) For this we return to the Fourth Gospel: "You will know the truth, and the truth will make you free" (John 8:32). "Knowing" retains here its biblical relationalism, often recognized as such with an Adam-knew-Eve wink. If truth is what sets us free, then we recognize truth as truth by its *liberating effects*. The Italian philosopher Gianni Vattimo puts it vigorously: "The truth that shall set us free is true precisely because it frees us. If it does not free us, we ought to throw it away."[31] Here was a proposition about truth that could unhinge any notion that truth is a correct proposition. For it claims that any claim about truth is tested by its living effect: it isn't true unless it is made true—by making us free.

> When healthy doctrine is added to useful terror not only to have light of truth scatter the darkness of error, but also that the force of terror may break bad habits, then as I said, we rejoice in the salvation of many.
> —JUAN GINÉS DE SEPÚLVEDA[29]

Maybe this one verse proposes a stable truth about truth. It is a proposition that deconstructs its own propositionalism: it scans for shibboleths, as for a virus.

It happens that the very day I started to write on this verse, my spouse had rented a movie he had been wanting me to see: *Brazil*, the ominously zany 1985 British update of George Orwell's *1984*.[32] In a darkly surreal London, we find ourselves inside a futuristic gothic skyscraper called the "Ministry of Information" (echoing Orwell's "Ministry of Truth"). It houses the State's center for "Information Retrieval," the euphemism for interrogation and torture. Torture of citizens is needed in the endless war against "the terrorists." A fascist-style statue in the foyer rises nightmarishly hundreds of feet high. The camera pans down to its base, where we read the caption: *The Truth Shall Make You Free.*

My heart sank. So much for my self-deconstructing proposition. Even this trusty proposal of liberation could be morphed into an emblem of the imperial truth-regime. This wasn't a filmmaker's cynicism. With satanic self-righteousness, John 8:32 was routinely cited in inquisitions and interrogations in the name of Christ. For a moment my project stumbled: Is *any* strong truth-talk destined to be used as a shibboleth of terror? Isn't the justification of torture even now "passed off as God's truth"? Is relativism after all the only honest out?

Satire *relativizes* absolutism. It exposes its solemn truth claims as truthiness. And often—as in *The Colbert Report*—the effect is not cynical but ethical. Before the fall of communism, *Brazil* was warning prophetically of the tendency of unchecked Western democratic capitalism to undergo a fascist metamorphosis, for which Christian codes would provide legitimacy. In another scene, demonstrators carry "Consumers for Christ" placards, while Christmas carols surge on the soundtrack.

It is not just that "truth stumbles in the public square" but that Truth is triumphantly erected in its place. I suspect we find no way out of the torturous dilemma except by way of the truth-process itself.

In Flesh and in Truth

The regimes of torture demand Truth, and shrug if they happen to hear any. Truth isn't a proposition that will set you free because you say it or believe it. It isn't a neon revelation but a revealing illumination. It isn't a shibboleth that will win you passage across the river Jordan, whether to safe haven or to heaven. But as you find yourself moving *in* the currents of the river, so you may recognize truth *in* its liberating effects. The Johannine truth that makes free is a truth that you *do*, that you make. It makes the space in which our complex relationships can breathe and thrive, beyond competition, suffocation, violence. In spirit and in truth.

"If our culture were to receive within itself the mystery of the other as an unavoidable and unsurmountable reality," the French philosopher Luce Irigaray notes, "there would open up a new age of thought, with a changed economy of truth and ethics."[34] That "other" is always reciprocally the self. In the altered "economy of truth," the dyad of objects opens indefinitely through the spirit into the multiple. Here activism is no longer the opposite of spirituality but its vibrant complement.

> Instead of being light opposed to darkness, or knowledge opposed to ignorance, truth is light which does not give up mystery . . . never total, never authoritarian or dogmatic, but light always shared between two subjects irreducible to one another.
>
> —LUCE IRIGARAY[33]

Theology, a densely wordy, propositional process, is slowly learning to support the activism of truth. One recent theologian, Mark Wallace, advances the helpful idea of "performative truth" as the "witness of the Spirit." The witness of the spirit echoes the testimonial character of truth in the Fourth Gospel. "The goal of theological truth-making," he writes, is to enable "compassionate engagement with the world in a manner that is enriching and transformative for self and other."[35] The open-ended interactivity of a truth-process flows precisely in this engagement. To perform truth is to transform our reality. We will be reflecting later on the theological meaning of compassion in the actualization of the possible. The feeling-together that is com/passion and the knowing-together that is con/sciousness collude in an inseparable interactivity.

Consider the above verse in its own context: "If you continue *in* my word, you are truly my disciples; and you will know the truth, and the truth will make you free . . ." (John 8:31-32). No cheap grace here: one must *persist* if one is to become free. Here indeed is the resolute. *To continue* in this truth, in this relationality, requires the critical fidelity that tests any testimony. Truth does not transcend its context but changes it. The Johannine sense of the testimonial truth of discipleship follows its Hebrew antecedent. "Lead me in your *emet,* and teach me. . . . All the paths of YHWH are steadfast love and *emet* . . ." (Ps. 25:5, 10). That resolute love is the biblical paradigm of ultimate concern. The truth-path is not liberation *from* our world but *in* it.

What about "my kingdom is not of this world"—uttered before Pilate? The word for "world" here does not signify the creation, the universe, but rather the world as status quo, the empire constructed by the torturing power before which he stands. To be in the Johannine testament "in but not of the world," in a testimony to one who "so loved the world," signifies the third way we seek: neither a delusional absolution from the creation; nor a dissolute identification with the world as it is. It is the way of resolute becoming.

Under the sign of "truth as process," we have considered several inflections of the concept of truth itself. As trust—a trust responsive to the path of *emet*—it opens us to risk testimony, to risk putting the truth as we know it on trial. The Johannine drama performs the truth of vulnerable, spirited flesh before the indifferent shrug of empire. It offers no shibboleths of salvation. And yet it refuses to dissolve in fear and subjugation. It persists in its witness, sometimes slight and often slant, but always in touch. It opens a wayward process, in which we—in our "infirm delight"—are invited consciously, knowingly and together, to continue. To move forward we now spiral backwards, into the context and the text of all processes, called Genesis.

CHAPTER 3

Be This Fish
Creation in Process

The universe in its persistent becoming is richer than all our dreamings.
—STUART KAUFFMAN[1]

Fishy Grace

A popular theologian of the late third century was preaching on the watery deep of the creation story. He was riffing on a verse from the first creation story: "Let the waters produce living things, and living things were born" (Gen. 1:20). "Imitate the fish," he proclaimed. Though this creature does not appear high on the pecking order, food chain, or hierarchy of creation, "it should appear to you a miracle." Bishop Ambrose turns the fish into a metaphor of all our struggles amidst chaos.

> He is in the sea and he is on the waves; he is in the sea and swims with the swell of the water. On the sea the storm rages, the winds scream out, but the fish swims; he is not swallowed up because he is used to swimming. To you, this world is the sea. Its currents uncertain, its waves deep, its storms fierce. And *you must be this fish*, that the waves of the world do not swallow you.[2]

In the wild waters of the world, the fish does not go under. It is in its element. Amidst the unpredictable it swims in grace. For us, says Ambrose, developing his allegory, "it has been reserved that water should regenerate you to grace." If it were my sermon I might continue: even when life seems to be flowing along calmly, its rhythms pleasingly supportive, currents of uncertainty ripple through my day. Waves of anxiety warn of some gathering storm amidst my relations or my obligations. The tempest may dissipate. Or it may blow in. It may be personal, it may be professional, it may be political. An undertow of chaos tugs at every moment. How I try to ignore, control, or flee that chaos.

What if instead we learn to swim right *through* its swells? This fishy grace is not just for the calamitous storms, when the monsters of the deep make their appearance. If we can practice our strokes during the calmer seas, we may be prepared to keep on swimming through raging storms. For Ambrose the oceanic regeneration is distilled into the baptismal font, with its ancient uterine form. His sermon was preached at a baptism: not a sprinkle upon a baby's forehead, then, but a ritual of spiritual rebirth following a rigorous training process. But in this chapter it is not the sacrament of baptism that will occupy us as such, but the cosmic con/text of Genesis 1, the genesis within which all generation and regeneration unfolds. That ancient narrative naturally enough often forms the starting point for the linear unfolding of a systematic theology.

We are pursuing a more wayward process. Therefore we come only now— soon enough!—to the current question of the universe and the ancient testimony to its creation. Its "in the beginning," its "God said," its "it is good," its "in the image of God" permeate the Western imagination of what we *are*. But we are also haunted by the waters of the deep. The mysterious imagery of a bottomless chaos from which the ordered world emerges has played, for reasons that will become apparent, a very minor role in theology until recently. Yet it plays a major role in the Genesis narrative: hidden in plain view! Our truth-quest, with its critical fidelity to scripture and its engagement of the most trusty knowing we can find about our shared reality, puts its hermeneutics to the test in this reading of Genesis 1. For in the primal waters is hidden, like treasure, a key not just to *what we are* but to *who we are becoming*. Recall that the very word *genesis* means literally "becoming."

Under the sign of "creation in process," we will consider more or less in sequence the mystery of the lost chaos, its mystical relation to the luminous dark, a vivid pagan creation myth that Genesis echoes and shifts, and the current scientific metaphor of "self-organizing complexity" as a device for rereading the emergence of the species in Genesis. We end in a "seascape of grace." But only after facing the bi-gendered "image of God" and the ecological meaning of the "dominion" text.

At stake in the hermeneutics of the bottomless deep, the *tehom* of Genesis 1:2, is mystery itself. So a theology of becoming both resists the literalizations of our knowledge—whether they are scientific or theological—and insists upon our creaturely knowing-together, our creativity, and our responsibility as spokespeople for what we may call the *genesis collective*.

Ex Nihilo or Nihilism?

The grace of the fish lies not in escaping the watery chaos but in moving with its currents. Such grace does not transcend the water (like the absolute), nor does it drown (like the dissolute): our little fish, swimming bravely on, is an icon of the resolute! If we want to practice this oceanic grace, we need here to open the way and the channel theologically. So as Ambrose was preaching from the already ancient symbols of Genesis to his living context, we also read the currents of the beginning chaos as our *current* element.

In other words, the chaos—the turbulence, the uncertainty, the storms, and the depths of our actual life-process—is all signified by the watery deep, the *tehom*, of Genesis. And from that womby chaos, in the symbolic codes of many ancient peoples, including the Hebrews, the universe itself is born. The first creation narrative of Genesis is of course also giving perpetual birth to the biblical canon itself.

The narrative itself has long suffered from two kinds of interpretive absolutism. The literalist interpretations, unlike the Ambrosian allegory, reduce it to a bit of primitive pseudo-science. Then it lends itself to every form of religious war against secular science, whether the six-day creationism that simply junks the spacetime of astrophysics, or the more sophisticated "intelligent design" campaign that tries understandably to resist neo-Darwinian reductionism but in doing so allies itself with the U.S. politics of fundamentalism.

Beyond the problems of biblical literalism, theology in general interprets the text as proof of God's creation of the world from absolutely nothing. Certainly the *creatio ex nihilo* is one possible interpretation of the text and of the universe. Both Testaments picture a creation through divine speech, a dramatic beginning of this universe rather than a static or cyclical creation. Theologians rightly argue that the radical novelty and contingency of the creation—as creation, and not just inert eternal stuff—sets it off from a purposeless universe. Yet theology usually then presumes that the *ex nihilo* version of the creation is the only alternative to nihilism.

But something is fishy in the history of interpretation! For we learn from biblical scholars that the *ex nihilo* doctrine has no basis in the letter of the text itself. The Bible narrates instead various versions of a more mysterious process: that of creation from the deep, known as the watery chaos. It inspires an alternative both to the absolutes of a top-down, once-for-all act of creation—and to the dissolutes of a mechanistic reductionism. The third way of an open-ended process of creation emerges in resistance to the presumption of a preprocessed creation. We may call this doctrinal alternative the *creatio ex profundis.*[3]

If in this chapter we reflect on the creation from the watery deep as a drama, big bang and all, that never stops, the immensity of the universe drip-drops into our every moment. As the theological tradition recognizes, the primal creativity persists: *creatio continua.* But our particular theology may either alienate us from this continuing creativity or empower us to participate in it actively, indeed interactively. The first chapter of Genesis can be locked down as a report on the absolute origin from nothing. It can be locked out as mere prescientific ignorance. But what if instead we open it up, almost like a parable, to suggest unexpected meanings for our lives in process now? As Ambrose suggests, the waters of genesis and regeneration, of creation and of new creation are inseparable. Every beginning is a beginning-again. We begin again with the poor harassed text—over-used and under-understood, constantly being literalized and being debunked—of all beginning.

A Magnificent Mess

Try to bracket everything you've been taught about God and creation as you reread the opening verses of the Bible. Notice that there is no nothingness, but a whole lot of not-quite-somethingness.

> *(1) When* Elohim *began to create the heaven and the earth—(2) the earth was* tohu va bohu *and darkness was upon the face of* tehom *and* ruach *was pulsing over the face of the waters—(3) then* Elohim *said let there be light . . .*

The second verse is the one of which the French Jewish translator and commentator Rashi wrote a thousand years ago: "This verse cries out, 'interpret me!'"[4] Poignant—the text itself is crying out to be interpreted, begging for what would later be called "hermeneutics." Genesis 1:2 opens close to home, but unrecognizably so.

If "earth" exists it can only be as the energy of a potential planet, its condition uninhabitable: *tohuvabohu*. That phrase, sometimes translated "waste and void" but better translated "waste and wild," was devised for its onomatopoetic rhythm and rhyme. "It is easy to specify the minimal redundancy, the initial repetition, incipient dawn above the waters of chaos; it is the echo," writes a French philosopher of science, thinking of chaos theory. "Languages like to articulate it in various ways; tohu-bohu or brouhaha."[5] French dictionaries contain the word *tohubohu*, and French moms scold kids for making one. The playful poetic repetition of the Hebrew may be of the essence of its meaning: for matter, as we are learning from a new physics, *is* at base rhythm. Indeed, superstring theory "suggests that the microscopic landscape is suffused with tiny strings whose vibrational patterns orchestrate the evolution of the cosmos."[6] The earth *tohuvabohu* suggests a rhyme that has not yet found its reason. And that is just—the beginning.

In the third metaphoric pair of the second verse, the *ruach Elohim*, the spirit/breath/wind of God, also pulses. Remember the whirlwind of Job, and John's uncontainable spirit blowing in truth, flowing as living water. The Hebrew *mrhpht* (often translated just "moved" or "hovered") connotes rather a spirit-rhythm as in the beating wings of a seabird, the oscillation of breath, or the ebb and flow of ocean. (Some scholars suggest that the verb *vibrate* best captures the range of its motile meanings.[7]) Flow in nature is a function not of a smooth continuous motion but of pulsation, as in the in- and out-take of breath keeping your supply of oxygen steady, as in the pump and pulse of your heart keeping your blood streaming, as in the ebb and flow of waves keeping the ocean moving.

It is the ocean that provides the primal metaphor of Genesis 1, as the *tehom*—the oceanic deep, later translated into Greek as *abyssos*, chaos. But the waters are also the more actualized sea, the *mayim*, over which the spirit vibrates, in exquisite attunement. Poetry synchs with the primal rhythm so much more effectively than our stilted propositions and theological abstractions. Or music: in the opening of Mahler's Third Symphony, a grand creation narrative in music, it is an eerie oscillation in the bass register that signifies the minimal gesture of genesis.[8]

There is surprising aquatic complexity in this brief text. Those spirit-waters (*mayim*) seem to flow from

> A careful reading of Genesis does not associate the formlessness, emptiness, darkness, the deep, or the waters with evil. . . . The creation story is a birth story, a story about the nativity of the earth and its creatures, including women and men. . . . A wildness, a free natural growth, is therefore part of all that lives.
>
> —KAREN BAKER-FLETCHER[9]

the darker waters of the deep, the *tehom*. Neither of these waters are identical with the terrestrial ocean that is produced by being divided from the deep above (an ancient cosmological picture, somewhat egg- or womb-like, of the darkness of the night sky and of the oceans as the two differentiated halves of the deep). These waters express the widespread myth of a primal chaos, an infinity of unformed and unfathomable potentiality. However we interpret them, the *tohubohu* of matter and the waters of the deep do not suggest some empty *nihil*.

If the cosmological intuition of the priestly writer of Genesis is not primitive ignorance, just waiting to be debunked by modern science and defended by modern fundamentalism, it is theopoetics more than theoscience. But does it therefore say nothing about the actual universe? Should we separate the stuff of science from the stories of religion, like the two halves of the deep?

What a wasted opportunity, just as science itself begins to outgrow its modern reductionism. "Story?" asks the biologist Stuart Kauffman. "Surely story is not the stuff of science. I'm not so sure. . . . If story is not the stuff of science yet is about how we get on with making our ever-changing livings, then science, not story, must change."[10] For not everything in science can be deduced. In its postmodern mode it recognizes itself as a model wrought of metaphors, relatively stabilized, on whose vibrant basis rigorous hypotheses and testable deductions can be made. Science is also on the mystery. Scientific reductionists have as difficult a time, of course, with such a paradigmatic shift as do religious absolutists. If we do not mistake the ancient biblical stories as pseudo-factual primitive science, if we do not abstract them into mere dogmas, we let the interpretive and inspiring power of the ancient stories come back into play, in our struggle to find our difficult way.

Lost Chaos of Creation

We may read the premodern poetry of Genesis as though it contains the intuitive germ of a postmodern science. We can read here, for instance, an inspiration for a chaos theory of creation. For it is in the chaos math and science of the last several decades that the West has begun to realize the meaning of "chaos"—of an iterative nonlinear process, not of pure disorder but rather of an alternative order, a process unfolding unpredictably and yet with organization, like the bifurcation of a tree's branches, the motion of a whirlwind, the spiral of galaxies. The iteration of a fractal algorithm depicts not a predictable continuity of sameness, but a rhythm of repetition with a difference. Fractal "self-similarity" unfolds at different scales, like the whole enfolded in each part, the macrocosm in the microcosm. Thus it captures with greater precision than had been geometrically possible the vortex of a whirlwind. It models the way the veins of a leaf replicate the form of the branches, and each branch with its twigs iterates the form of the tree. Or similarly, the rocks, and the peaks, and the mountain range as a whole are iterations of pattern at different scales.

The algorithms of chaos mathematics depict not some formless disorder but the complex forms of flow, too complex precisely in their fluidity, to be captured in linear formulae. They recur in the branching patterns of our lungs and of our circulatory system. Chaos theorists find this principle depicted in a head of broccoli, a population growth-pattern, in Hokusai's famous painting, *The Wave*—each drop of the curling froth of a great wave is itself a micro-wave. So perhaps the notion of creation from the vibratory field of the *tehom*, the primal chaos, expresses—precisely as poetic metaphor—a rhythm and a truth of the universe itself.

> A planet like the Earth is bathed in the flow of energy from a star, which makes the whole surface of the planet an open, dissipative system. All life on the surface of the Earth makes use of this energy to maintain itself far from equilibrium, on the edge of chaos.
>
> —JOHN GRIBBIN[11]

Or when we hear in recent astrophysics of a mysterious new "dark energy" pervading, indeed pushing outward, the universe, we might wonder at the resonance with the ancient intuition of "darkness upon the face of the deep." Such resonances themselves iterate if we let them. They do not threaten to collapse the distinction between the disciplines of science and theology, practices incommensurable in style, history, and intention. They do, however, encourage some healing interdisciplinary conversation. The conversation between religion and science is still developing, but there were always anticipatory forms of it. For instance, a great reformer such as John Wesley insisted that his ministers keep up with science, called then "natural philosophy." He directed them to ask themselves: "Do I understand natural philosophy? If I have not gone deep therein, have I digested the general grounds of it? Have I mastered Gravesande, Keill, Sir Isaac Newton's *Principia*, with his 'Theory of Light and Colours'? In order thereto, have I laid in some stock of mathematical knowledge? Am I master of the mathematical ABC of Euclid's

Elements? If I have not gone thus far, if I am such a novice still, what have I been about ever since I came from school?"[12]

Yet an abyss remains between the sensibilities of science and the language of faith. Theology cannot simply blame scientific reductionism for this breakdown in communication. The schism is symptomatic of the spiritual disease of supernaturalism: the attempt to dissociate spirit from matter. Hence we noted earlier that the religious absolute can have a *dissolute* effect on the world: truth out of touch. When theology insists upon creation/genesis from a mere void, it can render the embodiment in which we live every moment of our actual lives close to nothingness. Materiality becomes empty of value, little more than surface of carnal temptations and meaty decay to be passed through with as little contamination as possible.

Panentheism

Yet for the peoples of the book, the goodness of creation, human and nonhuman natures together, is a nonnegotiable value. It cannot be traded against any supernatural hope. The core doctrine of Christianity, the incarnation, celebrates the embodiment of God in the world. And the Hebrew story of creation illustrates God the Spirit pulsing intimately, touchingly, upon the face of the uncreated waters. The fluidity of an emergent universe is the process of a becoming world. For a theology of becoming/*genesis* matter matters to the spirit. Spirit *matters:* it takes on flesh. It is not just a matter of the single incarnation, but of an enfleshment always and everywhere taking place, and always differently.

> [God's] goodness fills all his creatures and all his blessed works full, and endlessly overflows in them. . . . God is everything which is good, as I see, and the goodness which everything has is God.
>
> —JULIAN OF NORWICH[13]

This is the implication of Wesley's return to the mystical Christian sense that God is the spirit of the world, the *anima mundi.* "God is in all things, and . . . we are to see the Creator in the glass of every creature." From this all-presence he draws ecological as well as theological inferences: "we should use and look upon nothing as separate from God, which indeed is a kind of practical Atheism."[14] Similarly, in traditions close to process theology, the universe may be named "the body of God."[15] This is not to *identify* God as spirit with the body of the world, as in pantheism ("all is divine"). Instead, process theology speaks of "panentheism," to retrieve the classical vision that "all is *in* God." Such radical incarnationalism does not diminish the distinction between the material world and divine mystery but rather intensifies the open-ended interaction between them.

In a documentary by Bill Moyers about the greening of evangelical Christianity,[16] an Appalachian churchwoman is seen speaking at a demonstration against the coal-extraction process called "mountain top removal." This voracious destruction of an entire landscape is decried—not so surprisingly—as a desecration of God's creation. But one is startled to hear her announce: "The earth is God's body."[17]

Environmental spirituality, or ecotheology, as well as conversations with natural science, are examples of emerging ways to *re*associate theology with what matters. Might we awaken our culture from the sense that the matter at hand is some dull, opaque stuff, some lifeless and unfeeling substratum that we with our computer-like brains can manipulate however we please? The materialities of our lives—in the mysteries of the subatomic and the astrophysical energies, in the urgencies of the flesh, the subtleties of moods, the formation of social roles, the distribution of resources, the endangerment of the carrying capacity of the earth, the sacraments of the church—bespeak our most *spirited* interactions.

Over Our Heads

On the face of the deep: a profound potentiality for theology itself faces us. Its very darkness is mysterious to some, terrifying to others. Indeed, many theologians have identified this chaos with evil itself. Karl Barth interpreted the deep as the nothingness to which God said a primordial "no" by the very act of creation: on them, "even the Spirit of Elohim is condemned . . . to the complete impotence of a bird hovering or brooding over shoreless or sterile waters."[19] For him Genesis 1:2 reads as a parody of pagan mother-goddess imagery. Yet for most Jews and Christians it reads differently, as a mysterious fold within a dignified liturgy of cosmic beginnings. In much of the theological heritage, the relation of the divine spirit to the dark waters seemed far from menacing.

Augustine, like his mentor Ambrose, deploys the deep for a baptismal theology: "This is the spirit which from the beginning 'moved upon the face of the waters.' For *neither can the Spirit act without the water, nor the water without the Spirit.*"[20] As the genesis-flow moves in Augustine's imaginary between creation and baptism, it cannot refer only to the creation as a cosmic singularity or point of origin, but rather to the ongoing process of creation. The elemental interaction of airy spirit and living water infuses the process of genesis as a whole, and so of every new creation, every renewal of life, every new beginning—like that "living water" of regeneration we glimpsed in the story of the woman at the well.

> Thou has thy mighty wings
> outspread
> And brooding o'er the
> chaos shed
> Thy life into the impregn'd
> abyss
> Thy vital principal infused
> And out of nothing's
> womb produced
> The heav'n and earth and
> all that is
>
> —CHARLES WESLEY[18]

To return to our sermon: when you make a fresh start—perhaps just getting up after a night of dark dreams, or starting to write after a spell of blockage, or loving after a time of loneliness, or living after a great loss—you have faced the dark waters. But are they evil? Or are they rather more ambiguous, chaotic, turbulent, surging with still unformed potentials along with deformed pasts? There may be evil mixed in, as often in what Augustine called a fallen world there will be. But the tehomic depth, for all its chaotic risk, is not evil. The open-ended interactivity of the process of creation exposes us to suffering and evil. And to great good. And sometimes it will take great discernment to tell the difference. It will take great spirit. We are always in over (our) heads.

Yet the spirit continues to move upon our waters. The *ruach*, this breathing, pulsing, hovering spirit—your spirit somehow, yet somehow more and other than "you"—have you felt it moving? Have you found yourself drawn into its rhythm, into the creative brooding, the oscillation of risk and promise? If so, then this creation metaphor is neither opaque in its darkness nor neon in its illumination.

A Luminous Darkness

In the mystical tradition the interplay of darkness and light takes on another intensity. It becomes symbolic of the interplay of unknowing and knowing in our language about the ultimate: in our theology. Nicholas of Cusa, the fifteenth-century mystic with radical intuitions about God and the universe, was a polymath who kept current with the latest mathematics and science. Announcing that there is no center in the universe, he was ahead of Copernicus and Galileo, who merely claimed that the sun and not the earth was its center. Over a century later, in the more defensive era of the Counter-Reformation, Giordano Bruno got burnt at the stake for espousing in a more flamboyant tone similar ideas about the infinity and omnipresence of God in the "contracted infinity" of the universe. In the first chapter we noted that for Cusa the only predicate that can literally be applied to God is the negative "infinite." In this tradition of negative theology the darkness is not evil but mystery, the space of the unknowable that nonetheless calls us, reveals something of itself to us, invites our response. Similarly, Gregory of Nyssa writes in the second century: "When therefore Moses grew in knowledge, he declared that he had seen God in the darkness, that is, that he had then come to know that what is divine is beyond all knowledge and comprehension, for the text says, Moses approached the dark cloud where God was."[22] Pseudo-Dionysius, who coined the phrase *negative theology*, invokes God in a poem as the "luminous darkness."[23]

In their writings these authors wander knowingly, in reverent adventure, on the mystery. In terms of the sign of creation, they could not directly question the orthodox doctrine of *creatio ex nihilo*. But we might now ask: Is the uncreated "darkness on the face the deep" the very bottomlessness of the divine? A depth of which finite creatures can have no knowledge—only an inkling, a hint garnered at the edge of awareness, where our most radiant capacity trails into oblivion? Where our deductions break down, our certainty dissipates, our cognitive fuses blow? Thus Cusa writes of negative theology: "this whom it worships as inaccessible light is not light as is corporeal light, whose opposite

> According to the theology of negation, nothing other than infinity is found in God. Consequently, negative theology holds that God is unknowable either in this world or in the world to come, for in this respect every creature is darkness, which cannot comprehend infinite light, but God is known to God alone.
>
> —NICHOLAS OF CUSA[21]

is darkness, but is most simple and infinite light, in which darkness is infinite light; and that this infinite light always shines in the darkness of our ignorance but the darkness cannot comprehend it."[24] That darkness of our unknowing is not sin but an inevitable limitation.

So exegetically we may read the "darkness on the face of the deep" as that darkness from which at another moment *Elohim* differentiates the light: "God separated the light from the darkness" (1:4). In other words the original dark *is* also original light, a depth that contains both darkness and light, or more precisely, transcends that distinction: it would be none other than the "luminous dark." It is like a picture of the immensity of the universe—vast darkness indeed—through which ripple invisible waves of light-energy. Only with certain instruments, or within the galactic neighborhoods of stars, as with our sun, can the light be distinguished. But Genesis is a theopoetics, not an astrophysics, of light born from this dark.

Still, one may retort: Why does God call the light good, and not the dark? Doesn't that prove that Barth is right on this—darkness biblically is evil?

I don't see how. *Elohim* exclaims with delight at the light—it is the new thing, the unfolding of a new order, the explication by word of this universe. How does that make the *implicate* order, the mysterious potentiality, from which it comes *bad*? Is the womb evil because the infant snatched lovingly from it is "good"?

Besides, surely we can no longer blithely use the adjective *dark* as synonymous with "evil." The light-supremacism of our spiritual traditions has reinforced white-supremacism, making it easy to associate dark skins with spiritual darkness, with chaos and evil.[25] We have missed the bright white evils of *order*: for example, in the unparalleled orderliness of fascism, of totalitarianism, and more currently, of the slick transnational homogenization of the face of our world. The corporatocracy erects throughout Asia, Africa, and Latin America the idols of white beauty. People of color—the variegated shades of our embodiment as human creatures—thus internalize bodily ideals they can never match: "not quite, not white." Such inflicted order violates the very process and mystery of creation. The depth questions of mysticism appear on the surfaces of our living relationships. Truth touches upon our very skins. Spirit *matters*.

Of Wombs and Warriors

We are reading the face of the deep. We touch its ancient tracery of wrinkles. The semitic relative of the Hebrew *tehom* is the Sumerian *Tiamat*, meaning also salt water, deep, chaos. Both are grammatically feminine. But in the cuneiform of the oldest creation epic, the *Enuma Elish*, Tiamat is very much a woman. She is the Grand Mother, the creator-goddess, of a tradition the Hebrews would have encountered during their Babylonian exile. Before the beginning, Tiamat mingles her waters with her mate Apsu, "abyss." From their union the gods precipitate. She is the fluid matrix in which this new life develops. As the story goes, the children then begot a third and boisterous generation.

Now begins the trouble (interesting how most narratives of origin tell of some kind of "fall"). Apsu wants to kill the noisy grandchildren: "By day I cannot rest, by night I cannot sleep; I will destroy them . . . and then let us sleep!" Agonized, Tiamat protests, sounding a way of nonviolence poignantly at odds with her writers' culture: "Why should we destroy that which we ourselves have brought forth? Their way is indeed very painful, but let us take it good-naturedly!"[26] He goes on with his scheme. The grandchildren kill him first. After a bout of mythico-clinical depression, Tiamat gets in touch with her anger. Breeding monsters, the poet transmutes her into a symbol of pure evil: quite a demotion! The loving mother of reality is turned into the monster of the deep.

Evil can now for the first time be identified with femininity: "it is only a female thing you fear," sneers the great warrior god Marduk at his peers, who were afraid to confront her. He successfully manipulates their terror, frames Tiamat as primal terrorist, and slaughters her. He then rises to rule the universe he constructs from her bleeding corpse. Creation, in other words, is a work of matricide. However, he produces the world in a sequence that Genesis echoes. The text of Genesis 1, after all, had been composed in response to the Babylonian exile and all the loss it meant for the Jews. Babylon's rulers were honored as incarnations of Marduk. While the city-state of Babylon was becoming the paradigm of aggressive empire building, its poets crafted the paradigm of creation by destruction.

Given the parallels, may we read the Genesis *tehom* as an allusion to Tiamat, and *Elohim* to Marduk? Biblical scholars draw on divine warrior motifs in Isaiah and the psalms to make a case that the biblical God does create through violence, that the chaos is evil, and that God creates and redeems *not from nothing* but from the struggle with the sea monster, sometimes called Leviathan.[27] Some Jewish and Christian interpreters thus discover in Genesis 1:2 a quiet replay of creation by murder. Is *this* then the mystery of the lost chaos? Must it be hidden because it echoes a bloody patriarchal warrior myth?

Certainly there are biblical texts that demonize the deep and its monsters: "You divided the sea by your might/you broke the heads of the dragons in the waters. / You crushed the heads of Leviathan" (Ps. 74:13-14). This is a poignant theopolitical response to invasion by Babylon. Such a fearful response is perfectly human. The psalmist hopes—as the poets of Babylon also hoped—for the most powerful force of all, the strong arm of the Divine Warrior, to come to the rescue. To save us from all that we fear. From imperial enemies out there and intimate threats within. Fear of whatever shadows our light, whatever transgresses boundaries, leaks across categories, sneaks out of closets, whatever she-sea might suddenly flood our fragile confidence. Fear of the "female thing." Of all things too deep and too fluid: we may call this fear *tehomophobia*.

The primal feminine waters metaphorically iterate the salt waters of the womb. And the heroic warrior-ethos of the occident is based on a cosmic matricide. Of course, the Hebrews mimicked and mirrored the patriarchy of the ancient environment. Not only does biblical monotheism inevitably make God male, but the divine warrior recurs in the Bible in misogynist form. Preeminently he appears in the Christian Apocalypse, where Tiamat the horror of Babylon appears transmogrified into the Whore of Babylon. Thus salvation entails "no more sea."

Robin Morgan's feminist stanza—"I am a monster/and I am proud"[28]—runs like a chant at the back of my mind whenever I hear of great warriors, gods or men, slaying their various dragons. So it is not insignificant that the text of Genesis 1 does not even hint at violence, let alone matricide. And there may be a certain mockery of the pagan myth, if in a different sense than Barth meant it. The priestly narrative can be read as parody of the imperial model of creation by violence that had wreaked such horrors upon Israel. The text implicitly counters any ideology that demonizes chaos to justify a brutal *order*. So in Genesis the watery chaos does not signify an evil to be conquered by a good God reigning high and dry above it. It is more like the very womb of the world. Thus Job's whirlwind God returns to the same scene:

> Were you there when I stopped the waters / As they issued gushing from the womb? / When I wrapped the ocean in clouds / and swaddled the sea in shadows? (Job 38)[29]

Similarly, the great creation poem, Psalm 104, celebrates the oceanic: the monster Leviathan is exalted as a "playmate of God," where "the great sea monsters" are a source of joy to the creator, no scarier in Genesis 1:23 than all the fishy life that "swarms in the sea." This biblical counterculture does not romanticize the chaos. But like the whirlwind, like Genesis 1, it celebrates the fishy grace of the deep: we may call this alternative sensibility *tehomophilia*. Embracing the depths of life, in which are mingled the depths of divinity itself, we participate in an open-ended creativity. We no longer huddle within the frozen order of an absolute power, waiting to be saved from the creation itself. We are called into a process of interaction with our fellow creatures—and with the one who calls us forth.

Genesis and Genetics

Already in the beginning, we are called to take responsibility for our worlds. In the story, we are created as collaborators in the creativity, in the image of the creator. Yet this cooperation in creation is not solely human. On the contrary, it is first of all the earth and the sea that are called to *put forth* or *bring forth* the species that will inhabit them. Both earth and sea are depicted as entities response-able to the divine invitation to generate life. "Let the earth put forth vegetation: plants yielding seed, and fruit trees of every kind on earth that bear fruit with the seed in it" (Gen. 1:11). And it does, with all that botanical specificity repeated, beginning to overwhelm this short, liturgical chapter, and insistently so. It is surely no coincidence that the much longer *Enuma Elish* lacks any reference to the flora and fauna of creation, but leaps right from the stars and planets to the humans, who appear alone, created to be slaves of the gods.

"And God saw that it was good" (Gen. 1:13). An intuition comes through here of divine pleasure in the results: As though God's suggestions, the content later to be called "the word," and even later "the lure," have yielded not altogether predictable fruit. God *sees*, not *says*, that it is good. The element of surprise, of real perception of something new, has been theologically too little perceived. Then "Let the waters bring forth swarms of living creatures . . ." (1:20). So they do, those mysterious waters, responding to zoological cues. And oh it is good. Once again, the earth brings forth—narrated with more of the loving, repetitive lists

> The extravagant gesture is the very stuff of creation. After the one extravagant gesture of creation in the first place, the universe has continued to deal exclusively in extravagances, flinging intricacies and colossi down aeons of emptiness, heaping profusions on profligacies with ever fresh vigor. The whole show has been on fire from the word go!
>
> —ANNIE DILLARD[30]

of biodiversity. And that is how the creation takes place, through the co-creative action of the creatures: ". . . the waters dance in cocreative activity with God."[31]

If we quit looking for an omniscient report, we may discern in the text a quasi-evolutionary intuition into what biologists call "emergence." The various populations thrive within the earth and the sea from which they emerge. The earth and the sea appear as super-organisms, anticipating the twentieth-century Gaia Hypothesis of the earth as a single complex ecosystem rather than just the sum of mechanisms more characteristic of modern taxonomies. They are creative creatures of integrity and responsiveness.

Is God the composer calling forth an ensemble to play with? An ensemble of ensembles? *Elohim* calls forth art, like the music of a jazz ensemble, with multiple solos and constant reintegration, with ever more complex riffs on the elemental themes, sounded in the depths. Primal themes, like $E = mc^2$ and the law of gravity, seem to express the law or *logos* of this universe. Then when biology happens, ACGT—the letters representing the four nucleic acids comprising the gene—sound the primal theme. The variations on those four will branch out into the thirty thousand genes making up the human genome (close in number and constitution to a chimp) and account for the unfathomable diversity of life. No wonder the science writer Matt Ridley cannot help exclaiming, "In the beginning was the word!"[32]

The *logos* of John 1.1, echoing the Elohimic utterance of Genesis, here becomes a metaphor for genes. If ACGT is itself a primal theme upon which we creatures riff at a collective level way beneath consciousness, is it not also a possible metaphor of the divine word? Here genesis and genetics are one. Yet only a reductionist science, imagining a deterministically programmed genome, will shut down the open-ended interactivity. As Ridley demonstrates in his aptly titled *Nature Via Nurture*, "genes are not puppet masters or blueprints. Nor are they just carriers of heredity. They are active during life; they switch each other on and off; they *respond to the environment.*"[33] Our genes not only order our potentiality, but absorb the influence of formative experiences. Contrary to the nothing-buts of either genetic biology or social environment, our embodied life is an intensely relational process.

For as John 1 riffs on Genesis 1: without the word "not one thing came into being." Neither text suggests that the word is *all* that it takes! For without the co-creativity of the earth and sea and all the other creatures in the evolutionary process, this particular world would also not be made. But then we are speaking theologically, not scientifically, imagining our relationship as creatures to the creator.

Self-Organizing Creation

The metaphor of a God who speaks, who calls, who creates intentionally, surely implies some notion of a designing intelligence. But are we then ipso facto implicated in a theology of "intelligent design" (ID)? Advocates of ID claim that complexity of the universe and of living things can only be explained by an intelligent cause, not a random process such as natural selection. While in attempting to make scientific arguments, they avoid explicit theology, "God" in the classical sense of the first cause is of course the designer. I actually agree with the ID advocates when they announce: "We are skeptical of claims for the ability of random mutation and natural selection to account for the complexity of life. Careful examination of the evidence for Darwinian theory should be encouraged."[35] A 1950s-style neo-Darwinian reduction of life to the interplay of chance and natural law is a theological conversation-stopper. Yet as Ridley suggests, such reductionism is also an increasingly marginal kind of biology. Besides, as the first chapter was at pains to communicate, the reassertion of a theological absolute is not the best response to a reductionist dissolute.

> The creative Wisdom of all things has established marvelous and ineffable harmonies by which all things come together in a concord or friendship or peace or love or however else the union of all things can be designated.
>
> —JOHN THE SCOT[34]

The ID proponents project the old picture of a Creator-God, sitting in heaven planning and directing the structure and course of the universe. Not only is such creationism too anthropomorphic. It does not account for the spontaneous interactivity of the creatures with each other and with the creator. It reinscribes the notion of a supernatural master plan delivered by an omnipotent and unilateral providence. The problematic moral presuppositions of such a view of divine power, beyond its sheer noncredibility to so many thoughtful people of faith, will be the subject of the next chapter. For now suffice it to say that with its monarchical view of God, it cannot take into account the self-organizing complexity by which life in fact emerges. Such theology offers a preplanned, preprocessed creation, rather than a creation in process.

One scholar of science and religion, reflecting on the above divine commands to bring forth, suggests that God *continually creates* through self-organizing systems. Drawing on Ilya Prigogine and Stuart Kauffman in their work on the emergence of complexity and order in nonlinear systems, Ian Barbour proposes that God acts as a "structuring cause," influencing the range of possibilities within which creatures act. Many share his understanding of God as "designer of a self-organizing process."[36] Or one might privilege the biblical metaphors of divine *logos* or *sophia*, word or wisdom, to express the ancient intuition into what Whitehead, in his philosophical reconciliation of science and religion, considers God: the ground of order and novelty, offering an "initial aim" or "lure" to each emerging occasion. Rather than Intelligent Design we might speak of Creative Wisdom. The wisdom does not impose order but calls forth self-organizing complexity.

Contrary then to any vision of a linear designer-universe, the creation is not portrayed in Genesis as God's solo-performance. One can only read there a process of cosmic collaboration. Not a thing-like creation but a complex interactive process is called forth: we may call it the *genesis collective*. Emerging from the mysterious *tehom*, the very matrix of differentiation, creatures become, like infants, increasingly other from the mother, capable of relationship—but never altogether separate. Genesis involves generations of forth-coming, multiplying creatures. The gathering cooperation unfolds as a rhythm, a cosmic liturgy: divine lure, creaturely improvisation, and divine reception—ooh, good!

When the level of order, of what biologists call "self-organizing complexity," reaches a new level, so does the risk of chaos! But since complexity theory teaches that creativity in the universe—the evolutionary leaps in organic versatility—emerges "at the edge of chaos," this risk also expresses the creative wisdom. The creation called forth in genesis is a *kosmos*, in the Greek sense of a decorative order. But unlike classical, symmetrical aesthetic, this cosmos unfolds an art of flows, waves, disruptions, and surprises. A disciplined improvisation is called forth in creatures—at great risk. Genesis names not a static and settled cosmos, but something more like what James Joyce playfully dubbed "chaosmos." In the interplay of formlessness and form, chaos and order, emergence and collapse, the possibilities in what process theology calls the "divine lure" find actualization. The genesis collective thus continues, moment by moment, amidst all its losses, to emerge.

> How manifold are your works! In wisdom you have made them all.
>
> —PS. 104:24

Male, Female, and Talkative

Out of the corner of my eye I see a familiar creature jumping up and down, crying, "What about *me*?" I've been trying to defer that one's entry, for it has dominated every discussion of creation so far, and is usually impatient to get past all those seedy, fishy, fruity, creeping, and crawling things—to me-me-me! The human. Well, ok. Even in the interest of widening our theological, cosmological, and ecological attention span I cannot really keep us out of the discussion any longer.

The primal art does seem (to *us*, I must add) to reach a new level in the creation of the human. For we are able to participate in the self-organizational complexity of the genesis collective with a self-conscious creativity. That self-consciousness is both our gift and our curse. It can fill us with ourselves—me-me-me—and therefore cancel out the *imago dei*: the consciousness of the multiplicity of creation that we share with the creator. So here begin all the painful self-contradictions of human history: self-organizing complexity tangling us up in ourselves.

The creation narrative of Genesis itself, that one little chapter, has had an extraordinary and indeed self-contradicting impact on human self-organization. For instance, the same microtext encodes *both* the possibility of gender equity among humans—*and* the exploitation of nonhuman species to the point of extinction:

> Then God said, 'Let us make humankind [adam] in our image, according to our likeness; and let them have dominion over the fish of the sea, and over the birds of the air, and over the cattle, and over all the wild animals of the earth, and over every creeping thing that creeps upon the earth.' So God created humankind in [God's] image . . . ; male and female [God] created them. (1:26-27)

This fleeting reference to "our image," doctrinally known as the *imago dei*, is the single most influential articulation of human identity in the Bible. We who are *adam*—humanity—derived from earth, *adamah*, we are created "in the image" of *Elohim*, earth-and-sky-maker. The human is properly translated: the *earthling*. Humble human humus. But how could the earthling come in the image of something that does not have a body or a sex, something that remains always invisible? The visible "image [*eikon*] of the invisible God"? (Col. 1:15) The incarnation is imagined as the "second Adam," an image of the attempt to correct what would go wrong with the first when it got clogged with its "me-me-me." As to that obstruction, we might consider the difference between a stereotypical male ego and feminine dependency, a separative Adam and a soluble Eve. If the third way is that of a "connective self," it requires the reimagining of our embodied interactivity.[37] The incarnation saves us precisely through our carnality, through the materiality that we share with all creatures, through the sexuality we share with many. *Saving* is the opposite not of *damning* but of *wasting*. The human experiment has long been at risk of wasting itself—a mystery of divine embodiment already working before any concept of "the incarnation" arises—the very materialization of the universe from the deep can be read as the birth of a cosmic body from the womb of the infinite. The universe as the body of God makes our creation in God's image all the more plausible—but no more mysterious. For we cannot discern God apart from the creatures, in whom God is ubiquitously, infinitely present. If, like Job, we may say "now my eye sees you" (42:5)—it may be after the whirlwind has cleared it of our anthropomorphic projections. What we see is: the rest of the creation. For our entire capacity to discern is creaturely. To discern divinity is not to see or hear something separable from the creation—except by theological abstraction.

However, part of our capacity is language. The primary genre of human creativity for the peoples of the book is doubtless language. So for us God's speaking *is* God's creating. *Elohim* creates *us* as an analogy to "themselves." Yes, the word *Elohim* is actually the plural form of *eloh*, God. The notion of *one* God was gradually folding the many gods into itself. But really only gradually. Worried interpreters try to make sense of this "we" as a council of angels, or an anticipation of the Trinity. And then (as though to keep us on this mystery of many in one) a plural grammar is inscribed in the all-important moment of the *imago*: "let *us* make . . ." The royal *we* was not Hebrew usage. This "we" of the creator suggests, as does the Trinity much later, that God is not a *simple* but rather a *multiple* One. Multiplicity is a many folded together as a complexity. The divine multiplicity hints at a complexity in the creator that unfolds into what William James, an ancestor of process theology, called "the pluralistic universe." *Elohim* here still resists "the logic of the One" that will come to dominate more conventionalized monotheism. A tehomic theology of creation celebrates rather than fears the fecund mystery of this multiplicity.

In the image of this divine Many-one, we humans aren't just anyone! Our multiplicity is assured through our sexual difference. The text does not require each human being to procreate. Genesis 1 is no more homophobic than it is tehomophobic. It describes a species that like other animals multiplies sexually. What distinguishes us is not our procreative equipment. It is this: that in the image of the We-God, we are created, male and female, without any difference of power or rank. Again, the chapter seems to counter the misogynist Babylonian epic, in which no such equality is declared. "For feminist readers of scriptures, no more interesting and telegraphic comment exists on the nature of being human and on the nature of God."[38] Try as some do to collapse the first into the second creation story, that of Eden with its troubling view of the woman, the message of Genesis 1 remains unambiguously gender-egalitarian.

Kabash the Earth?

At the same time, the same text seems to telegraph a formidable anti-ecological code. Both genders are granted "dominion" to "fill and subdue" (the Hebrew verb is *kabash!*) the earth. That *dominion* has been read as a warrant for *domination*. It is the prime shibboleth now justifying our exploitation of the earth and its elements. It is the password legitimating our overheating of that upper atmosphere called "the heavens" in Genesis, and our devastation of other species, to the point of not using, but using them *up*—at the rate of whole populations, and possibly dozens, going extinct every day.

Could there be a greater mockery of the narrative of Genesis 1? The rumor that dominion lets us do whatever we please to other earth-creatures conveniently bolsters an economics of unrestrained global growth—the corporatocracy we mentioned in our opening chapter.[39] Here the religious absolute of dominion merges with the secular dissolute of amoral corporate greed. For instance, just as many evangelicals begin to embrace creation-care, the Southern Baptist Convention put out a statement rejecting government-mandated limits on carbon dioxide and other emissions as "very dangerous" because they could lead to government interference in business and "major economic hardships" worldwide.[40] Yet the convention supports precisely the economic policies of predatory global corporations that are causing the major economic hardships. As in the Cornwall Declaration cited earlier, this contradiction shows how religious absolutism fuses with a morally dissolute greed. This anti-environmentalism is particularly histrionic at this moment, as it is attempting to stop the tendency toward a greening of more conservative evangelical Christians.[41]

Could this exploitative, exterminist domination possibly be what the authors of Genesis had in mind?

Well, if not, you may wonder, why "dominion"? Indeed, why the command to "be fruitful, multiply, fill the earth and *kabash* it?" My old teacher John Cobb, a prophet of the Christian ecological movement, smiles when this is put to him. "Yes," he says, "this is the only commandment of the Bible that we have managed to obey!"[42] Certainly the priestly narrator was writing in the context of expansive empires, with their entrenched patterns of domination. Despite some lingering fears of snakes, wolves, and other predators in the countryside, humans were already established as the dominant species. So could the purpose of the text conceivably be to flatter humans for being at the apex of creation and to encourage their destruction of the wild things God just deemed so "good"? Well, respond the anti-environmentalists, only humans are "very good." The answer to that is sorry, that isn't what the Bible says. It says, "God saw everything that he had made, and indeed, it was very good" (1:31). *We humans* are not very good; we are *part of* a very good genesis collective. Indeed, the under-quoted text immediately following the over-quoted declaration of our dominion, announces that we, just like the other animals can have every kind of plant to eat. Our Genesis 1 dominion is strictly vegetarian!

How could dominion in the con/text of Genesis 1 mean anything but *to call this gifted and aggressive earthling to responsibility?* Does not our "right" of dominion mean precisely *responsible care-taking?* But aren't we also invited into creativity, novelty, excess, "life abundant"? Surely. But then wouldn't the life-loving wisdom be calling us to a creativity that must be fundamentally opposed to an amoral, greed-driven, productivity? How can our creativity in the image of God mean anything but an emulation of the cooperative process of creation itself? Would the creative wisdom want us to help save or to help waste the world? In the image of the creator we are invited to a *creative response-ability*—an ability to respond in appreciative relation to the others, human and nonhuman. To respond not just dutifully but resourcefully, in the flow of creativity and in the beauty of grace.

Seascapes of Grace

Much has been lost, inconceivably and irreversibly lost. We grieve our losses so that we ourselves will not get lost. Already in the grieving the generativity of genesis, the flow of becoming, begins. The undertow of *tehom* can be painful. The pull of new beginning may seem to add insult to injury: to rub in our faces not just in dead actualities but the lost possibilities, all that might have been but cannot be.[44] The waters wear a dark face: we are mirrored mysteriously back to ourselves, deformed and aswirl. We are out of our depths. Faith does not mean "you can be anything you want to be." The world is not your oyster. It is your ocean.

> In a droplet—say how can this be?—The whole ocean of God flows into me.
>
> —ANGELUS SILESIUS[43]

Theology is here and there beginning—just beginning—to discern the face of the deep as the edge of our life's chaos. "Recovering the luminous possibilities of seascape, dwelling at the edge of the sea's mysteries—not forgetting its tragic aspects—is one way of experiencing the graced possibilities of sacramental poetics." So theologian and ecological activist Mary Grey reflects on that moment of the Easter Vigil, the moment of the rising sun/son, when the candle symbolizing the resurrection is unsqueamishly plunged into the baptismal font: here the tradition has not lost "the fertile promise of the watery depths of chaos."[45]

Amidst the undulations of uncertainty and the riptides of loss, can we discern the possibility that is *good* for us? So many potentials end up dead in the water. The *creatio ex profundis* may still seem fishy. When the *ex nihilo* loosens its absolute grip, does the dogma of an all-controlling providence also lose its traction? The next chapter will explore the question and the reconstruction of divine power.

If the world is the great ocean, as Ambrose preached it, life remains a creative risk. But we may trust in the divine process. If we unclench the needy greedy ego and let it "let be." In spirit and in truth, it will not do our swimming for us, but may guide us within a depth that even now bears and births us. There is in the process of genesis a generosity that never ceases to offer regeneration.

"And you must be this fish, that the waves of the world do not swallow you."

Ha Shem

. . . .

While creation groans
With constant plea
From bayou to bay
And from bay to the sea
And the winds prophesy
What a meager repentance
Such blasphemous offerings
And what mocking remembrance
Of secret waters
Rippling with mirth
Spirit hovering
Over depths
Meeting earth
Dancing in love
With wind
From above
Panting
Then Pulsing
'Til the first cry
Of birth
Alpha
And
Omega
Thus speaks
Ha-Shem.
—KAREN BAKER-FLETCHER[46]

CHAPTER 4

After Omnipotence
Power as Process

The power of God is the worship he inspires.

—ALFRED NORTH WHITEHEAD[1]

Power Flashes

Flashback 1: Taking a lunch break, I turned on the radio for company. On NPR's *Fresh Air*, Terry Gross was interviewing John Lind, the director of the Presidential Prayer Team, an Internet organization born in response to the collapse of the Twin Towers.[2] Their mandate is to pray for the president—that he may be upheld in wisdom, strength, and guidance under pressure. Sounds like a good idea. Asked if he believes that God chose this president, he hesitates for a moment (the PPT denies that it is partisan). "Yes," he says. President Bush is the right man for the crisis. Pressed, he admits they are also praying for this president's reelection. "What if the other candidate wins?" Gross asks. "Would that also be God's will?" "Yes. God's will is God's will."[3]

Flashback 2: Way back in the twentieth century. I was fourteen. Between classes, I was walking with a much older schoolmate (he may have been almost seventeen!). I was drawn to his gaunt soulfulness. I was trying to interest him in visiting my youth group at the United Methodist Church. I told him that our weekly discussion group is really interesting—that we talk about God and relationships and stuff. (Maybe I had an upcoming hayride in mind.) He interrupted me explosively. "Don't talk to me about God! My little sister died when she was nine. It was horrible. She had leukemia and she suffered on and on. If there is a God, how could he let this happen?" He stomped off, not waiting for an answer I couldn't have had anyway. So much for the hayride.

The Logic of Omnipotence

What do these two theological scenes have in common? Both are responses to catastrophic suffering. But Lind and my old schoolmate espouse strictly opposite views. One is public and unquestioningly theistic; the other is personal, experiential, and atheist. The Presidential Prayer Team reinforces the idea that God is in control: whatever happens is the eternal will of a changeless God. Yet it is all about praying to God to influence things. The second apprehends the contradiction. Disillusioned, it gives up on God altogether. But isn't the God it gives up pretty much the same God to whom the Team prays?

Terry Gross was worried that the Prayer Team represents a growing threat to the separation of church and state. Yet this Internet-based prayer group was not demanding to pray in public schools. I was not worried (in this instance) about the constitutional issues. It was the *theology* that disturbed me. "God's will is God's will"—an indisputable tautology—was supposed to have the self-evident meaning that whatever happens, happens *because* God wills it. *To will*, in this logic, is the same as *to cause*. I was hoping that Terry Gross would ask, "Is God responsible for all election outcomes?" The answer would be *yes*. So, the outcome of the German elections of 1933, as well? The logic is unambiguous: Hitler had to be God's choice. The 9/11 attacks? God's will is God's will. What is surprising is that such theological absolutism inspires political activism at all, given that "He" is both changeless and in total control. Doesn't "He" cause the suffering that we are praying against in the first place?

As to my classmate—he shared this theo-logic, but from the poignant perspective of bitter disappointment. The dissolution of a past faith was still turbulent and in process. His question—How could God?—silenced me then. But it lodged itself in a deep place. Looks like I'm still trying to answer it. I have heard it many times since, as you probably have too, in so many forms. "Why me?" "What did I/she/he do to deserve . . . ?" The chaos of suffering continues to provoke the perfectly lucid question: How can a good God *let* bad things happen? Or, worse, *cause* them?

In the case of the Prayer Team, we may recognize a standard logic of theological absolutism; in the second, a common reason for secular dissolution. But hopefully the reader is now suspicious of such binary oppositions. For it turns out that both partake of the same theo-logic. Both the theist and the atheist assume that God's will explains whatever happens.

What kind of God do both of the above flashbacks exhibit? The answer is simple: in the words of a common liturgy, this is "the Lord of power and might."[4] This God sits enthroned in the theo-logic of omnipotence. It is not a marginal logic among the monotheisms. It comes very close to what many—believers and unbelievers—think "God" means. God's omnipotence is often taken to mean an arbitrary power to do anything.[5] It usually gets softened and evaded by adding some modern feeling of "free will." For of course we presume our freedom in every choice we make, to have milk in my coffee or to argue with this proposition. Indeed, the very activity of prayer presupposes a freedom to relate in new ways to a God who is free to respond in new ways. Normally, of course, Christians don't get a chance to recognize the contradiction between their presumed free will and their belief that whatever happens, happens by the will of God. Often it takes a shattering experience in their lives to raise the question. But the heat of a crisis hardly permits careful reflection.

Cool-headed theologians have framed the problem as one of theo-logic: If God is all-powerful, God could prevent bad things from happening. Is God therefore not good? Or is God not all-powerful? Or is God—*not*? Three questions in one: they add up to the classic problem of *theodicy*, the term coined three centuries ago by a philosopher and mathematician named Gottfried Leibniz: "the justification of God" in response to the charge that the world's evil is incompatible with the existence of a good God.

The syllogism goes thus: *A.* God is omnipotent—nothing happens apart from the will of God. *B.* God is good—and wills only good for every creature. *C.* Evil happens—really bad stuff, without which the creation would be a better place. *D.* Therefore: there is no God.

But of course the questions that lie behind the syllogism do not comprise a mere intellectual exercise, as if the problem of suffering might be solved by a correct belief. In its best-selling articulation in history, the problem emerged from the suffering of another child's unbearable and terminal disease, that of the son of Rabbi Harold Kushner, who then penned *When Bad Things Happen to Good People.* The problem also works in the obverse, as a student in my intro class quipped wickedly: "Why do good

> The word of God continues to be heard. So does the silence of his dead children.
>
> —ELIE WIESEL[6]

things happen to bad people?" The people of Israel verbalized both forms of this searing problem. It inspired the dark poetry of Job and, thousands of years later, the literature of the Holocaust.

In this chapter, under the sign of divine power, we consider the classical theological problem of suffering: How can a God who is all-powerful and all-good let so much unfair suffering happen? We raise the question of theodicy in this chapter with reference to Job's whirlwind vision, Calvin's doctrine of God's omnipotence, and Paul's concept of God's weakness. But what good, folk wonder, would be a God without the power to rescue us? Why pray to a vulnerable, sensitive God who cannot step in and make things right? We raise the question, the questions, of theodicy, not in the heat of trauma but under the shade-tree of reflection. For although theology cannot "solve" the problem of suffering, it might mitigate the suffering by removing another theological log from our eye. Well-meaning theological shibboleths like "God's will is God's will" can—and have—made suffering worse. More than addressing the human causes of suffering, they have tended to blame the victims. They have disempowered the kind of relations that might alleviate suffering, and empowered those that intensify it. So our discernment cannot proceed without putting on trial/in process the theological meaning of power.

> Deep calls to deep at the
> thunder of your cataracts;
> all your waves and your
> billows have gone over me
> —PS. 42:7

Crashing Waves

The waves of creation—always uncertain, always risky—sometimes swell to unbearable violence in our lives. The *tehom* becomes the flood. In this millennium's early experiences of natural disaster (the Southeast Asian tsunami, Hurricane Katrina) the mythic flood has displayed a face of horrifying literalism. Faith gets cast upon the waters of chaos. It may not return. The sense of shock, of disorientation, of disbelief, leads theists spontaneously to ask: Surely God does not *will, does not want,* such tragedy? Or—*why?* Why all these unfathomable horrors? The God who creates and calls all creatures must *somehow* be within those threatening, crashing waves as well. But how?

When we think that for some inscrutable reason God is causing our tragedy, does this alleviate suffering? Perhaps for some it does. If they think God is testing or punishing them, at least there is meaning. But for many every bout of bad luck, every disaster or tragedy gets slicked over with resentment, with an alienated feeling of a cosmic injustice, indeed a divine betrayal. Many people just go numb in the face of this contradiction: they suspect the very God who has caused the tragedy is the one they worship. The one to whom they pray for relief.

In this numbness, grief gets repressed. I remember sitting and choking on my silent fury during the memorial service for a young colleague who had died of early-onset diabetes. What a waste—this was a gifted scholar and teacher, leading amazing educational projects in areas of Newark devastated by poverty. It wasn't God I was furious with—but with the minister offering the memorial sermon in my own seminary chapel. "Our friend has been called home to a happier place," he intoned. "If we have faith we do not grieve." I saw members of the immediate—and grieving—family squirming at these pronouncements. Thus is the grief process stifled in the name of faith. A shibboleth of faith.

This pat repression of sorrow comprises the precise opposite of the beatitude from the Sermon on the Mount: "Blessed are those who mourn, for they will be comforted" (Matt. 5:4). The comfort that is only possible when grief is allowed to flow and so to be shared and to find relief gets violently obstructed by this routine theological gesture. Clergy who are afraid of grief and loss themselves may be most prone to teach this attitude of anti-beatitude. Perhaps their theology keeps these well-meaning Christians trapped in the tangles of theodicy.

The biblical tradition, however, does not teach such frozen fear. Long before the beatitudes, it offers the rich variety of the psalms, poems passionately expressive of grief, of anxiety, of perplexity, even anger—often directed at God. "For you are the God in whom I take refuge; why have you cast me off?" (Ps. 43:2). Better to rage and plead with God openly than to be caught in a piously depressed alienation: then perhaps, in the flow of emotion, which after all is a *motion*, a new perspective can break through. A truth-process can take place. "How long, O LORD? Will you be angry forever?" (Ps. 79:5) is such a common cry. It does presume God's intense causal engagement in our life and history. But it reads that engagement not as one-way causation but as covenantal relationship, in which persuasion may work both ways. "Help us, O God of our salvation . . ." (79:9).

Biblical faith did concentrate immense power in the One God, Lord of Creation. The powers that were previously distributed throughout the multiplicities of divine and natural forces got gradually funneled into the single One of monotheism. Theologians have wanted to find there the doctrine of all-controlling power that formed the basis of their beliefs. Yet there is no formal doctrine of omnipotence in the Bible. Scriptural traditions must be warped into a later abstraction to imply that God is determining whatever happens. Otherwise how could the unique ethical genius of the Hebrew Bible have emerged? You cannot hold yourself accountable as a person or a people for your actions if they are being determined by an all-determining providence.

There are stories of an evolving and complicated relationship with a many-named deity whose effects were not reducible to any abstract propositions about power. Indeed, the very title "The Almighty," the only basis for an ascription of straight omnipotence to the biblical deity, is a mistranslation. As we noted earlier, the name in question is *El Shaddai*—"the Breasted One." Of course, this trace of God as "an infinite Mother" was getting erased by the Hebrews as well, but her memory, with "blessings of the breasts and of the womb," was not quite purged from the canon. [7] The Almighty, however, is a figment of a later doctrinal imagination.

More important to Hebrew sensibility than any divine determinism was the process of divine call and human response-ability. We observed a relationship of asymmetrical and yet reciprocal *trust*worthiness already narrated in the creation from the *tehom*, the infinite deep that calls to our own deepest realities. . . . Nonetheless, the temptation toward a pagan fatalism, a belief that anything that happens is the will of the gods, or of *moira*, fate, or that whatever we suffer is punishment for prior misdeeds, seeps into monotheistic forms. And when the One God seems to be functioning like a merciless, all-determining dictator—there is no way out. And so, within the force field of biblical honesty we witness wave after wave of the crash and crisis of that faith. "My God, my God, why have you forsaken me?" (Ps. 22:1). The paramount case of this despair is attributed as a citation to Jesus on the cross. Centuries before Jesus, however, it is the poet of the book of Job who pushes the power-question all the way to crisis.

Job's Leviathanic Epiphany

He breaks me down on every side, and I am gone,
he has uprooted my hope like a tree. (Job 19:10)

The poet—after citing the old legend of God's wager with his associate, the Satan—has Job asking the great questions of justice and demanding, impossibly, that God answer. "I am not answered; I call aloud, but there is no justice" (Job 19:7). Job's friends, who have sat in mourning with him for a week after the loss of all his children (more empathy than most anyone in our culture would offer a friend) before trying to explain away his outrage, try to convince him that his sufferings are for the good—that either he or his children must have sinned. For "who that was innocent ever perished?" (4:7). Perhaps Job doesn't realize what he did to deserve it. Job's friends sound familiar: we have heard these well-meaning "comforts": it was God's will; God wanted little Suzy for Himself. God doesn't inflict more than you can take. "Know then that God exacts of you less than your guilt deserves" (Job 11:6b). Job retorts: "Miserable comforters are you all / Have windy words no limit? Or what provokes you that you keep on talking?" (16:2b-3).

The drama of Job stages a shocking theological honesty: here is truthfulness deconstructing the shibboleths of belief. Sadly, most Christians never read the book of Job; they just hear the superficial Sunday school story of the Satan's wager with God and Job's final reward for staying faithful. But that is an old folk story adapted by the author of the book as a framing device; it provides the foil for his immense poetic satire, called by some the tragi-comedy of Job.[8] Indeed, the Sunday school Job represents the theology that he is questioning!

In response to Job's poignantly furious, at points comically pathetic, demand that God come and defend himself in writing, God does not offer any self-justifying theodicy. Job does, however, receive an answer. And in what form? The word of God comes in the *whirlwind:* another manifestation of the spirit that we have seen gusting through Genesis and John. The whirling wisdom takes no responsibility for the ills that befell Job. It never acknowledges the omnipotent control, with which Job (assuming like the folk story that God was responsible for his misery) had mounted his case. The very image of the voice from the whirlwind seems to blow away Job's juridical argument that the One in power has done this to him, unfairly. Job presumes belief in a heavenly Sovereignty using the catastrophes of history and nature to punish the wicked.

The divine mystery revealed in the whirlwind, in other words, seems to have nothing to do with the character's anthropomorphic and anthropocentric projections. In the blustering poem of creation, the divine voice claims responsibility for the broad sweep of the universe, the intricate wisdom of the specific astronomy and biology of heaven and earth—but not for any specific events in the lives of people. If the vision unfurls a great blustering amplification of the creation narrative, whirlwinds in meteorology exemplify the fractal amplification of a complex system at the edge of chaos. The whirlwind revelation celebrates the undomesticated creation, the wild things of the universe, from weather patterns to ostrich wings. But how does the creator's delight in the complexity of the nonhuman creation answer the question of unjust human suffering?

Certainly not in any tamely reassuring sense! What provides the grand finale of the divine self-revelation? None other than the great sea monster Leviathan. "I will not keep silence concerning its limbs, or its mighty strength, or its splendid frame . . ." (Job 41:12). And so forth for a full thirty verses of YHWH's unrestrained enthusiasm, indeed, even a bit of tehomic hilarity: "It makes the deep boil like a pot; it makes the sea like a pot of ointment" (41:31). Inspired by this Joban mood to write *Moby Dick*, Hermann Melville comments: "When Leviathan is the text, the case is altered."[9] So to Job's impassioned challenge of God's goodness the answer is: the monster of chaos! What clue does this grandly tehomophilic revelation have to offer a theology in process? Is it trying to tell us something about our losses, our finitudes, our creaturely vulnerability as woven into the inhuman fabric of creation itself?

Is this the truth of the whirlwind: that God, the "spirit of the world-wind," does not will our suffering—but does will a world, a living, whirling, open-system of a world?[10] That world happens to be *this* creation, this real world of finite creatures who live, feed, risk, exult, and die, a world of change and interdependence in which suffering is inevitable. Yet this genesis collective is so intensely alive, even or precisely in its chaos, that new life is also always happening. Therefore, even for one as tragically hurt as Job, new life can take place. This may only be possible because he has refused to suppress piously the turbulent truth of his own experience, but has grieved and raged and confronted the meaning of life. *Ex profundis.*

Calvin's *Decretum Horribile*

Some read the poem very differently. They hear in the Leviathan a final threat to Job, confirming God's omnipotence. See, I, the all-powerful Lord of Creation subdue even the sea monster, so hold your tongue, puny fool. Calvin was one of the latter group of interpreters. He found Job supremely edifying as a testimony to omnipotence. But it turns out that he is uncritically siding with Job's comforters, backing the theology that YHWH in the end disqualifies![11] Let us consider here Calvin's general doctrine of divine power. His lawyerly mind cuts to the heart of the problem. He helps us lay bare the logic of omnipotence.

For him it is the meaning of *divine providence* that is at stake. Imagine, writes Calvin, that "a man falls among thieves, or wild beasts; is shipwrecked at sea by a sudden gale . . ." Imagine that another man, "wandering through the desert finds help in his straits; having been tossed by the waves, reaches harbor; miraculously escapes death by a finger's breadth." Our common sense, what he calls "carnal reason," will ascribe either outcome to "fortune." This is what we call luck, or randomness. And with good reason he finds fortune an inadequate explanation for a Christian. "Anyone who has been taught by Christ's lips that all the hairs of his head are numbered [Matt. 10:30] will look farther afield for a cause, and will consider that all events are governed by God's secret plan."[12]

Calvin will permit no evasion of the full force of this providence. From his point of view much of the Christian tradition was a sloppy mix of explanations: omnipotence mixed with a cupful of randomness, a pint of natural law, and a dash of human freedom. "For he is deemed omnipotent, not because he can indeed act, yet sometimes ceases and sits in idleness, or continues by a general impulse that order of nature which he previously appointed." In other words, God's power is not a matter of sporadic interventions. Nor does it reduce to an initial creation followed by a sustaining natural law. Rather, he says, God is called omnipotent "because, governing heaven and earth by his providence, he *so regulates all things that nothing takes place without his deliberation.*"[13] That is a radical view among Christian options: God is determining everything that happens, including human decisions. Human freedom is a nonstarter for Calvin. He is right about what omnipotence means. With his legal rigor, he blasts away those incoherent and still common compromises that let believers presume divine control on the one hand, and on the other, talk of both chance and choice.

Calvin argues that the Gospel suggests something very different from a universe designed by God and then left to an indifferent randomness. Matthew points to a teaching of God's exquisite interest in each creature—down to the follicles! In context, Calvin is opposing the deism that was growing in popularity among thinkers in the Europe of early modernity. This is the clockmaker God, who produces the machine of the universe, sets it running, and leaves it alone. Calvin protests persuasively that "to make God a momentary Creator, who once for all finished his work, would be cold and barren." He wants us instead to "see the presence of divine power shining as much in the continuing state of the universe as in its inception."

So far he is doing good biblical theology. A theology of becoming also discerns this continuous "shining." It takes the chill off the cosmos. Calvin aptly cites Matthew 10 to argue that "faith ought to penetrate more deeply." God's agency is not exhausted in an initial production of a universe and its laws: but also "sustains, nourishes, and cares for, everything he has made, even to the least sparrow [cf. Matt. 10:29] . . ."[14] Far from indifference, the Gospel suggests a radical and continuing attention to difference. As in the whirlwind vision, creation *matters*—in every material detail—to the creator. And creation matters not as a past event but as a present relationship.

It is at this point, however, just as we are warmed by this all-permeating care, that Calvin's argument shoots into the full logic of omnipotence. From the very same gospel verse, he infers that "every success is God's blessing, and calamity and adversity his curse."[15] This is not a passing hyperbole. "It is certain," he insists, leaving no room for doubt or Jesuitical subtleties, "that *not a drop of rain falls without the express command of God.*"[16] More radically yet: God is the cause of all human actions, the evil ones included. For "men can accomplish nothing except by God's secret command, that they cannot by deliberating accomplish anything except what he has already decreed with himself and determines by his secret direction."[17] Secret, that is, to all but Calvin.

Yet some of us who have "been taught by Christ's lips" find this determinism as "cold and barren" as the deism it opposes. How can we grow and thrive, when our choices are made for us, indeed—chillingly—before we have been created? If Calvin's view were true, notes the theologian John Macquarrie, "it would make utter nonsense of any belief in human responsibility."[18]

What then does the Gospel in question actually offer? Coordinating the two Gospel versions of the sparrow teaching is in this instance key. Matthew's version is open-ended: "Not one sparrow can fall to the ground apart from your Father." Luke's version is more specific as to what this means: "Not even one of them is *forgotten*" (Luke 12:6). If every hair and sparrow is divinely "numbered," this means that every creature *counts*. Everyone matters. God is not apart, God is *with*, God is remembering: so God is said to be knowing, not to be *causing*.

Recall that to be con/scious is to know—*with*. The God of Jesus is *witness and with-ness*, is *with us*, caring intimately about the creation. Calvin's very proof-text for omnipotence fails to deliver it. Rather, the text itself invokes *omnipresence*, and indeed a certain qualified omniscience: a knowing not of the future, but of the present. This biblical "knowledge" does not mean objective cognition but rather a nurture that will liberate us, if we embrace it, from anxiety. We are freed to be as the lilies of the field, the birds of the air, emancipated from the needy greedy ego to be vibrantly present. This divinity is *loving* the creatures, human and nonhuman—not *controlling* us.

For the sake of this love, *we resist the simple identification of any success or any failure with God's providence.* The radiance of divine care for the creation is the gospel criterion for human choices. So if someone is "successfully" perpetrating policies not of care but of careless exploitation—policies not of *care* for the well-being of the birds and all fellow creatures but of *domination*—then this is precisely *not* the will of God. This is the *failure* to do the will of God. And our failure to change those policies is also not the will of God but our own failure.

So this is where the *compelling* logic of Calvinist omnipotence breaks down. For if God is in fact compelling the outcomes of all events—every holocaust included—what kind of care is this? It would signify a control that evacuates all meaning from the term *love*. Indeed, for Calvin most humans are "predestined to eternal damnation" before they are even created; heaven is thus shadowed by an eternal holocaust. A purely Calvinist God does not give a damn (in the original sense) whether I enact care for other creatures or sin against them. These human actions are all God's providence anyway. There follows inexorably the doctrine of "double predestination"—the teaching that Calvin did confess to be a *decretum horribile*—which has the Lord determining before the creation, for all eternity, who will be saved and who will be damned. While most Christians, indeed most Calvinists, would downplay this horror of a preprocessed and closed salvation, it nonetheless registers the impact of absolute power upon the biblical teaching of love.

Once the doctrine of divine all-control is locked in place, both the biblical concepts of divine love and of sin are undermined. Love and responsibility go down the tubes with the elimination of freedom and its open-ended process of interaction.

Sin and Power

Of course, Calvin does not intend to let us off the hook for sin. He thunders on about the "total depravity" of the human will. He means to reinforce a strong concept of "original sin." That concept hearkens to Augustine, who argued a millennium earlier that we are all born into a *massa perdita*, a lump of perdition. Certainly there are biblical indicators of the infection of humanity, indeed of the whole genesis collective, by sin. If one of us sins, sin passes through that one to all of us (Rom. 5:12). "Adam"—"earthling"—and "Eve"—"mother of life"—symbolize that familial relationality of our species. Sin is traditionally defined as separation from God, a delusional condition in which we turn in on ourselves, *curvatus en se*. We may follow Marjorie Suchocki, the process theologian, who argues that the sin

> Sin is not a contained act, but an extended event in an interdependent world. . . . Rebellion against creation constitutes humans as sinners, and even God feels the effects.
>
> —MARJORIE SUCHOCKI[19]

against the creator is that which manifests itself in our violence toward the creation. She is arguing against the focus on sin as a "rebellion against God," which removes our focus from our responsibility to each other.[20] This abstracts our relation to God from our relationships to the community and to the creation. Such abstraction of "sin" into a religious misdemeanor, often sexual in nature, distorts biblical attempts to protect us from each other. By defining sin as "the violence of rebellion against creation," she restores the prophetic emphasis on justice for the widow, the orphan, the stranger, the poor. It is in our delusional separation from each other that our separation from God *matters*—and matters to the God in whose image we share responsibility for each other.

Let me put the problem in a parable: a squabble breaks out in the kindergarten. A bully has hurt a smaller child, and all the *kinder* get into an uproar, throwing things, screaming, kicking, biting. What is the good kindergarten teacher concerned about: the kids hurting *her*?

The answer seems evident. And yet of course if the kids hurt each other, this *also* hurts the teacher. Talk of our relationship with God is empty in abstraction from our relations with each other: love God—and the neighbor *as yourself*. Because we are radically interdependent, we are unbearably vulnerable to each other. We are in each other's power. But power does not mean dominance. Power is manifest concretely in the flow of influence, the flow of me into your experience, of you into mine, by which we consciously and unconsciously affect each other. We may define power as the *energy of influence*: so it can be human or inhuman, benign or destructive. Power is that process whereby causal influence has effect: whereby any being has its effect on another. Within a relationship, the power flow is never altogether unilateral, however asymmetrical it may be. When we misuse the power that flows between us, when in our need and greed we collectively warp the very channels of that energy, the abuse of power becomes a disease that perpetuates itself "unto the seventh generation." Abuse begets abuse. And in this interdependence, power flows into the most intimate and the most public reaches of ourselves.

No part of ourselves remains pure or untouched by the disease that the tradition calls sin. Serene Jones succeeds in defending Calvin's notion of total depravity along these postmodern lines: because we are socially, culturally constructed creatures, no part of us remains unaffected by the collective sins of our species. No essence of us remains pure.[21] The violative influence infects the whole system, interpersonal, intrapersonal, transpersonal. My family's legacy of slaveholding, racism, the sense of entitlement, and the bitterness of its loss, for example, has influenced me, shaped my desires and my habits, before I can have any consciousness of what it is. This is why for the Pauline-Augustinian heritage that the Reformers radicalize, sin was "original," in some sense inherited and collective. Therefore, for Paul the metaphor of the body of Christ, in which we recognize that "we are members of one another," is the antidote for the human disease (Eph. 4:25).

Even *my will to heal my ill will is too ill* to start the healing process, as Augustine argued powerfully. But I am nonetheless *responsible* for my life—and called to become a responsive healer of others. It is at this point that Calvinism itself needs healing. The notion of total human depravity traditionally signals total dependence upon the untender mercies of the all-predestining God, that Sovereign Omnipotence who has already predetermined both our depravity and the names of those who will be saved from it! And so—startlingly—the biblical sense of sin as demanding repentance, reparation, and transformation is gutted by this radicalization of sin. Its emphasis is not to call our species to healing from our habits of violation, but to justify the omnipotent providence of God. Calvin sacrifices human freedom to divine omnipotence. Our capacity to use power well or to abuse it is swallowed by the image of an all-powerful Lord and absolute ruler of the universe: what the philosopher Deleuze, driven by this anti-democratic logic, as so many have been, to atheism, calls "God the fascist."

Calvin does solve the problem of theodicy. God's goodness no longer contradicts God's power.[22] For the goodness has been quietly replaced by the power.

Calvin is right that God is not sitting in a watchtower, impassively awaiting the blowback. God is there, in the midst of every event. But Calvin assumed that to *participate* in an event is to *control* it. Yes, the God of the gospel remembers every sparrow, numbers every hair. But the gospel ceases to be good news if God *wills* my hair to turn grey or my husband's to fall out—and everything else. God may rather be heard calling forth an unfathomably rich universe, full of laws and spaces for self-organizing complex systems. We can imagine this God willing the systems to thrive in such a way as to protect their finite, fleshly freedom. This God would have no use for a pretend universe, full of puppet-creatures; this God calls forth our freedom—and is, in ways that future chapters will discuss, therefore also vulnerable to our decisions, good and evil. For power is an interactive process; influence may be asymmetrical but is always somehow reciprocal. Whatever we become reverberates—in spirit and in truth—in the divine.

Blameworthy or Responsible?

I am arguing that the conventional logic of divine omnipotence offers at best a flawed vision of God's care. It makes God all-powerful by rendering the creature powerless. Thus we are found blameworthy because of Adam's sin, but not responsible. We can do nothing to effect salvation one way or the other. Yet the gospel suggests the opposite: for all the past sin of the world, however much it infects me and sickens my spirit—I am *not to blame, but responsible.* I am not to blame for the sins that precede me "Adamically": the oppressive systems advanced by my forebears, sins in my case of slave holding, of addiction, of wasted gifts and rebellion without a cause. Yet I am responsible to recognize the collective structures of injustice, to recycle my legacy for the better, to resist what *wastes* life and to take part in what *saves.* I am *able* in spirit to *respond.*

Yet Protestantism did not inspire quietism but stimulated immense and ambiguous worldly activity. Calvin and the other Reformers wrote at the dawn of Western modernity. The European will to power was about to be unleashed on the world. Max Weber's famous *Protestant Ethic and the Spirit of Capitalism* tracks the correlation of the explosion of capitalist economic development with the urban centers of Calvinism, especially in the German-, Dutch-, and English-speaking worlds. What a paradox: it is precisely the strong emphasis upon God's unilateral grace that stimulates the Protestant emphasis upon industry and earning.

Reinhold Niebuhr, that faithful Calvinist trained in the seminary where I studied, warned that a corrupt kind of Puritan Calvinism believes that our prosperity is the sign of God's favor. This most public U.S. theologian of the twentieth century warned half a century ago that we must unmask "our pretensions of innocency"—or face the apocalyptic consequences of our own messianic imperialism.[23] He was watching an American Empire arise from the ashes of the British, exercising an unprecedented global economic and military might. So its recent efficacy is not accidentally yoked to a fundamentalist echo of Calvinist theocracy. Far from constraining human power drives, the construct of an all-controlling omnipotence, to the contrary, seems to have fired them up. Powerlessness regarding the matter of salvation seems to have effected voracious worldly power.

Niebuhr took the Calvinist bull by the horns. He embraced the Calvinism that affirms "the grace of divine power, working without immediate regard for the virtues or defects of its recipients (as illustrated by the sun shining 'upon the evil and the good and the rain descending upon the just and the unjust')." And he shows how "any grateful acceptance of God's uncovenanted mercies is easily corrupted from gratitude to self-congratulation" when it "represents particular divine acts directly correlated to particular human and historical situations."[24] When, in other words, it yields to the logic of omnipotence.

Is there now any way—at least for the citizens of the current empire—to claim the "power of God" without gutting the gospel?

Let us return to the initial statement of the problem of theodicy. If God is *good* in any moral sense of the word; and if God is literally all-controlling; and there is real evil in the world: it follows that this God doesn't exist.

When Christianity quietly gives up on the *goodness* of God, it gains a forceful consistency, as exemplified by a religious right mobilized around such non-gospel themes as homosexuality and abortion. In the meantime, democratically minded people continue to give up on "God." And the muddling Christian middle remains adrift in the contradiction, unable to provide effective alternatives. Most theists don't actually believe in an absolute omnipotence. They presume some back-and-forth of genuine relationship with God. Yet without a serious theological alternative, they fancy that their relationship is with an all-powerful God, who *could* but usually does *not* step in to prevent even the most ungodly evils. To cover the illogic, they appeal to mystery. Okay. But I'm just saying that mystery needs to start sooner: in the presumption of the defining attributes (like omnipotence).

What if we let go of the specter of an all-controlling omnipotence? What if we *lose* God the emperor, puppeteer, micromanager, dictator, or father-knows-best? We may then be left with a goodness that corresponds to our best hopes, to our desire for justice and the renewal of all creaturely life—but with no guarantee that these dreams will be realized. What *good* is this God? Are we left with a cosmic care that enjoys our joys and suffers with our grief—but cannot rescue us from it? Is a weak God any more resonant with biblical discernment than an omnipotent one?

Perhaps the very opposition of "power" and "weakness" is misleading. Impotence is not the only alternative to a Calvinist omnipotence. A theology of becoming discerns its third way in the wisdom of open ends. Amidst indeterminacy and its complex determinations, the *sophia* of an alternative power slowly comes into our con/sciousness.

Thorny Confession

Toward the end of his correspondence with the community in Corinth, Paul makes a risky confession. He notes that the revelations he has received are of such "exceptional character" that even if he wished to boast, he would be "speaking the truth." (A proud humility, that . . .) Therefore, he says, "to keep me from being too elated, a thorn was given me in the flesh" (2 Cor. 12:7). He doesn't reveal, however, just what this ego-deflating "thorn" might be. He has prayed repeatedly, he says, that this "messenger of Satan" be taken away. One thinks of how some Christians today pray in torment that their homosexual impulses be removed. Into the nature of this suggestively shaped "thorn" we need not pry. The answer that finally comes to him refuses any "fix." And it offers an important clue for any theology in process.

> But the divinity of the truly divine God is to be displayed neither in a display of magic by Jesus or his heavenly Father, nor in the secret hope that the Father is going to square the accounts for him in an afterlife and give these Roman soldiers their comeuppance in the world to come. The divinity is rather that his very death and humiliation rise up in protest against the world, rise up above power . . .
>
> —JOHN D. CAPUTO[25]

What he heard "the Lord" say to him is this: "My grace is sufficient for you, for power is made perfect in weakness" (12:9). Some versions read just "for my power is made perfect in weakness." So, says Paul, "I will boast all the more gladly of my weaknesses, so that the power of Christ may dwell in me." This is an extraordinary correlation of his own fleshly weakness with a divine weakness. Yet this weakness does not signify the opposite of strength: to the contrary, the divine voice suggests that a power which is divine gets "made perfect," brought to fruition, to realization, *through* this weakness. A deconstruction of the standard model of power seems to be in process here. "The perverse core of Christianity," writes John Caputo approvingly, "lies in being a weak force."[26]

To make sense of this nearly unspeakable intuition of divine vulnerability, Paul moves right to the cross: "For he was crucified in weakness, but lives by the power of God" (2 Cor. 13:4a). This is a terribly difficult association Paul is attempting: of his own challenging flesh with Jesus' crucified flesh. And the point would be that the vulnerability of the flesh—whether to an unwanted temptation or to an agonizing death—cannot be wished away. But an honest embrace of our vulnerabilities may turn them into sources of empowerment. For those weaknesses seem to lie close to our strengths: our disorganization lies close to our creativity, for example, or our insensitivity close to our decisiveness. If the honest struggle with oneself that Paul recommends is engaged, the weakness that shames us can become a laboratory in a new kind of power. Our worst vulnerability can become, rather than a site of personal dissolution, the opening into an illimitable interactivity.

If the message of divine vulnerability shatters the idol of absolute and impassive control, it does not idealize weakness and passivity. To do so would merely entrap us in patterns of unjust suffering. "Predicating suffering of God in such a way that suffering becomes a value in itself, or that God becomes essentially weak or powerless, and then holding up this model for emulation," warns Elizabeth Johnson, "is a trap that ensnares women's struggle for equality and full humanity . . ."[27] We noticed this in Rebecca Parker's story of the abusive Christology in chapter 1. I would argue that it equally ensnares men's struggle for a full humanity—which requires vulnerability to their own sometimes masked interdependence.

A "power made perfect in weakness" is neither omnipotence nor impotence. Paul is straining to give voice to a new idea of incarnational vulnerability: the idea of a God who participates in human flesh, and therefore in all of our human sensitivity and pain. And the point is not that God is *causing* or even willing the pain. In the Nazi prison cell, Dietrich Bonhoeffer was approaching this insight when he wrote also of the weakness of the God manifest in the crucified Christ, "God at the mercy of the world."[28] Even under the most horrific circumstances, where our vulnerability becomes the site of our torment, it may not be impossible to experience the love that empowers, the life that resurrects. The teaching of nonviolence as a mode of courageous confrontation—never seeking martyrdom but sometimes risking it—as iconically exemplified in Mahatma Gandhi, Martin Luther King Jr.,[29] and Oscar Romero—suggests the political potential of this power of vulnerability, when organized. The power made perfect in weakness may belong to a congregation that loses members because of a courageous stance. The open-ended interactivity of power means that change happens at the edge of chaos. Hope takes its next step, even if a very small one—a tipping point of spirit. This is a power that does not overpower but empowers.

Double Crossed

Of course, any theology of the cross may conjure the specter of a Father who wills the torture and death of his Son; whose appetite for "justice" can only be sated by blood.[31] Then once again the will of the emperor and his executioners is mistaken for the will of God. Such theology itself shrugs like Pilate. It can misread Paul's "power perfected in weakness" to mean that our weakness and Jesus' crucifixion merely demonstrate our total dependence on God's lordly power. Christians have been taught to imagine that Jesus is choosing to die, thinks that God wills his death; or that Jesus in some simple way "is" God on the cross, just going through the motions of suffering, essentially above it all. We confuse the crown of thorns for the imperial crown of domination. The power made perfect in weakness becomes a power merely disguised as weakness. Christendom has dangerously and repeatedly crossed the power lines of divinity with those of domination. And so we get terribly tangled up in these live wires. For domination is at shocking cross-purposes with the gospel itself.

> Sophia-God is in solidarity with those who suffer as a mystery of empowerment. With moral indignation, concern for broken creation, and a sympathy calling for justice, the power of God's compassionate love enters the pain of the world to transform it from within.
>
> —ELIZABETH JOHNSON[30]

Concerning the conversion of the Roman Empire to Christianity, Alfred North Whitehead wrote of "the deeper idolatry," an idolatry exceeding that of pagan polytheism. By this he meant "the fashioning of God in the image of the Egyptian, Persian, and Roman imperial rulers." Pointing out one effect of this idolatry, he said that the resulting doctrine of "a transcendent creator, at whose fiat the world came into being, and whose imposed will it obeys, is the fallacy which has infused tragedy into the histories of Christianity and of [Islam]." Then comes a great moment of Western self-recognition: "The church gave unto God the attributes that belonged exclusively to Caesar."[32] The cross is still brandished as a sword; the double-crossing of the gospel continues.

God is there with Jesus on the cross. Sure. Not as the one who wills the atrocity as a means to the good. But otherwise: as the one who is indeed *in* Jesus, suffering what he suffers. Feeling the full horror of the human condition, feeling its helplessness before its own apparatus of violence. Feeling our immense sensitivity, intelligence, and hope, reduced to this evil. And yet feeling—nonetheless—love for humanity. And this God will lure good from the evil whenever possible. What makes it possible may be precisely the prayerful attunement of our will to the divine will.

So a theology of becoming discerns the weakness of Jesus on the cross in the light of Jesus' prayer in Gethsemane: "Remove this cup from me." He *really* did not want to die. He *still, painfully,* hoped some other outcome, some other way, might be possible. "But your will be done" does *not* need to mean: if you want me to die, Lord, so be it. Have at me. We may instead read it thus: "Not my will but yours be done," no matter what happens (Luke 22:42). If there is no good way out of this impending horror, let me live it in love. If our hiding place has been betrayed, if I cannot escape this time without betraying the movement, then let my suffering not be in vain. Let me somehow realize your will—right through my dying and my death. Let good be made of this evil.

By twisting the cross itself into a symbol of victory, we short-circuit the symbol of the resurrection. For then we also deny death; we repress our horror at the injustice that renders finitude unbearable; and so we obstruct the Good Friday, the good grief, by which release comes. And so we are left with the omnipotence that eclipses the revelation of the empowering power. But only in the stretch of love beyond what seems humanly possible—the realization of power in weakness—can the cross yield to resurrection. In the crossover between life and death a way of new life might open. This is not an idealization of weakness. It is a revelation of a strength operating *within* weakness, *within* vulnerability. We glimpse a passion that cannot be killed: "love is strong as death" (Song of Songs 8:6). We cannot lose death, but we might lose its sting.

God of Letting Be

We have barely begun to answer our opening question. What is the good of a vulnerable God? Of a God who cannot do our bidding? Of the one Jürgen Moltmann calls "the Crucified God"? Of a God who calls forth a universe of irrevocable open-endedness, indeterminacy, and freedom? And then experiences it all—*Emmanuel*—with us? The ancient voices of Job and Paul provide clues, hints, revelations at the edge of their own bubbling abyss. On the mystery.

The possible truth of the third way, the way of becoming in relation, depends on an alternative theo-logic: the "power perfected in weakness" may not be "weak" at all. Or, more precisely, it is weak by the standards of external force—either of amoral nature or of immoral empire. Then we would no more imagine a God "in control" than a universe "out of control." We worship neither an invulnerable power nor a powerless vulnerability. God's will need no longer be confused with—whatever happens. Most of what happens happens through the complex combinations of indeterminacy, chance, natural law, and human freedom that comprise life on the earth. To discern the divine influence within that complexity of influences is the work of the next chapter. Suffice it for now to say that the open-ended interactivity would be protected by a loving deity, in the way that a parent protects a child's freedom.

A friend describes a process she learned as a mother. "I never did try to control my kids, there were too many of them to do that. I had three children in two years, and it became very clear early on (such as day one), that control was not possible. Instead of getting in their way and trying to run their play, I had to arrive at some other mode of being with them as they are." So she invited friends over for them to play with, and the chaos mounted. But this is what she observed: "If I were willing and able to let the four or five very young children jostle, mess around, explore for about forty-five minutes—with the ground rules of not hurting each other or the home—if I just let them go through whatever procedures they needed to go through, they would come up with something that they loved to do together. They would arrive at some game, project, make-believe . . . that would keep them positively, joyfully engaged for up to three hours. All of them."[33] She could even rely on some time for her own reading.

This is a humble parable of creation from chaos. It illustrates uncontrolling love. Parents and all who relate in love have to *let be*. So do good teachers, pastors, and leaders. As *Elohim* "let be" the light? Macquarrie defines "letting be" as something much more positive than just leaving alone: "as enabling to be, empowering to be, or bringing into being."[34] Thus our experience of "letting-be" may serve as an analogy of "the ultimate letting-be." Love does not control. It opens a space of becoming. The space is not without protective boundaries, not without rules. The healthy parent is not merely permissive, but constantly teaching ideals of fairness, cooperation, and creative development. This space comprises neither rampant disorder nor imposed order. It opens at the edge of chaos, without plunging into the abyss. It supports the free play of relations—and satisfies desires of both parent and children. This uncontrolling care empowers the children to construct their own "complex self-organizing system." At least temporarily!

If we may push our parable a bit further, the desired interplay is not about a private "me and my God" relation but a love opened out into a fuller sociality. "Two or more gathered in my name." In the communality of genesis things are risky, noisy, messy. But fresh order continues to emerge from the chaos. And while its equilibria do not last forever—"love never ends" (1 Cor. 13:8).

If I have mainly argued what God *is not*, or *does not*, this is the mark of negative theology: it pushes open dis/closive freedom from theological control by such notions as omnipotence. Yet such metaphors as the good mother make affirmative, if nonliteral, claims. We have had so much idealization of a bad parenting model (that of a stern father more concerned with his authoritative order than with the children's development) that alternative parental metaphors need to come into play. But the analogy of parental love for God remains problematic.

It imports an anthropomorphic and infantilizing image, in which dominance is barely withheld. Mommy can fortunately always step in and keep Bobby from hitting Mary again.

God, it would seem, does not. Does that mean that God *cannot*? Does God just *choose* not to interfere with our freedom? The so-called free-will defense of God's goodness and omnipotence tries that middle road: God permits, but does not cause, evil, and so leaves us our freedom. This is close to the chilly deism Calvin railed against. But usually those who hold this reasonable view also hold out for occasional special or miraculous interventions on God's part. But then: Why didn't God manipulate the vote just a bit so that Hitler would lose the election? Or, for that matter, heal my friend's little sister's leukemia? Or excise that bad gene in the first place? Or all bad genes?

The free-will defense only works if held consistently. But that is hard to do. To say that God "permits" evil for the sake of our freedom implies that God *could* step in at any time, and as far as history demonstrates, just chooses not to. Accordingly, God protects human freedom (for the sake of the moral good that is possible only in voluntary relationships), but could and does occasionally intervene. Then why must so many billions of lives be sacrificed without having any experience of that good? While this free-will theodicy makes sympathetic moves, I think it is still too anthropomorphic a notion of God's own freedom: as though God considers a choice between micromanaging the world and designing a more autonomous universe. And then chooses occasionally to intervene even if s/he chooses the latter.

If it is a divine choice not to control, a choice to *let be*, then perhaps we need to understand this choice as the very meaning of what we call "God": the letting-be at the heart of the universe. Or starting up a universe, as Genesis 1 poetically captures it. And this divine freedom to create depends upon the responsive freedom of the creatures, the lapping and overlapping of influences flowing upon the face of the deep.

The alternative to omnipotence lies in the risky interactivity of relationship. It does not toss the creatures into a deistic void, chilled but autonomous. It continues to call them forth, to invite. In the language of process theology, it "lures" them collectively and individually toward self-actualization. The power of God, if it is a response-able power, *empowers* the others—to respond. In their freedom. God's will is indeed God's will! But the term *will* derives from *voluntas*, from which also comes "voluntary," which means not control but *desire*. What God *wants*. That wanting, that desiring, has a decisive element, limiting in advance what is possible for this universe. And within those limits Torah, covenant, and the whole apparatus of redemption suggest that God's will seeks to *be done.* On earth. But *to want* is not the same as *to cause.* "Your will be done" is nothing we would have any reason to say, if we were just telling an omnipotent God to please go ahead and do whatever you intend to do anyway. We are praying that we may satisfy rather than obstruct the divine desire for abundant life.

In what sense then is the divine process *powerful?* It can perhaps even be called all-powerful, if that language for the biblical God seems indispensable to some, in this sense: God has "all the power" that a good God, a God who fosters and delights in the goodness of the creation, could have or *want* to have. But the point is that this is not the unilateral power to command things to happen out of nothing and then to control them under threat of nothingness. It is another kind of power altogether, a *qualitatively different power*—a power that seems weak when dominance is the ideal. The metaphor of "power perfected in weakness" tried to make comprehensible the difficult alternative to coercive force: the contagious influence that flows from a radically vulnerable strength. Two thousand years later, we have made limited collective progress in its realization. Perhaps experiments in social democracy, in which persuasion is favored over coercion, and care valued as a supreme public strength, hint at the alternative. Perhaps experiments in gender equality and nonviolent parenting are also advancing, here and there, our metaphoric reservoir.

God the Spirit in whom her children grow in wisdom. God the Wisdom who lets-be her children, in whom she delights. God the Word of testimony, witnessing in utter weakness to a truth whose power will flow through centuries of influence. God the voice of the Whirlwind, who—having absorbed our rage, our disappointment, our grief—blows away our theodicidal projections and opens our eyes anew. We glimpse the radiant beauty of the creation in which we are called to be most dignified, most beloved participants.

The One who calls forth good even from the ashes of evil, a good that requires—indeed commands—but cannot coerce our cooperation. A power that *makes possible* our response. "Only this God is the God of love, for love is precisely his self-giving and letting be." Such a God pours forth into creation in a self-giving that risks itself: "the more love (letting-be) exposes itself in risk, the more it accomplishes in conferring being . . ."[35]

To break open the false logic of theodicy we would not surrender to the absolutism of loveless power; we would not dissolve into the relativisms of impotent love. What would be the third way? If love and power do not contradict each other in the divine nature, we have the clue we need. On the mystery, the alternative power would be precisely the power of love.

CHAPTER 5

Risk the Adventure
Passion in Process

My distress is great and unknown to men.
They are cruel to me, for they wish to dissuade me
From all that the forces of Love urge me to.
They do not understand it, and I cannot explain it to them.
I must then live out what I am;
What Love counsels my spirit,
In this is my being: for this reason I will do my best.

—HADEWIJCH[1]

The previous chapter suggested that the theological alternative to the standard version of divine omnipotence is the power of love. But then what do we do with the saccharine sentimentality and the passionate destructiveness of love? What strength can we find in such an over-processed notion? How can a Hallmarked and Hollywooden culture yield any honest theological metaphor of love? How should the power of love, even Love Supreme (to cite Coltrane), resist the forces of destruction, empower the powerless, and embolden the meek?

Anyway, when I think of "love" an intimate collage of disparate images flicker across my psychic screen. The ghosts of young passions blow by, wasteful intensities mixed with sweet affirmations, my own greedy-needy ego too fragile and too forceful, hurting me and others. Then I think of those who reached into the turbulence of that evolving "me" to touch something spirited, something loveable. There was the elder peace leader at a camp, finding me at fourteen weeping, feeling rejected by my peers as too intense, serious, "heavy." He said with a divine grin: "Anyone who thinks you are heavy, honey, is a lightweight." And my trust in the gifts of older love still grows, grateful for an evolving capacity that is never mine in isolation, at once the most transient and the most sustaining of forces . . .

I may "do my best." But I wouldn't recognize the divinity within the love-process on my own. For the metaphoric depth of this Love, we reach deep beneath our present tense.

Indeed, we might temporarily slip out of our epoch altogether, back to an intriguing theological teacher from the early thirteenth century named Hadewijch. Our wayward journey loops frequently into the diverse pasts of Christianity. In the medieval mysticism of love, women first come to voice theologically. And we find in this particular voice a startling poetic freshness—and an antecedent for the amorous vision of process theology to be unfolded later in this chapter.

Hadewijch was a visionary and poet among the Flemish Beguines, the medieval movement of women who formed ascetic communities while refusing the veil, seclusion, and ecclesial supervision. Her Love was no sappy sentimentality, no tender illusion: "love comes and consoles us; she goes away and knocks us down. This initiates our adventure."[2] Her poems passionately, relentlessly, pursue the joys and the griefs of this love.

"All that the forces of Love urge me to." What are these forces that *do not force but urge*—so *urgently* that this gifted mystic took great risks in relation to the church patriarchs of her age? What is this "counsel" in which she finds her "being," her sense of spirit and self? "Love," the counselor in this poem, is her favorite name for God. She used the grammatically feminine term *Minne*, which had the courtly associations in Flemish of a new culture of respect for women.[3] Feminism was, of course, no possibility in this context; yet when she reinforces that metaphoric femininity with a wide range of female personifications, we cannot help but notice the adventure of her very language. For a woman of her time, the very use of this passionate language, expressive of such an unstereotypically female strength of self, already poses a dare to any theological absolutism.

Whoever, she writes, "dares the wilderness of Love / Shall understand Love: / Her coming, her going." This Love quickly shatters any idols of popular romance or pious sentimentality. It, or she, can seem elusive, withdrawn, even cruel at times, making us "stray in a wild desert." And so Hadewijch counsels courage: "*O soul, creature, And noble image, Risk the adventure!*"[4] This may be an unprecedented moment in theology: in the name of our humanity in the image of God, we are empowered not to lord it over others, nor to settle into a serene and dispassionate piety, but to risk an adventure? To go off on an uncertain journey? To take untoward chances? She seems quietly to have reclaimed the ennobling egalitarianism of Genesis 1:28, as we discussed it in chapter 3. But beyond a transgressive femininity, she recoups from the doctrine of creation the profound and turbulent *creativity* so often lost in Christian translation. If we are created in the image of one who creates amorously, and not without chaos, she intuits the passion that makes us human.

In the name of this *imago dei* and in the spirit of this adventure, the same poem urges us to persist—"ever keep on to the end / In love." Between the dissolute and the absolute, the resolute appears once again at the edge. This resolve expresses a daring suggestive of the very etymology of "courage," from the French *coeur*, "heart." The connection of courage and love has been dimmed: but we still use the locution "take heart." It is not just that loving always has an element of risk, but that the courage to take a risk takes heart: it presumes a love, a passion. Only in Love, Hadewijch implies, do we actualize our potentiality as humans: only in the wilds of Love do we truly come *to be*. Does it "let be" in the active sense of the creative process we have been examining in our reconstructions of creation and of divine power? Does it suggest a third way for love itself: neither the eros rendered dissolute by loveless sexual conquests, nor the moralistic "love" that knows no holy eros?

Intriguingly, in none of her theopoetic writings does the Beguine oppose her Love to any other kind of love. She draws no prim boundaries between the Love that is divine, indeed that is God, and the lower loves that urge, shake, and devastate us. It is Love itself, somehow there calling to us in and through all of our loving; in and through the hope, heartbreak, and high-risk vulnerability of human openness. To persist in Love is to learn that it can never be restricted to a relationship between two humans—though it may tarry there. For Hadewijch this Love is fully divine and fully human. Yet she writes as a poet and not as a scholastic; she does not offer dogmatic definitions. Anyone who has loved anyone passionately could be lured into her poetry. This is not a faith of formulae but of adventurous becoming.

"O powerful, wonderful Love, You who can conquer all with wonder!"[5] In this atmosphere, which will be intensified through a brief reading of the biblical prototype of love mysticism, the Song of Songs, we will consider what a theology in process means by "divine power" when love is taken as the Christian priority. Yet the love at stake displays a surprisingly sharp, even political edge. Under the sign of love transliterated as passion, we will also undertake a more explicit consideration of process theology. What John Cobb calls the "creative love of God," developing Whitehead's concept of "the divine lure," will allow us to articulate the interplay of creaturely and divine passions, and to begin to ensconce both theologically in a larger divine adventure of becoming.

In Control or In Love?

Love in theology names at once a *relationship* to the divine, and the divine itself. Love reveals the personal face and force of God. So the question still presses: if power means the exercise of influence, what kind of power is poetically encrypted in "the forces of love"? Love will always seem to weaken any doctrine of divine *power*—as long as the standard is *control.* As we analyzed it in the last chapter, a tyrant's power then appears as vastly and unquestionably greater than that of a loving partner or parent.

So then which would be the more suitable symbolism for divine power? The Bible as a whole offers no easy answer. Blustering images of dominion and lyrical invocations of love mix confusingly together in both Testaments. But it isn't a matter of dumping the metaphors of divine power. It is a matter of theological priority. So we may further ask: Is love to be measured by power? Or is power to be measured by love?

When it comes to the gospel standard, the answer is unambiguous. The New Testament never says, "God is power." It does say, "God is love" (1 John 4:8). Therefore the power Christians attribute to God must meet the standard of love—even the high standard of what we call "Christian love." Not vice versa. If divine power is in process, love itself puts power—and all images of power—on trial. It is not that power needs love to balance it out, that the stern lordly power of divine domination is softened and complemented by the gospel of love. It would rather be that love *is* the power, the energy, the style of influence, of God. But this strong claim can be quickly deformed to mean: whatever God does to us is for our own good, like the punishments of a stern but loving Father. And then we are back to where we started. We are back to defining love in terms of power, not power in terms of love. When power is the priority, love remains icing on the cake: God may sternly cause tsunamis with one hand and then tenderly comfort the survivors with the other.

Unlike the insurance companies, a theology in process does not read earthquakes and hurricanes as "acts of God." They would be side effects of the complex self-organizing systems of the creation that God has—in the immense and risky adventure of the universe—lured forth. A God who is infinite, who is everywhere, even in the underworld of *sheol*, according to the psalmist, is also present *in* the tsunami. But as I hope the previous chapter made clear, contra Calvin, *being within* an event is not the same as *causing* it. God's will cannot be read off the surface of events. The divine love-force can be discerned in the continuing capacity of the earth—tectonic plates and all—to nurture life as it spins gracefully in its orbit: "the Love that moves the sun and the other stars."[6] In a very different way, it can be discerned in the post-disaster moments of human care for strangers. But God is no more forcing us to care than the earth to turn or to shake.

Enemy Love: Not for Wimps

When it comes to theologizing the power of love, we face not just the problem of omnipotence vis-à-vis power, but the problem of sentimentality vis-à-vis love. Christian love may conjure a Victorian Jesus of flowing auburn locks and moist eyes, turning a cheek in a manner suggestive not of daring but of victimization. It seems to dissociate God from the nonhuman universe, from the wilderness patches, the *tohuvabohu* and *leviathan* of things. The unflinching Calvinist omnipotence, with its tyrannical Lord causing everything that happens, may provide a kind of dark counterpoint. But these images of impotence and omnipotence are complementary, held together in a certain scenario of the dispassionate Father who sends the Son to his death for our sake. The causal omnipotence has not been effectively mitigated by the standard version of Christ's passion.

The "forces of Love" suggest another path, no less Christian, for theology. They imply neither omnipotence nor impotence. They are forceful but do not directly "cause" this or that disaster or rescue from disaster. Hadewijch anticipates process theology when she hints at a force that "urges" and "counsels." Its power of attraction will help us to articulate the alternative force. It "has *swayed everything that lives*."[7] This language anticipates the "divine lure" we will consider shortly. Indeed, it is suggestive in its passion not just of the Christ-like suffering, but also of the desirous force of eros. And indeed, Whitehead reintroduced in the twentieth century the metaphor of the divine Eros.

Hadewijch's love mysticism is alluring because it invokes that flooding, fiery force of nature that we can indeed link with erotic love: It is infinite in its intimacies, embracing the full range of embodied experiences and sensitive feelings. But we misunderstand the mystical eros if we decouple it from the austere ethics of the gospel. And by the same token, we may be misunderstanding Christian love when we split it from its elemental passion!

For what is more elemental than the foremost gospel icon of divine love: to practice love in the image of God, we are told, is to stream like the sun and the rain, to shine, to flow, out into the other. Though this is the great gospel proposition of love of the enemy, there is nothing self-victimizing or masochistic in its solar radiance, its fertile downpour. "But I say to you, Love your enemies and pray for those who persecute you, so that you may be children of your Father in heaven; for he makes his sun rise on the evil and on the good, and sends rain on the righteous and on the unrighteous" (Matt. 5:44-45). We saw it cited by Niebuhr to emphasize the best in Calvinism. It does not convey powerlessness, and certainly not control, but a certain kind of power nonetheless. The double image of elemental flow is not accidentally invoked. It indeed evokes an elemental in/fluence, an influx and permeation.

> To be an Afro-American, or an American black, is to be in the situation, intolerably exaggerated, of all those who have ever found themselves part of a civilization which they could in no wise honorably defend—which they were compelled, indeed, endlessly to attack and condemn—and who yet spoke out of the most passionate love, hoping to make the kingdom new, to make it honorable and worthy of life.
>
> —JAMES BALDWIN[8]

Such outflow in love is risky. We flow into the unknown, the unpredictable. For at some level we remain opaque to each other, strange even in our intimacies. Sometimes enmity charges that opacity with danger. So love of the enemy—the test case of Christian love—takes courage, not hatred. In the mood of Hadewijch we recognize that the gospel advocates no domesticated virtue but an elemental streaming, an amorous adventure.

That adventure lies upon the same erotic spectrum as James Baldwin's angry passion. To "love" a civilization shaped by white racism as a strategy of hope, "to make the kingdom new, to make it honorable and worthy of life"—does this, rather than some dishonorable surrender to the intolerable, not illustrate what Jesus had in mind with love of the enemy? This hope echoes the good but bracing news of the *basileia*, the "kingdom of God," that will occupy our next chapters.

The gospel invites us to risk our best possible response to the irritating neighbor, the scary stranger, the random fellow creature, the immoral society—regardless of whether or when those others will give back. The metaphor of streaming love makes it possible for us to relate to the unknowable deep of reality. Its infinite, impersonal mystery gets personal. In spirit and in truth: we find ourselves permeated by love. We may realize that we are *in* Love. Or is Love in us—inviting, drawing, desiring?

Sin and Love

We do not readily sustain the passion of love's larger challenge. No wonder. It always wants too much from us. Ultimately, perhaps nothing less than the delicate, long-term work of reorganizing our planet for a more sustainable adventure in human becoming: "to make the kingdom new." We gifted souls seem, on the whole, more or less numb to the urge, unswayed by the counsel. The space of dis/closure shuts down so quickly. Possibilities that had seemed so very tangible, that were beginning to be actualized, suddenly become impossible: intimacy between lovers, joy within a family, esteem between friends, respect between competitors, justice between peoples, balance between species. We routinely betray that larger love—in the name of all manner of needy greedy desires. What violations are not performed in the name of "love"? "Love complains of this to loftiest Fidelity, / and Fidelity must look down on us with love."[9] Even our abuses of love do not make us unloveable.

The problem referred to in archaic language as the "hardness of the heart" suggests a numbness that comes from too much privilege, too much violence, or just too much habit. It dissociates from the complex multiplicity of its interdependence. How can such a heart feel the lure? This heart may satisfy its craving for adventure through cruelty, even terror—in a movie or a war—to feel fully alive. The good news of an amorous gospel will, to the hardened heart, seem boring, unless maybe it comes drenched in the bloody special effects of Mel Gibson's *The Passion of the Christ* or the apocalyptic massacres of *Left Behind*.[10]

Among the more sensitive, the resistance is not hardness but, to the contrary, fragility, a sense of woundedness that just as surely shuts down the soulful adventure. It blocks the relational process. In Korea this suffering is called *han*, a notion that has entered the vocabulary of global Christianity.[11] Both the numbed dissociation and the wounded vulnerability cause blockage. And we tend to pass that unhealed *han* on to others. The violated may come to violate.

From a theological perspective we call this violence *sin*, because it is never just between humans—as conversely, love is never just between us either. The attitude toward our fellow creatures is the test and trial of our attitude toward the source of all creatures. For the *han*/sin pattern begins to imprint us individually and collectively from the earliest beginnings of our lives. It comes mixed in with the care that lets us live. If we are formed and deformed "originally," "Adamically," preconsciously, its stereotyped habits of violation, its loveless cycles of heterosexism, racism, and greed remain tediously unoriginal. Our very relationships damage our capacity to relate. The power that rolls forth from the past, the power of the creation, exercises devastatingly ambiguous influence.

Yet here is a hopeful fact: while most who abuse, have been abused, most of those who have been abused do not go on to abuse. We are not powerless to change, nor unable to respond. "I must then live out what I am." Love, writes Hadewijch, never ceases to counsel "my spirit."[12] But beyond responsibility, she was an ecstatic who threw her life into the God-relation. In an ever more distracted, drugged, digitalized, overfed, and info-tained culture, how can the amorous invitations even register?

We return to the nagging question, then: What kind of counterinfluence, beyond our own deformed patterns, is operative? What kind of "power" or efficacy does the divine have in the world? What sort of synergy does it require? How could it reopen systems closed in on themselves, cycling in delusional absolutes and addictive dissolutes? For as we have seen, absolute power, all the more frightening when given religious sanction, fuses in a kind of codependency with an indifferent relativism. How can the power of love displace the love of power?

It is in attempting to answer these questions with both honesty and faithfulness that the tradition of process theology becomes indispensable. It is admittedly odd to let a theology based in a very rational philosophy, indeed one of the primary models for the dialogue between religion and science, regroup under the banner of Passion. But perhaps more systematically than any other theology, it has deconstructed the classical tradition of an omnipotent, impassive God, an unmoved mover who causes suffering but does not suffer, who gives joy but does not enjoy. It recognizes that Western culture has made itself in the image of an idol of power. And it sets forth its construction of an alternative divine power, vastly subtler than the projections of royal force onto the heavens: that of the divine Eros.

God in Process: Lure and Response

Process theology speaks of two aspects of divine activity in the world: the "creative love of God" and the "responsive love of God."[13] In this chapter we are focusing on the first. We might also call this creative love *desire*, or the divine *passion*. Alfred North Whitehead had called it "the Eros of the Universe." He had in mind a cosmic appetite for becoming, for beauty and intensity of experience. The divine Eros is felt in each creature as the "initial aim"—or the "lure." It is a lure to our own becoming, a call to actualize the possibilities for greater beauty and intensity in our own lives. The responsive love, by contrast, can be called the *divine Agape*. The Eros *attracts, it calls*: it is the *invitation*. The Agape *responds* to whatever we have become; in com/passion it feels our feelings: it is the *reception*. They are different gestures of divine relationality—yet their motions are *in spirit* inseparable, in constant oscillation.

We will consider this dual love-concept as a constructive alternative to omnipotence. For neither the passion nor the com/passion, neither the call nor the reception *force* us. These complementary motions map onto a single moment of our becoming. For this is what is *actual*: this becoming moment. Of, say, you, there, now. In its past and its future you *collect* yourself—in recollecting past becomings and in anticipation of future ones. Apart from this moment of actualization, the past and the future remain abstractions. But for process theology this becoming moment, the "actual occasion," is key to the cosmos: it is the individual creature here/now, emerging within the matrix of all creaturely relations.

Locate yourself as though in a guided meditation: you are feeling yourself here now, reading within a field of relations more or less chosen, edgy or warm, heavy with past—the past of all that has shaped you, including the various theological perspectives that vie for your attention even now. You emerge—now—in a dense collective of nature and nurture, turbulent with memories, anxieties, and hopes. Still, here, now, you feel lungs opening, drawing breath, air shared by all the breathers near and far, breathing the same air as those near you, those whose feelings you sense, breathing together with all creatures, sealed in an ozone layer enveloping our rich atmosphere, swirling gracefully amidst the choreography of the planets, turning amidst the liturgy of the galaxies: there you are. The elemental magnitudes of relation, the force fields of creation, shoot through this moment so tangibly that they can almost be felt connecting you-there-now to me-here-then.

Imagine this moment as a wave of the waters of creation: a wave of the becoming that is at one and the same time your becoming yourself—and the collective emergence of our shared creaturely life. The matrix of our cosmic interrelations bottoms into an infinite depth. That depth lacks the personal relatedness of what we name Love, or God. Yet the infinity, as we have meditated upon it earlier, within the doctrinal symbol of the creation, may be called the *depth* of Godself, the creative womb of all that is. Whitehead called it "creativity."

That infinity enters into relations with the finite beings surfacing on the face of the deep: we creatures, called forth amidst the swirling choreography of it All.

Called forth, born—natured, nurtured—at every moment. That call, that invitation is the creative Eros: the amorous desire of God for life, and more life. Life not for the sake of my life alone but for the sake of the evolving network of relations in which my life is worth living—*worthy-scipe*, lived as an act of worship.[14]

The "creative love of God" conveys the *logos*, the *sophia*, that seeks incarnation in the world. Not just once, but always and everywhere. As even the father of orthodoxy, Athanasius, put this "thing most marvelous": the *logos* "contained all things himself; and just as while present in the whole of creation, he is at once distinct in being from the universe, and present in all things . . ."[15] In this classical panentheistic vision, the divine will for all creatures seeks embodiment in every wave of becoming. This is God-in-love: *willing* in the original sense of the word—wanting, desiring, urging.

"God is the poet of the world, with tender patience leading it," wrote Whitehead, in a "vision of truth, beauty, and goodness."[16] These values are pure possibilities, only actualized in the particular becomings of the creation. The content of the divine aim for the particular creature is that moment's best possibility. Thus the divine is within each of us, as an influence, an influx of desire—whether or not we share that desire as our own. In this sense the aim is like the ancient concept of prevenient grace. Amidst the mess of our past stuff and present inclinations, God calls. Love lures and lets be. Our mess becomes our potential. And we creatures be-come, come forth. You this moment come forth, a wave freshly breaking on the face of the deep. In an ocean of overlapping waves, all new, all different.

Perhaps every creature in a creature's own way is *called*. Persons personally, animals bestially, plants vegetably. . . . Among persons, a tinge of consciousness of this lure lets us choose—to grasp a fresh possibility, or not.

The lure is not like a memo dictating to us our best course of action. We are called to improvise. We are invited to risk the adventure. For our adventure is inseparable from the divine creativity: the unfolding world is not a preprogrammed drama. How dreary it would be for God to be able to predict it all. Yet neither are we quite on our own with these choices, these risks.

Here is the question, perhaps finally the only question that matters: In this moment, will you somehow *materialize* the possibility? Will you in traditional language heed God's will? Like a wave cresting, turning, might you sense the wisdom for this moment? Do you begin, however minutely, to embody the love that is possible—in this moment, this time, this place? (Even now, in how you read.) Amidst the array of divergent, conflictual influences from which you are becoming—you might sense the mysterious magnetism of possibility. In your "heart's desire"—is there an echo of the larger love-life of the world?

Arise, My Love

Perhaps loving each other requires that we look at the invisible together, that we abandon the sight of it to the breath of the heart, of the soul, that we preserve it in its carnality, without staring upon it fixedly as a target.

—LUCE IRIGARAY[17]

We might meet this Love in any of her creaturely embodiments. In her elusive excess, she ignites a desire that drives beyond our grasping ego. "For this reason I will do my best," wrote Hadewijch. The love-process morphs power into actions of care, of justice, of celebration. Of poetry. These are all actualizations of the possible. They express the infinite desire for incarnation. But also, still and often, does our most carnal desire. The divine Eros may be transcendently irreducible to sexuality: but after all it calls forth the immanent life of the creation by means of sex. Our creaturely carnality cries out in and beyond sex for disclosure in love, not the closure of possession. "A body that is in love," writes Luce Irigary, a contemporary philosopher who hails from the same region as Hadewijch, "does not endure being fixed as an object."[18]

As we meditate on the lure, let us supplement the poetics of Hadewijch with the biblical text from which flowed so much love mysticism, that of the Song of Songs.

The voice of my beloved!
Look, he comes,
leaping upon the mountains,
Bounding over the hills.
My beloved is like a gazelle
or a young stag.
Look, there he stands
behind our wall,
gazing in at the windows,
looking through the lattice.
My beloved speaks and says to me:

"Arise, my love, my fair one,
and come away . . ." (2:8-10)

The Song was subject to all manner of allegorization: as the love between God and Israel favored by rabbis, or the love between God and the soul, or between Christ and the church, favored by Christian celibates.

As in the poetry of Hadewijch, love's shadows appear. "Upon my bed at night I sought him whom my soul loves; / I sought him, but found him not" (Song 3:1). How readily the dark night of the lover's absence would echo in later traditions of the dark night of the soul: the experience of the absence of God. Mystics faced rather than denied or numbed this peculiar suffering, one that in a more numbed age yields simple atheism. Hear the echo of the Song in St. John of the Cross:

One dark night
Fired with love's urgent longings
—Ah, the sheer grace!—
I went out unseen,
My house being now all stilled.[19]

The dark night remains fiery with desire. Yet we may now receive this spirituality without confining its biblical prototype to the house of a purely celibate allegory. For the text itself offers no transcendent, desexualizing signals. It bears witness to ancient poetics of very human passion, replete with images of transgression. No nice Jewish boy would peek through the lattice of the women's quarters, luring his lover to "come away" with him! As one commentator writes, "the powerful erotic charge of many of the amorous idioms defies any purely allegorical interpretation: 'His left arm is under my head and his right makes love to me' (2:6 and 8:2); . . . 'his fountain makes the garden fertile' (4:15); or 'my beloved thrust his hand / through the hole in the door; / I trembled to the core of my being' (5:4)."[20] Why would we want to lose the rare instance—almost unique in biblical and Christian literature—of the celebration of a woman's sexual passion? "I adjure you, O daughters of Jerusalem, if you find my beloved, tell him this: I am faint with love" (5:8).

Yet for all these tantalizing scraps of narrative, the poem is notoriously non-narrative, its own meaning as elusive as the Lover. It is lyric poetry rather than narrative, and thus of interest in form as well as content for theology. The very rhythms and riffs of the poetry—both in the Hebrew and in the translation, in this case—themselves perform the power of a lure. Music, poetry, and liturgy hew close to the eros of an alternative spirit, still vibrating over the waters. Perhaps, as another commentator writes of the Song of Songs, "the forms of poetry do more than just give shape to an existing theological content, but have the potential to give rise to genuinely new theological possibilities."[21] Also meditating upon the Song, the Roman Catholic philosopher Richard Kearney suggests that the new theological possibility, beyond established content indeed, is not just a possibility for theology, but a theology of possibility. "What we have here is a story of *transfiguring eros as the making possible of the impossible*."[22]

These commentators on the Song inadvertently illumine the process theological idea of the divine lure: for as noted above, the content of the initial aim is precisely the *possible*. It is the possibility of something that would remain impossible apart from the amorous gift of the possible itself. A possibility that we are being invited to actualize—or in more theological language, to embody in our carnal reality, to make flesh—to incarnate.

Rather than allegorizing away the fleshly passions, we may instead include them as an elemental layer of a multilayered tissue of textual meanings. Mystical readings may displace or transfigure sexual energies, but need not repress them. Think of the perennial appeal of Augustine's *Confessions*. He may have sworn off sex for life, he may find dissolute the promiscuous homoerotic and heterosexual excesses of his youth, but he hardly represses them! The erotic pulsations of his recollections infuse his theology with a dazzling intensity: "I both shudder and glow with passion." But for a discerning relationalism, something more is at stake than outgrowing Christian moralism, and then having to outgrow defiant rebellions *against* Christian moralism.

> In the beginning, O God, you made heaven and earth in your Word, in your Son, in your Power, in your Wisdom, in your Truth, speaking in a wondrous way and working in a wondrous way. Who shall comprehend it? Who shall declare it? What is that which shines through me and strikes my heart without injuring it? I both shudder and glow with passion: I shudder, in as much as I am unlike it; I glow with passion in as much as I am like to it.
>
> —AUGUSTINE[23]

The divine Eros itself, the desirous will of God, may not be discernible when we are revolted by the erotic energies that pulse through the creation. For what we *are* and can become as creatures, whatever possibilities of relationship, in bed or out of bed, we choose to actualize, is inescapably embedded in the living, dying, sexuate "flesh of the world" (Merleau Ponty). If, as the tradition insists, the infinite divinity permeates every ounce and atom of the material world, indeed, if we may imagine the universe as God's very body, all our matter *matters*. How we cherish and inhabit it matters. As Shug in *The Color Purple* puts it, teasing Celie about sex, the divine "love all them feelings."[24]

Can we hear the voice of the beloved, the divine lure, promiscuously inviting us *all*, even now, to come, to "come away"? To become who we did not know we could be?

"Invisible Attractions": Law and Love

The lure suggests then the experience of a divine desire that, sweetly or dangerously, in flesh and in spirit, *attracts* us. The touch of truth is not heavy-handed until humans try to force it. So this divine passion influences us not by a power of coercion, from the outside, but by a power of attraction flowing into us. It invites *from within*. In process theology this "initial aim" takes the place of what is called traditionally the power of the creator or the will of God. So the atmosphere of divine Eros has strikingly little to do with some grimly pious obedience. It is not a matter of following a top-down dictum—not even of a right-on liberation or feminist or ecological variety! But shall we then dispense with the scriptural symbols of command?

> The drawing of this Love
> and the voice of this
> Calling.
>
> —T. S. ELIOT[25]

The commandments of justice and mercy, indeed of love or the golden rule, have after all inspired historic resistance to lawless aggressions and to oppressive law. The Torah, the Jewish law, is not reducible to legalism or exclusivism, but supports the "struggle for justice and mercy."[26] Perhaps it is a matter of infusing the commandments within the atmosphere of the Eros: "Arise my love, and come away" is also an imperative—a *proposition* in the sense suggested in our earlier discussion of truth-claims! After all, the ethics of "should and should not" may also encode, *should* also encode the divine lure. For without strong supportive structures of community, society, liturgy, theology, the chances are minute that we can individually or collectively even *discern* the initial aim.

The interiority in which the lure is felt is not the inside of a bounded and autonomous subjectivity but of a social individual, emergent within the reciprocities of open systems. The "still, small voice" may be calling from within to our freedom—badly and variously compromised as it is by the habits of fear, greed, and dominance we call "sin," painfully constrained by the multitude of biological and social forces that limit our potential. But as Paul made clear, mere ethics will never motivate its own fulfillment. Ethics itself can become part of the love-blockage, part of the *han*/sin pattern, when it stifles rather than stirs fresh possibility. The law becomes legalism when it freezes into the absolute; when in fear of the dissolute, it loses the porous flexibility of an open system. When it merely stifles desire, rather than stirring life-affirming desire.

How does this unforcing force work? By sparking *your desire*: desire ignites desire. This sparking process takes place largely beneath and before our consciousness. Sometimes glimpsed in a dream, in a stranger's face, in a flow of grief, a comforting embrace, a surge of music, a private illumination, a public act of truth. In conscience, shame, guilt, awe at a random sunset. The spark is what we hope for in prayer, meditation, worship. We infer it—and cannot in truth make any certain claims about it, as in "God told me this or that; God wills this or that for me." For it comes already coated in our experience, in our own subjectivity, in the aims of our own socialized desire.

Passion in process is also on trial. Human passion, precisely in its relational intensity, can be the most selfish of all powers. This is why the New Testament is careful not to pit love against the law, but to offer a law of love: "I give you a new commandment, that you love each other" (John 13:34).[27] But doesn't "commandment" imply the coercive power? In context it does quite the opposite: it suggests that there is an imperative at play within our interactivity, a demand that we treat others with the noncoercive care with which we want to be treated. "Love does no wrong to a neighbor; therefore, love is the fulfilling of the law" (Rom. 13:10). In other words we are "commanded"—shall we say urgently invited—to coordinate our personal desires with the well-being of our larger world. The love-commandment reminds us to attend with discipline, not just with whim, to the new possibility for a shared flourishing.

"Behold, I do a new thing!" The Hebrews had a genius for novelty, thus for *history* as the scene of the new, the irreversible, the "acts of God." Newness marks the irruption of possibility out of the impossible. "Let us sing a new song." [28] The impossible exercises no influence. The possible just *might. . . .* This newness of the initial aim may be just a stirring of freshness, a wisp of hope. It does not belong to a model of an omnipotent *creatio ex nihilo.* It offers rather the newness of *creatio ex profundis:* genesis from the relational *complexity, the bottomless and irreducible past influence, the fluency of the very waters of creation,* in our con/fusing historical lives. In process thought, you and I are comprised not of skin-encapsulated subjectivities, not of atoms or of substances, nor of any fixed natures, sexual or otherwise. We are *processes* of relationship, members of multiple incomplete collectives, human and nonhuman.

"By strong though invisible attractions," wrote Charles Wesley, God "draws some souls through their intercourse with others. The sympathies formed by grace far surpass those formed by nature."[29] The founder of Methodism, who pioneered the development of a movement through small-group formation, knew that faith does not consist in one-to-one intimacy with God, but always includes "two or more." By sympathies that are formed by grace, Wesley is indicating the loves that exceed familial patterns and just laws, the wider, freer intimacies in which we experience spiritual growth. Within the multiple attractions that lure us toward one another are manifestations of the divine lure. These sympathies connect us in pathos-with, in fellow feeling, for new patterns of influent relation, new collectives of grace.

As we become unblocked we *feel* our interdependence as creatures of an intricately interwoven creation. We might have a sense like Shug in *The Color Purple* that "if I cut the tree, my arm will bleed."[30] On the same principle, Jesus inserts himself in the future community: "I am the vine, you are the branches . . ." (John 15:5).

In the dense matrix of relatedness that scripture brings to bear upon our flighty spirits, creative newness is not disconnection, but new connection. Transcendence does not belong to a lone spirit soaring free of the creation and all of its constrained, chaotic creatureliness, but to a flow of spirit *within* the open-ended creation. Transcendence is the transformation of power *within* the process of creative, influent interrelation.

The relationships composing our memory, body, family, community, ecology, and world form the material, largely unconscious, of our ongoing genesis. And these very relationships can close in on our spirit, close us down, usually in the name of morality or tradition. They can suffocate the talent, the promise, the possibility that we are called to realize. As Hadewijch complains, they try "to dissuade me [f]rom all that the forces of Love urge me to." It is not just heartless or selfish obtuseness that seeks to dissuade us. Jesus' family tried "to restrain him" and to get him to come home too (Mark 3:21). They saw the risk for him. The countercultural counsels of this Love may expose me, or my family, or my whole community, to turbulence, to break-ups and break-outs.

Nonetheless, the ambiguous matrix of our relationships also constitutes the material through which spirit *matters*. In resistance to structures that have formed and deformed relationship itself, but only in and through these relations, can I "live out what I am."

Between Eros and Agape

So to some degree we actualize the possible. To some degree, sometimes very minimally, sometimes just by taking a breath, we embody the divine passion. We respond, by default or by embrace. Then what?

Then—and this is not a "then" at the end of linear time, but the other side of each moment—we are *received*. This is what Cobb and Griffin call "the responsive love of God."[32] It is in fact a response to our response to the creative love, the Eros. This response would be the divine hospitality: we are invited; we come as we are; and we are received, as we have become. At any given moment this may not be a pretty picture. Our adventures may flop. Yet the parable of the prodigal son suggests not humiliation for his dissolute behavior but a joyful reception. But only because the prodigal has heeded the lure.

All the metaphors of judgment suggest that no happy homecoming is guaranteed. This love is not coercive; it is nonetheless *demanding*. As Cobb and Griffin put it, "there is a tension between oneself and one's experience of what ideally would be, between what one is and the rightness in things that one dimly discerns. Hence the divine presence is experienced as an other, sometimes recognized as gracious, often felt as judge."[33]

> The worship of God is not a rule of safety—it is an adventure of the spirit, a flight after the unattainable. The death of religion comes with the repression of the high hope of adventure.
>
> —ALFRED NORTH WHITEHEAD[31]

Remember, however, that in this model we are talking of something going on always, at the edge of every event of becoming, not just the end of a life or of time. Here is the heart of the co-creative process: we are called forth, we may creatively cooperate, we are received. For Whitehead this reception is called "the consequent nature of God." It will resemble what we will be discussing in subsequent chapters as the kingdom of God. This cosmic com/

passion will feel like judgment when we are out of sync with it. Creation and salvation are inseparable in this model, two moments of the same ongoing, open-ended, process.

God's *passion* flows into us—and our response, responsible or not, is met by God's *com/passion*. And in these two gestures of the love that is God, there is intimate interaction, there is an empowerment of the creature to return and redistribute love. These are the complementary loves of eros and agape. And still there is no divine coercion. God takes us in in such a way that we become part of the divine experience, part of Godself. But that means that God's self has altered in this moment, not ceasing to be all that God was but now enriched—and sometimes at the same time perhaps impoverished—by all that happens, here and in the other one hundred billion galaxies. And then this agape "floods back again into the world."[34] That flow is the eros for the next moment, bearing some fresh possibility—sometimes only for another breath of survival; sometimes for that kingdom materializing already and not yet, within and among, in this world and beyond it.

Yet for all this flow of influence, for all this fluency of passion, the divine power in play remains vulnerable to the forces of violence. It does not meet coercion with coercion. Neither does it idealize victimization—even when it results in a cruciform passion. The amatory power cannot be measured on the scale of dominance and subjugation, win and lose.

> I look at you as at the passage of the word into flesh, of the flesh into word, a lasting incarnation, the fulfillment of which is not perceptible by whoever does not keep his or her gaze upon the invisible.
>
> —LUCE IRIGARAY[35]

As we get free of the projection of a controlling omnipotence, we may sense the divine desire for a thriving, adventurous, beautiful world—for God's sake, not only for ours. We miss the intensity of this urging if we imagine God off in some Other World, a Heaven removed. The omni-amorous God[36] everywhere and invisibly inhabits the matter of *this* world. The power of love flows from the risk of the larger love—sometimes, only sometimes, at the cost of self-sacrifice. For what connects the infinite to the finite but the incarnations of love? In the next chapter we will explore further the character of that difficult love. It will appear as the com/passion that enfolds our passionate adventures. Free of the deadlock of the absolute and the dissolute, it is Hadewijch who reveals by name the way of the *resolute*:

> Since I gave myself to Love's service,
> Whether I lose or win,
> I am resolved:
> I will always give her thanks,
> Whether I lose or win;
> I will stand in her power.[37]

CHAPTER 6

Sticky Justice
Com/Passion in Process

I took my other hand and placed it on top of hers, and she moved her free hand on top of it, so we had this black-and-white stack of hands resting upon my chest.

"When you're unsure of yourself," she said, "when you start pulling back into doubt and small living, she's the one inside you saying, 'Get up from there and live like the glorious girl you are.' She's the power inside you, you understand?"

Her hands stayed where they were but released their pressure.

"And whatever it is that keeps widening your heart, that's Mary, too, not only the power inside you but the love. And when you get down to it, Lily, that's the only purpose grand enough for a human life. Not just to love—but to *persist* in love."

—SUE MONK KIDD[1]

Liberating Com/Passion

This moment of epiphany—a dis/closure of power, glory, and love at the heart of human life—takes place in South Carolina of 1964. It is the fierce desire of an adolescent girl for freedom from abuse and shame that kicks the plot of this novel, *The Secret Life of Bees*, into motion. Her violent father blames her for the shooting death of her mother when the child was a toddler. Lily's hope for liberation has been sparked by a series of mysterious signs: a visitation of bees, strange dreams, an old photo of her mother found in the attic, the label "Black Madonna" on a line of honey products—and then as powerfully embodied by the maker of those products, the beekeeper herself, August. These signs come like trail markers in a wilderness of social and psychological change.

Might the divine lure take such enigmatic forms, in its inviting action?

Lily takes some terrifying risks to free herself, along with her caregiver, who has been imprisoned on a trumped-up charge. Might she be acting on that daring passion we discussed in the last chapter? Desire pervades the novel, as it does our lives, in very specific and diverse forms: for the lost mother, for the love of her surrogate mother, for a talented and endangered young male, and ultimately for the hospitable wisdom of August. She is revealed to be the spiritual leader of a small community gathered liturgically around a statue that has been passed down from the time of slavery. This little ecclesia, called the Daughters of Mary (including one son as well), has developed its own litany:

> "The people called her Our Lady of Chains. They called her that not because she wore chains…"
>
> "*Not because she wore chains*," the Daughters chanted.
>
> "They called her Our Lady of Chains because *she broke them*."[2]

The Lady is a rough wooden icon of emancipation. In one ritual the Daughters coat her with honey, both for its metaphoric and its preservative properties. This is no conventional, let alone Roman Catholic, devotion to the Virgin Mary. Our Lady of Chains signifies, as has often been the case in actual Marian devotion, something more than a merely human mother of a divine male.[3] In the novel, she appears as a female symbol of the divine. The Black Madonna dis/closes for her community the ultimate face of Love.

If in chapter 5 we considered the lure as the divine Eros, as process theology's "creative love of God," we might say that the adventurous passion of Lily, the motherless child, is sparked by that Eros. We began to explore a complementary process of relationship, initiated through the invisible attraction of a new possibility. Whatever becomes actual, process theology suggests, is received back into "the responsive love of God." Both August and the statue can both be read as icons of that responsive com/passion.

Only in the difficult interplay of these two styles or modes of Love in the world, which we may call eros and agape, does life take on its fullness. Both can be fully human; both can be fully divine. Yet we do not experience the amorous divinity directly, as something or some One separate from the movements of passion and compassion in our creaturely relations. We experience the loves of our life, in all their intensities and their extensities. From them we draw the best metaphors possible to us for language about the mystery that exceeds language. A work of fiction may so economically narrate a world of human experience as to advance our spiritual discernment. With the help of *The Secret Life of Bees*, we focus in this chapter on the meaning of the ideal of agape in relation to the theological eros we have discussed; and we face its surprising implications for the concept of God.

Just Love

"Not just to love . . ." Love is not enough for a theology in process, either. Our own loving feelings might not issue in transforming action. And indeed, the attractive will of God does not by itself make justice or change the world. The love-lure may provoke a liberating passion—as it provokes the young protagonist Lily to her own exodus from oppression. It may provoke brave and joyous moments of resistance to the need-greed system that enmeshes us all in relations of violation.

". . . But to persist in love." If these moments are to have lasting effects, if they are to build up wide and supportive structures in history, then resistance is not enough.

Persistence in love: this, according to August, is worthy of human life. It reverberates with the "steadfast love" discussed earlier as the Hebrew connotation of "truth." And perhaps this persistence can provide us a worthy theological analogy for the divine Agape, the love that patiently, stubbornly, continues. We have been considering how the elemental love of the Gospels, in an unconditional radiance that embraces neighbor, stranger, or even enemy, suggests something utterly different from the self-demeaning, abuse-accepting passivity so many have mistaken for Christian love.[4] Through the passion that issues in compassion, love *persists*. And therefore justice in our world has a chance.

"Whatever it is that keeps widening your heart": here we recognize an agape that complements eros. The Lutheran theologian Anders Nygren had, however, made the opposite case: "Eros and Agape belong originally to two entirely separate spiritual worlds, between which no direct communication is possible."[5] He argued that only agape is divine, indeed it is only divine. Eros, even in its mystical forms, remains a self-centered, grasping degradation of love, a form of self love, not love of the other. But a relational theology does not accept the polarization of self love and love of the other: the divine Eros invites a coordination of self and its influent others. So we have already located a certain eros as the divine desire itself.[6] Therefore we are thinking them in tandem, as two motions of one amorous energy. Agape in God or in humanity is not *higher* than this eros. But agape is *wider*. For it collects the multiplicity of passions into the complexity of compassion.

Still, it is difficult to use the word *compassion* without conjuring either a self-demeaning sacrifice or an other-demeaning pity. Feminist theology has helped to highlight the problems of agape, defined as self-sacrifice.[7] For the ideal of self-sacrificial love has been privileged at the expense of the self-affirming dignity that women and members of other traditionally subordinate collectives may most need from their faith. A certain controlling power-play had come to light in the agapic: as God gives himself/his Son in unilateral love, so "should" we sacrifice ourselves for the other (as in the case of the abused wife). Read: so should women subjugate their lives to their men, servants to their masters, and so forth. The symbolization of agape as divine love reduced eros to the merely and sinfully human, thus contributing to the alienation of our desires, especially of our sexuality.

Feminist theology has often therefore preferred the language of eros to that of agape, when it comes to love. More widely, progressive theology has made the ideal of *justice* its foundation. It has in this taken Reinhold Niebuhr's assessment in the 1950s seriously: "American Christianity tends to be irrelevant to the problems of justice because it persists in presenting the law of love as a simple solution for every communal problem."[8] Agapic or compassionate love has seemed sentimental, ineffectual, patronizing. It prefers charity to structural change. In response we can only insist: those who are oppressed don't want our compassion, they *just* want justice. They want a shift in the structures of power that block their possibilities, that shut down their life process.

And rightly so. The question is how the work of that justice happens, beyond the routine applications of established law. I am arguing it does *not*, without the amorous stretch. In its holding together of our multiple passions, the com/passion holds open a solidaristic space. It widens the context of our relationships. It fosters a persistence beyond the hope of the moment. Does this motion recall the testimony of a truth in process and on trial—the witness to a love that infinitely exceeds our sentiment, our individual affiliations, and our personal feeling? This stretching of my context, in the honesty of our interdependence, *implicates* me in the lives of alien others. It involves me in what Niebuhr called "the spirit of justice."[9] That spirit enfolds me, across painful difference, in a shared world. And so, as we saw, it gets fulfilled, not superseded, by the law of love. Love makes justice *matter* for me, materialize as part of my own life. It does not remain a matter only of obligation. It adds desire to duty—and both are changed. The passion for justice finds fulfillment in a just love that renews and stretches the passion itself.

Network of Mutuality

The agapic stretch deepens who I *am*, who I am becoming, amidst my living relations. And what I become influences what you may become. It was Martin Luther King's premise that "all life is interrelated."[11] One can argue that he was actualizing a unique, black Baptist activist version of process theology. In his doctoral studies at Boston University, he had intensively engaged the work of Henry Nelson Wieman, an early process theologian.[12] Quite apart from his world-transforming leadership, King's grasp of the relational structure of creation was way ahead of most thinkers. But of course his practice is inseparable from his philosophy. To live in consciousness of this width of relation means to honor that "inescapable network." For the movement, it entailed an increasingly global cosmopolitanism: "Never again can we afford to live with the narrow, provincial 'outside agitator' idea."[13] Such a practice of mutuality requires a depth of self, my well-being gets caught up willy-nilly in that of the others. So my vulnerability also deepens. As King put it, speaking from his disheartening experience with white moderates: "There can be no deep disappointment where there is not deep love."[14]

> "Injustice anywhere is a threat to justice everywhere. We are caught in an inescapable network of mutuality tied in a single garment of destiny. Whatever affects one directly, affects all indirectly."
>
> —MARTIN LUTHER KING, JR.[10]

This depth only accrues through an agapic *persistence*. Without the persistent stretch of our relationality there is *no sustainable motion from eros to justice*. It is not a matter of shifting from love into justice, like changing gears, but rather of *letting passion grow into the justice of com/passion*. For this reason I keep the slash in the word—as soon as I take it out, the passion seems to drain away. For it is precisely not a matter of replacing our passions with a tepid concern for others, but of letting our passion grow. It is not a matter of diminishing eros but of enlarging its perspective.

For compassion is literally *passion-with* the other—even first of all with the very other whom one most intensely desires. Eros is a much wider concept than sex. But think of this even sexually: in a relationship in which I cannot empathize with the desires of the other, how long is the sex likely to be sustainable?

And how long can any relationship last, if I do not practice com/passion for this other in his or her disappointing limitations? Without this com/passion for the love-object don't I make her or him my idol—who soon shatters? (Along with a heart or two.) There is an analogy for faith, here, as we shall see.

The point is that passion is only sustainable in as much as it modulates into com/passion. It does not cease to be passion. It does not therefore lose the element of self-love: love the other *like* you love yourself! Not because the other is like you—not even because you *like* the other! If agape sacrifices the fullness of our selves, it is a false agape, lacking self-esteem and therefore lacking, precisely, the power of persistence. It does not offer cheap grace to the violator but a chance of transformation: forgiveness is not an excuse to continue to violate but a chance to interrupt the cycle of violence. If Christian love enables violators to continue to violate, it violates the gospel law of love.

Agape—when it has not been dissociated from eros—regenerates a common life. Our mutual influence bleeds through the walls meant on one side to protect the violator from justice, on the other to protect the violated from the violator. Justice itself requires a system of firm boundaries. Yet theology cannot lose sight of that "inescapable network" that crosscuts all our boundaries. For instance, the leading proponent of black theology, James Cone, comments that Martin's vision remains suspect to those more inspired by Malcolm X. They worry at the depoliticizing and disempowering effects of Christian love-teaching on so many blacks. Yet Cone teaches that "the human family is as important as the black family, because we either learn to live together with others, or we will perish together."[15]

We blossom only as *knowingly* interdependent creatures of a good creation. If "all life is interrelated," justice for the *others* is—in spirit and in truth—a mode of *self*-care. But I can treat that interdependence with indifference, with scorn, or with love. If I can embrace ever more of the other, ever more others, the character of my desire evolves. It enters into wider coordinations. Agape does not give up pleasure, it stretches it. It stretches *you.* There is an eerie beauty in the stretch. Love *becomes* you. Agapic love is never purely for the other.

Any effective family life fosters the needy greedy impulses into wider cares. One hopes for the accomplishment of this socialization without repression. But normally maturity in our civilization yields an ego striving for separateness more than for connection. Traditionally this is the male ego, with the feminine self clinging too dependently to connection. As John Cobb has mapped out in his *Christ in a Pluralistic Age*, the book that lured me on to graduate school, another self-structure is possible, in which my ego will be transformed by my intentional empathy with the desires of others. He found Buddhism, with its notion of the emptying of the ego, a great dialogical tool for the creative transformation of Christianity, and paradoxically for renewing the doctrine of Christian love.

Disciplined empathy is not self-dissolving but self-opening. It reshapes my own desire, not lessening it but strengthening, clarifying—widening it. For example, my unhappiness about a particular loss may require a lot of compassion from my friends, perhaps more than they have to give. But if on the longer run I remain open to the fuller life of my friends, if I let their experience become part of my own, then their joys will be not a cause of envy but of actual enjoyment. Their sufferings will not compete with mine for attention but will rather give me needed distraction and proportion. If the passions of others flow through me, relativizing my own and involving theirs, I will not feel mired in my loss nearly as deeply and as long. For my sorrow is not repressed but massaged into a wider, richer tapestry of experience. And loss only remains unbearable when such width is lacking. Then life shrinks to the size of the wound.

For, after all, "I" am this moment of becoming afresh. "I am" is co-constituted by the entire network that is my past, my world, my relations. The currents of all my relations flow into this wave of my becoming, now, for good and for ill. What I do with all that material, how I collect myself from it, how I compose myself: all this comprises my *response* to the divine lure. And reciprocally, the self I become in this moment will then flow into the collectivity of my relations as part of *their* future.

Agapic Justice

I can grow with or against the relational grain of our interdependent becoming. This collectivity comprises the social structure of any self. We may be more or less in sync with this structure, or in violation of it. The structure exceeds any individual life, though it is a mere abstraction apart from the individuals who realize it. When it corresponds to the lure that calls us each into the creative coordination of our desires, it also protects us from each other. Its boundaries will be supportive but permeable, subject to continual negotiation and critique.

This coordination amidst the flux of uncertain and conflictual relations is what we mean by *justice*. Amidst the self-organizing structure of complex human interactions, justice is the gauge of collective well-being. In this justice reflects the structure of creation itself, read as we did in terms of the emergence of order at the edge of chaos. And it may be precisely the underdeveloped relationality of justice that my colleague, Professor Isasi-Díaz, calls the logic of solicitude, involving a surprising element of tenderness, that can keep social systems open.

In other words, an agapic justice supports the emergence of social complexity in its turbulent, democratizing process. Justice is hardly an issue where life is simple, without the competition of imbalanced interests, conflicting passions, and systemic violence. But conversely, just order is impossible where the disorderly conduct of uncoordinated eros is not tolerated. For justice can only maintain its structural sensibility in the face of chaos through the peculiar fluency of love, its resilience, its patience. It may persist against intolerable odds. And in the face of its enemies it will still insist on their humanity. Inasmuch as justice can be distinguished from retribution, it is a disciplined com/passion that sustains the collective passion for justice. Thus love keeps justice itself *en procès*, on trial and in process: and justice tests love for its power of persistence. Agape, always translating the "steadfast love" of the Hebrew truth-tradition, stretches the passion of love into the work of justice: the com/passion of the resolute.

> I believe that if societies continue to view fairness, equality, and merit as the characteristics of justice, injustice will continue to prevail everywhere. I believe we need a new logic focusing on relationality made explicit in solicitude or care, characterized by tenderness and resulting in reconciliatory praxis.
>
> —ADA MARÍA ISASI-DÍAZ[16]

Community of Compound Passions

Western modernity grew rapidly, aggressively, with spurts of tolerance for the chaotic diversities of its own fledgling democracies. This modernity has released some magnificent creativity along the way, gestating the potentiality for a democracy capable of structuring compassion beyond theocratic and clannish forms of community. But in the reaction against religious absolutism, democratic development fostered an eros liberated *from* rather than *to* community. It emphasized the values of an individual alone, free from the endless social web of the other creatures and finally from the Creator. A great gift of critical thinking comes from the struggle of this truth-process. When we criticize it, we are borrowing its resources of self-criticism. But if we fail to criticize our highly developed Western individualism, "justice," as in the words of Isaiah, "is turned back." For Western "Man" has in the name of Freedom pursued his [sic] own passion and profit at any expense to others. Indeed "Freedom" may be today the most dangerous shibboleth of them all. If the "others" are non-European, nonwhite, let alone nonmale and nonstraight, they still, massively, fall outside the boundaries of "the Man" and his justice.

> Like the deer, we have sensed the 'living waters' from afar; and now we run toward them, but with no certitudes . . . barely allowing our goal to keep us alive, to keep us dreaming and to prepare us for the next step on the way.
>
> —IVONE GEBARA[17]

Over the past several decades, the theologies of liberation began to translate Christianity into a prophetic call for justice and for sustainability. These movements have also suffered setbacks from within and without. New forms of what Kwok Pui-lan calls "the postcolonial imagination" are needed to decolonize the (Christian) mind and complexify our liberation struggles.[18] The liberation legacy may depend upon a capacity to "persist in love," to widen the flow of love beyond any single "subject" of liberation (based on a unifying social identity like class, or gender, or sex, or race, and even or especially "religion" . . .).

More complex expressions of the liberation passion, with the potential for a persistent com/passion, have been emerging. For instance, the Latin American liberation and ecofeminist theologian (a designation already indicative of the complexity that is at stake!) Ivone Gebara captures the eros for justice with the psalmist's fluid metaphor: "As the deer longs for living waters." This longing takes on a depth that flows beyond any single issue, that dissolves the absolutes of certainty even as it replenishes a fluent hope.

The Johannine story of the woman at the well drew on these same living waters. Living and working amidst the poorest of the poor, Gebara has challenged the disembodied, desexualized ideal of Christian love that haunts even the liberation movements. They have never outgrown their anthropomorphic and andromorphic God. This Sister of Notre Dame, dwelling in the slums of Recife, offers her "song/lament" as "one who seeks, despite everything, the beauty of the ephemeral, of that 'something' that always escapes us, even when we insist on trying to hold it fast. *It is the song of one who seeks to rediscover arms and embraces, love poems, and reasons for beginning to hope once again. It is the song that is born of the body, and born of the earth . . ."*[19]

The song of earthly yearning, in which there is no longer any separation of eros and agape, suggests the planetary width of love. It opens a way that respects our most intimate desires—and invites them into a spiral of widening embodiment. For the com/passion of becoming does not subtract but compounds our own passions. Its just love is charged with the beauty of our co-creative becoming. Its hope *becomes* us.

Perhaps Gebara's song of the earth will help us to update Paul's vision for the church as the "body of Christ." Singing the song born of the body, rediscovering arms and embraces, we become in truth "members one of another." Not first of all members of an institution! Rather, we become part of each other in the interdependence of the body, a body "called out," ek-*klesia*, from the status quo of numbed disembodiment and bonds that block. And yet how prissy, how prohibitive, becomes all this agapic imagery if we read it as a matter of giving up our own honest passions, our adventurous spirits, for the sake of "the church," or "family values," or "the order of creation," or some other absolute demanding conformity. To joy in each other's joys, as Paul writes, and to help carry each other's burdens—this is the way of liberation, not of repression.

Yet along the way this wider adventure opens up too many loves, empathies, risks, and hopes for any one self to coordinate. For invariably, even in our smallest communities, the many desires come into contradiction. Therefore, the movement of widening requires for itself an ever-evolving structure of justice. Its ethical orders keep open the flow, they conduct and coordinate it. If the structure becomes rigid, the "running water" dries up. But the flow of life and love will dissipate without the structures of justice. (We are, needless to say, still finding our way between the absolute and the dissolute.) These structures allow us to negotiate our differences, to contest and to coordinate our desires. Therefore the structures themselves must always be in a process of adjustment, of social evolution.

In the Hebrew tradition, the law included the codes of mercy. Mercy is another name for compassion in its salt-watery flow of a tender womb, *rechem*. Indeed, the word *rachamim* ("mercy") is a coupling of *rechem + mayim*, the primordial sea of Genesis 1:2. Without mercy the law is mere maintenance of power, and justice—even revolutionary justice—a means of vengeance.

Even in intimate community, love never guarantees justice. But without this love widened in justice, we lack ethical persistence. The passion of resistance is followed too soon by bitterness and burn-out. The chains will be broken, and soon soldered into new ones. Thus the icon of Our Lady of Chains is meaningless apart from her community of care. Its depth of historical connection strengthens to risk—not recklessly but wisely—the other and the new. If our projects of justice are to persist in history, they will need to be not only motivated by passion but sustained by compassion.

Creativity signifies at every level, as suggested by our earlier discussion of creation itself, the self-organizing complexity of creatures living lives on the edge of chaos. At that edge, institutions remain necessary, offering enough rock, enough Petrine stability, for the growth of more complex interrelations. At the same time they remain flexible, structured by auto-critical "checks and balances" against the injustice to which every self-perpetuating organization is tempted. For a relational theology it is the oscillation between eros and agape that energizes and sustains the self-organizing complexity.

Love, Politics, Enemies

At this point in history perhaps neither progressive religion nor progressive politics can *progress* without a serious—not merely tactical—consideration of agape. I think this is why even such secular political theorists as Hardt and Negri have called for "a politics of love." Such a politics emerges from the passion for a vibrant and just planetary life, a passion *with* the neighboring others, their different priorities, issues, agendas, commitment levels, with whom we must make common cause.

A political love will test its politics in its ability to extend to those true others, those on the *other* side of our most passionately felt divides: the enemies. We began to consider the imperative of enemy love in the last chapter, as an implication of the passion for justice. It can however only become explicit in the work of com/passion. This does not mean that we should agree with them or even like them. "Agape," wrote Martin Luther King Jr.—who started out skeptical about the power of love—means "understanding, creative, redemptive,

> People today seem unable to understand love as a political concept, but a concept of love is just what we need to grasp the constituent power of the multitude.
>
> —MICHAEL HARDT AND ANTONIO NEGRI[20]

good will to all . . ." He continues: "I'm very happy that [Jesus] didn't say like your enemies . . ."[21]

If we cultivate whatever understanding we can of their human suffering and their human desire, we will—at the very least—gain a strategic edge. As Paul said, quoting Proverbs, "if your enemies are hungry, feed them . . . for by doing this you will heap burning coals on their heads" (Rom. 12:20). Obviously pure motives are not the issue here! "Reconciliatory praxis" may be served by whatever lowers the threshold of hate. But often more is possible. Through courageous negotiation, the patterns of enmity can be softened, tilted toward some common humanity.

Hardt and Negri write that "we need to recuperate the public and political conception of love common to premodern traditions. Christianity and Judaism, for example, both conceive love as a political act that constructs the multitude."[22] They add reassuringly that "this does not mean you cannot love your spouse, your mother and your child. It only means that your love does not end there, that love serves as the basis for our political projects in common and the construction of a new society. Without this love, we are nothing."[23] It will help if Christianity itself will collaborate in this recuperation. We will then help to foster the spiritual growth from personal to political love—without for a moment downgrading the eros that drives the growth itself.

In the case of our fictional young protagonist, some "mysterious attraction" seems at each stage to lure the girl toward liberation. It does not do so through some literal God-to-girl communication, but through signs, portents, and a widening matrix of relations, friends and enemies included. It keeps her on the mystery. In the dangerous racial context of the South at the dawn of civil rights legislation, each of these relations requires risk on the part of this white girl on the run, and of the African Americans with whom she finds refuge. Amidst these buzzing connections she collects herself, even as the community collects her into itself. In this little ecclesia, a collective "called out" from the racist and patriarchal forms of society and religion, she is given sanctuary. A chance not just to hide but to grieve, indeed to mope for a while, to learn about herself, her history personal and social, the impact of the civil rights movement, the intimate complexities of inter-race relations. And how to keep honeybees, of course.

August Wisdom

While the motherless Lily is driven by turbulent and transforming desires, the Beekeeper embodies an immense and persistent love. Her com/passion for the girl and for the eccentric little community she has gathered is not without desire, but it is a desire transfigured. It is no longer rent by needs and greeds. It is a desire beyond obsession, vibrantly tuned to the possibilities for creativity and healing among those she has gathered. Often it is com/passion for them as they suffer the throes of their various and conflicting passions. She offers neither charitable pity nor self-sacrifice. These characters do not need to learn about self-sacrifice, submission, and service. Indeed, a self-sacrificial agape would be a misplaced ideal for this narrative in which two very different southern black women figure prominently.

Both women have occupied the surrogacy relationship of "nanny" to white children characteristic of slavery and its aftermath. The (august) womanist theologian Delores Williams has critically examined the christological implications of precisely such surrogate, or substitutionary, care.[25] There has been, as mentioned earlier, a lively feminist and womanist challenge to the doctrinal emphasis upon

> Light dawns, courage is renewed, tears are wiped away, a new moment of life arises. Toward that end, speaking about suffering Sophia-God of powerful compassionate love serves as an ally of resistance and a wellspring of hope. But it does so under the rule of darkness and broken words.
>
> —ELIZABETH JOHNSON[24]

atonement as self-sacrifice. It questions any idealization of suffering, even or especially a suffering performed as stand-in for others. The point is not that sacrifice is always self-demeaning, avoidable, or best avoided, but rather that the sacrifice itself is not the purpose.

It is not Jesus' death that transforms but his *life*—a love-life that had the power to persist beyond death, as the stories of the resurrection mysteriously suggest. Granted, that mystery has been almost ruined by dogmatic "I believes." But for those with ears to hear afresh—the purpose of a Christian life is not whatever sacrifices it entails. That purpose is a way, a life, and a truth. It will entail sacrifices of various kinds, and sometimes, in the face of Pontius power, terrifying ones. But they are never the purpose. They are the *risk*. No more than Jesus did Gandhi, King, or Romero *want* or *seek* to die. Even when they could predict their imminent death, as each seems to have done, they were not choosing to die but to *persist in love*. Love "risks the adventure."

To stay with our local story: there is no self-demeaning or other-demeaning gesture in August's relationships. She mentors the community in the creative power of love to liberate from the effects of violation—effects that reach wide into the world and deep into the soul. Her skillful empathy does not manipulate or overwhelm those around her. It is a love that lets be. It participates in the primal let-there-be of genesis and regeneration. August never forces growth but patiently and truthfully empowers it. Sometimes growth fails. Indeed, one beloved and long-suffering sister kills herself. Then August sustains the surviving members and re/members the dead Daughter. She helps them not to lose heart. But she also plants clues—lures.

In her radiant self-esteem, she can nurture the girl's epiphanic discoveries of self and of (m)other, of the divinity in and beyond both. Her big, hot-pink house serves in every sense as sanctuary. August, as her name suggests, is a mature figure of resolute compassion. This is desire ripened into an inordinate width of passion, moved by many lives, moving many lives. It is this double motion, as a figure for the divine love, that troubles us now.

Love Rhythm

We have imagined in this chapter and the last a dual motion of love as a template of the "love divine, all loves excelling" (Charles Wesley). The divine Eros calls us to act, to actualize the possible; and the agape picks up the pieces of our limited efforts. It gathers us in. This oscillation between the intensity of passion and the width of com/passion is the figure of the divine life in its relationship to us at any moment. The eros lures us with its desire, which may become our own ("thy will be done"). It invites us to the infinite hospitality signified as the divine Agape. So the passion in which we may participate contains also a lure *toward* com/passion, toward an ever-wider connectivity.

Agape as the divine compassion is that unconditional care that reveals its prodigality in the life and teaching of Jesus. It is, of course, therefore agape that is traditionally meant by "Christian love": of God, of neighbor, of enemy. Here pumps the radical heart of the faith: no matter how lost, inadequate, messed up, bursting with unrealized intentions and unrequited loves, indeed how repulsive I feel, I matter infinitely. I am esteemed of the infinite. To say "God loves me" is to say I am therefore, in spite of what anyone else may say, loveable. I might pick up my bed and walk. I might shake off my doldrums and kick into action. I might stop waiting for the perfect lover, the perfect family, the perfect community, and as Josiah Royce put it, anticipating King: "Since you cannot *find* the universal and beloved community, *create* it."[26] The co-creativity to which we are together lured produces more than togetherness: it effects the structures of justice that will support the creativity of an ever-diversifying togetherness.

Our actions, our experiences, would be thus together collected into a divine movement, an embrace that re/collects the whole variegated, struggling collective of creation.

In us this primal rhythm of call and response, eros and agape, like breathing, lets us take in the possible, realize it as best we can, if at all, and breathe forth the actual, into the world. Viewed theologically, this means that whatever we become registers *in* the divine. We can imagine an infinite intimacy: the divine breathing out, unfolding, into the world, into us, in passion for becoming; and breathing in, folding us back into God-self, in the cosmic compassion for all creatures.

The creative love provokes *movement*—the movement that the world *is*, that you in particular this moment *are*. The responsive love is *moved*. And that latter thought has been *verboten* by classical orthodoxy.

Dispassion or Compassion?

Christians may unhesitatingly refer to God's love as self-giving, outpouring generosity. But have we *gotten* the gift theologically? Do we realize what is at stake in affirming a com/passionate God—that is, One who *feels/with* us?

Classical orthodoxy, dependent upon Greek metaphysics, in fact systematically denies that God can feel with us—that God can be *moved*. It understood God as both immutable and impassive, without change and without passion. For a "passion" is a movement of the soul; and to be moved means to be affected, subject to suffering and change. The term *passion* shares the same root as "paschal" or "suffering"; and as *pass*-ive. To be acted upon, to be in the receptive position, was seen in antiquity as already a form of vulnerability and therefore suffering. By contrast to the subservient femininity defined as passive and passionate—in other words, irrational—masculinity was defined as activity. The Greek metaphysical tradition identified the divine with pure changeless Being, eternally self-same, and therefore unaffected by the world: *dispassionate*. This rational dispassion, literally called *apatheia*, formed the Greco-Roman ideal of manhood as well as Godhood. The Christian God had gotten defined very early in terms of Aristotle's "Unmoved Mover." And Christian theology naturally enough absorbed this ideology as part of the hermeneutical process of translating the biblical witness into the language of the empire.

Indeed, the dispassionate ideal did important conceptual work for theology. It helped in those first centuries to counter the popular anthropomorphism, both biblical and pagan, that depicted God as all too human. If Plato had wanted "to throw the poets out of the kingdom" half a century earlier, it was because of the Homeric portrayal of the dissolute passions of the gods. But theologians could also use the platonic-Aristotelian ideal of dispassion to counter tendencies toward *biblical* literalism: less-educated Christians in the ambience of the pagan gods were all too prone to take the narratives of the Lord's more unseemly outbursts (in jealousy, rage, or vengeance) as factual depictions of his emotional life.

> Indeed, God seems to be the archetype of the dominant, inflexible, unemotional, completely independent (read 'strong') male. Process theology denies the existence of this God.
>
> —JOHN B. COBB JR. AND DAVID RAY GRIFFIN[27]

But beyond the real need for theology to resist literalisms that veer toward idolatry, a profound theological tension injects itself into Christian thought. For quite apart from the anthropomorphic excesses of some narratives, the biblical metaphors of God's relationship to the world remain rather insistently—relational. That is, they suggest a true interactivity, in which emotion plays just as important a role as reason. For instance, in the light of our systemic abusiveness, we read "And the Lord was sorry that He made humankind on earth." That may carry some anthropomorphic projection of our appropriate guilt. But the sentence continues: "it grieved Him to His heart" (Gen. 6:6).[28] Can we in good faith erase such poetic witness to the "responsive love of God"? When, centuries later, the New Testament intensifies the emphasis on divine love, do we really want to translate compassion into dispassion? Does love then mean anything at all?

Medieval theologians struggled valiantly with this dilemma. Anselm in *Proslogium* (1077–1078) addresses God directly on this matter: "Although it is better for thee to be [both] compassionate and passionless, than not to be these things; how art thou . . . compassionate, and at the same time passionless? For, if thou art passionless, thou dost not feel sympathy; and if thou dost not feel sympathy, thy heart is not wretched from sympathy for the wretched; but this it is to be compassionate."

Having so precisely captured this two-horned dilemma, he proceeds to a brilliant solution: "Thou art compassionate in terms of our experience, and not compassionate in terms of thy being."[29] In other words, God only *appears* to us to be compassionate; God is not *really* compassionate! For God to love means that He [sic] just does what is best for us, not that He feels for us.

Thomas Aquinas paraphrases the problematic logic thus: "For in God there are no passions. Now love is a passion. Therefore love is not in God." In his own way and context, he sought a third way beyond the two-horned polarity of love vs. apathy. His solution takes the bull by the horns: "God loves without passion."[30] Humans love with passion, they are moved; but God is beyond passion and change, loving the world dispassionately. A smart solution, for one who could no more question the classical presuppositions than the biblical authority.

The classical tradition is onto something. Who needs a God who is overwhelmed by every human tragedy? I don't even want a counselor, pastor, or friend to lose it when I share my suffering. I don't want them to become wretched—then I have to worry about them! But can they help me if they remain stoically unmoved by my wretchedness? Only perhaps if they can "fix" the problem. But then by that analogy wouldn't we be back in the zone of the omnipotent intervention rather than the loving influence? And indeed, when God can be defined only as *actus purus*, pure act, with no receptivity, a classical fantasy of power has surely trumped the vision of love.

Moved Mover

Process theology, along with a few other twentieth-century theologies, has insisted that the biblical vision requires a God who suffers with our suffering, who shares our vulnerability.[31] Its God is indeed moved: that is called the "responsive love of God."[32] For its God is truly in process. God in a process of becoming is not *capriciously changing but consistently responding*: the care is for every sparrow, every hair. Some will object that any change in God makes God less than perfect. But as Charles Hartshorne has shown, a faulty "logic of perfection" is at work in that assumption—as though change means improvement over something inferior. Are the most iconic people we know in our lives, the ones through whom we imagine the divine image, the ones who never change? Or the ones who continuously evolve, interested, growing, responsive into their oldest age?

"God enjoys our enjoyments, and suffers with our sufferings," write Cobb and Griffin. "This is the kind of responsiveness which is truly divine and belongs to the very nature of perfection." In this process theology hews closer to the biblical tradition than can classical orthodoxy. For there is no immutable or impassive deity in the Bible. There is no metaphysical changelessness. There is to the contrary "steadfast love": not absolute immobility but resolute relationality. Each relation contributes something, if only a smudge of failure and tragedy, to the divine experience. So God in this vision is not a metaphysical Being but a process of becoming: not changeless but faithful in change. "Upon this basis," continue Cobb and Griffin, "Christian agape can come to have the element of sympathy, of compassion for the present situation of others, which it should have had all along."[33]

A moved mover, then, who lures us into becoming and receives what we become—and is therefore affected by that shared becoming. But, of course, this does not mean that the divinity suffers in the way that we suffer. God, for instance, may share our vulnerabilities, even to the point of experiencing the cross from within—but does not therefore die on it. It would indeed be another form of theolatry to imagine God fully absorbed in any one act of suffering, for instance, in the way we ourselves become wrapped in our own strong sensations. For if God is everywhere always, then God is experiencing a war and torture and the death of children in Iraq—yet is no less present to the children laughing on the swing with ice cream down my street.

Still, some consider any idea of divine receptivity, or suffering—com/passion—to be unworthy of worship. They will find any pathos on God's part—pathetic. And so by whatever language they revert to the classical stoic ideal of divine *apatheia*. They miss the theological meaning of Paul's "body of Christ"—in which, in emulation of the divine love, the members *feel with* each other's feelings.

The third way of a love in process means that the com/passionate divinity is truly involved in an open-ended interactivity with all of us creatures. This doesn't make the divine mystery any more knowable. It does make it more—incarnate. For it means that when we draw upon metaphors of God as Love, knowing them to be mere metaphors, analogies, or poems, we are drawing on the best metaphors of our experience. We would then be affirming that com/passionate love would be a higher ideal than either control or apathy.

Yet I think we must also exercise a certain sympathy with the thinking of the great medieval theologians. In their resistance to literalism, and particularly the degraded notion of a capricious and unfair sort of God, who intervenes for his elect favorites and has temper tantrums and forgives all rather arbitrarily, the idea of dispassion is not without merit.

Perhaps we may concur in this way: an infinite com/passion will resemble no finite passion. But this is not because God's love is really some transcendent abstraction, but rather because it takes in *all the passions* of the universe at every moment. It therefore exceeds each and all creaturely passions so utterly as to be

ultimately indistinguishable from an agapic dispassion. But this would be a dispassion not of an unmoved transcendence but of an infinitely mobile sensitivity.
Theologian Kathryn Tanner captures this third space elegantly: "Immanence
and transcendence, closeness and difference, are simply not at odds in God's
relations with us."[34]

The omni-amorous One transcends the world only by embracing it.
"Dispassion"—inasmuch as it connotes a sterile isolation or an immaterial
transcendence—does not well capture this perspective in which all creatures
matter altogether. All together.

The idea of *wisdom* better suggests the serenity of this dispassionate com/
passion. Wisdom connotes the caring, nonjudgmental, nonneedy sort of attention that we hope for from others. We want from them neither a rational
detachment from our feelings, nor a sloppy over-identification with them, but
a discerning empathy. For instance, in the novel August suffers one terrible loss
and several heart-pounding crises. The beekeeper grieves, she feels, but she does
not panic. She does not seem long overwhelmed, and thus can provide harbor for
others who do. One might say that she retains always an element of dispassion in
her com/passionate involvement in the passions of all she comes to love.

Imagining God differently allows new images of the human to emerge—
which in turn enrich the theological imagination. When the idea of God is alive
and in process, it yields a divinity in process, close and different, interacting in
the open-endedness of infinity. This God "saves the world as it passes into the
immediacy of his own life."[35] As Whitehead articulates responsive love, or the
"consequent nature of God": "It is the judgment of a tenderness which loses
nothing that can be saved. It is also the judgment of a wisdom which uses what
in the temporal world is mere wreckage."[36] This love seems to operate a kind of
cosmic recycling process, an ecology of salvation. But theology only lives if its
metaphors are helping us to salvage our own world from the wreckage.

Sticky Gift

The beekeeper tells Lily that graffiti of bees appear in the ancient catacombs
as symbols of resurrection. She is helping the girl undergo her passage from
deadly fear and loss to a new life, a life buzzing with possibilities, winged with
freedom, honeyed with gracious relations. The resurrection was for the early
Christians not just a promise about the future but a cure for the fear of death,
now. Awareness of our mortality can paralyze us. So the courage born of resurrection is a gift of rebirth in the now, a baptismal *present* that opens the end in
hope. Otherwise the resurrection is just another "I believe" shibboleth.

In the interknit members of the Body of Christ, an already once-risen body, we begin to live in the newness of life *now*—if we can *accept* the promiscuous gift of its love-life. I am loved as I am. This is the agapic prodigality. But this gift remains difficult to accept. For it requires, as Paul Tillich put it, that we accept that we are accepted.[38] The gift is not a donation: as though the honey were presented to the bee readymade. *The gift is the reception.* I am taken into the divine process as I am. So this acceptance of myself poses a great spiritual challenge: I must cut through both my false self-assurance and my false humility. Only so can I accept and therefore *actualize* my specific and present gift, my calling, my potential.

> The image—and it is but an image—the image under which this operative growth of God's nature is best conceived, is that of a tender care that nothing be lost.
>
> —ALFRED NORTH WHITEHEAD[37]

Self-actualization, however, is never just a self-relation. Its activity is not "pure act" but porous interactivity. It exposes me to the uncertainties and contradictions of my open networks of relationship. "I" become who I will be within that network of relations, rooting in the nonhuman, blossoming in the intimate, branching into the unknown.

I may fear losing myself in all those relations. That fear echoes the fear of death. For in relation to my mortality and to my dependencies I experience a threat to my boundaries.

In the context of her theology of the cross, Anne Wonhee Joh has written of the fear of relational stickiness. She notes that Jean-Paul Sartre characterized eros as a child who sticks his hand into the honeypot. "Its stickiness is a trap, it clings like a leech, it attacks the boundary between it and myself." Joh shows how disgust with sticky feelings, identified with femininity, is a symptom of patriarchy East and West. She writes that love—which she symbolizes with the Korean word *jeong*, connectivity—"is a threat in a culture that values individualism and separation while devaluing communal interdependence and the interconnectedness of all."[39]

The adventure of a becoming self will get sticky. For of course some relationships, both individual and social, really do threaten to trap us. The truth that frees may sometimes spring a dramatic escape, like that of Lily from abuse. But as we grow in confidence, liberation also happens through giving up a fear, a grudge, a rage. This giving is forgiving. Lily, who becomes a skilled collector of honey in the novel, says that "people, in general, would rather die than forgive."[40] So we lock our passion in to our anger. Here a bit of dispassion may be just the ticket! Yet the virtue of forgiveness, like cheek-turning, became a moralism that demeans either myself or the other. It releases oppressors from responsibility as often as it works to interrupt the oppression. But we are learning to unsay the shibboleths of processed love. When we embark on the amorous adventure of a larger love, even forgiveness opens into the third way of resolute becoming.

The becoming that is our self flows with all of our relations into the divine becoming, where we are being recycled even now. This "tender care that nothing be lost"—not a swallow, not a hair—does not save us from our mortal lives. But *through* them. Whitehead's "intuition of permanence in fluency and of fluency in permanence"[41] puts all of life—permanently—into process.

Its fluidity sometimes thick, a little sticky, this love begins to absolve you of what is empty and dissolute; to dissolve for you what is hard and absolute. It retunes us to our inescapable interdependence and releases us to life again. No matter what.

"Get up from there and live like the glorious girl you are."

CHAPTER 7

Jesus the Parable
Christ as Process

I will open my mouth to speak in parables;
I will utter things hidden from the foundation of the world.
—MATT. 13:35 [1]

We have been moving within the forcefield of the Gospels all along the path of this book. But why only now, so indirectly and rather late, get around to the sign of "Christ" as such? Isn't this a rather wayward approach to the Way?

No doubt. When it comes to the heart of Christian theology, which is Christology, the doctrine of Christ, the only way that I can follow the way of Christ, the way that *is* Christ, is through a backdoor. For the front entrance is still patrolled by border guards: "Do you believe that Jesus Christ is your Lord and Savior?" The Jesus Christs, uttered breathlessly and without mystery, are breathless and legion.

In truth: Jesus would not have passed.

Here is a parable *about* Christology itself.

A man died. The people who knew him gathered to share memories. Finally a portrait was commissioned. But as generations passed the painting did not seem fine enough. The heirs of the portrait, who had become wealthy, created a new golden frame, immense, carved with motifs from the portrait and encrusted with jewels. People began to feel that the old portrait of that dark fellow with the haunting eyes pulled the effect down. As it began to peel from age, they extended the frame inward. One day the frame covered the whole canvas.

133

Missing Jesus

No wonder so many thinking Christians have found in the Gospel Jesus a tool for deconstructing the absolutes of Christology. For instance, Robert McElvaine, not a biblical scholar or a theologian, has written of "Jesusfree" Christianity. He calls "a spayed Christianity a spayed Christianity." Its basic contention, he writes satirically, is "simple: Accept Jesus as your Lord and Savior and then you can do whatever the hell you want."[2] Well, within limits: practice war, hatred, greed, sexual hypocrisy, and destruction of the earth. But this "Christianity Lite" deploys its Christ for an anti-gay, anti-abortion agenda that claims to be the literal biblical truth—and has literally zero basis in the Gospels. It weighs so little because it is conveniently devoid of Jesus.

Whatever their political motives, most New Testament scholars would concur that the symbolic Christ has from the earliest stages of textual transmission overshadowed the traces of the historical Jesus. Scratching beneath the overedited surface of the text in search of the gaunt Jew still living in his skin, the textual excavation of the Gospels has proceeded for well over a century. With its help, we might be tempted, whether for political, historical, or theological reasons, to give up on *Christ*—in the name of *Jesus*. Such a reversal would be a neat and modern solution. But in the early twentieth century the great New Testament scholar Rudolph Bultmann tried, as others had and do, to "demythologize" the Gospels, and so in effect to cleanse the human figure of Jesus of the christological accretions added to the text after the fact. What he found, however, was not a factual biography but the post-Easter proclamation of the early community.

A Christless Jesus would represent a self-dissolving solution for Christians. For the four Gospel accounts of Jesus do not resolve into any kind of objective, historical unity: Does his family come from Bethlehem or Nazareth? What does he say on the cross? To whom does he appear in the resurrection? Moreover, the Gospels are hardly Christless, nor, as the Gospel of John with its incarnate Word testifies, free of the divinization of Jesus as the Christ. In Paul the divinization of the messianic figure of the Christ was simultaneously intensifying; but it would be during the following centuries of mission within the Roman Empire that the deification of the Christ would eclipse the true humanity—nonetheless always confessed—of Jesus.

We have in the Gospels to do with four very different portraits, the fourth really different from the first three, which are called the Synoptics. A portrait is not a photograph. It is painted from a perspective, with particular emphases and particular omissions, with a style that already "frames" its subject.

If the story of Jesus remains irreducible to a single account, we can never escape the feedback loops of interpretation. Does that make biblical interpretation just relativism after all?

Indeed, the quest for the historical Jesus can lead one to the critic's shrug, not so distant from Pilate's "What is truth?" But for all its frustrations, the quest for the historical Jesus and the *non*rhetorical question of the Gospel Jesus himself ("Who do *you* say that I am?") may draw us deeper into the truth-process. Biblical interpretation also is *en procès*, on trial and in process. And no honest theology can escape the process.

The four testimonies together form the *evangel*, the "good news," of the Testament Christians call "new." We need not seek that newness in distinction from the Testament that Jews do not find "old." Its novelty rather distinguishes it from what we must call the *processed Christ*. That dispiriting—breathless—construction is produced by abstraction not only from the historical context of Jesus himself, but from the context with which he was ultimately concerned: that which he called the *basileia tou theou*, the "kingdom" of God (or of heaven, in Matthew, who preferred not to speak directly of "God"). This radically relational metaphor, the subject of Jesus' parables, proposes nothing resembling any historical kingship, empire, patrilineage dictatorship, or top-down power, let alone the ahistorical place that came to be meant by "heaven."

In order to avoid the misunderstandings to which "kingdom" can now give rise, I often stay with the original Greek term. The *basileia* is not a political programme. But neither does it leave politics alone—especially when a contemporary empire draws upon Christ for legitimation. "The best English translation," argues John Cobb, "may be 'commonwealth.' This term, besides not emphasizing the controlling power of a ruler, suggests that the realm may be organized for the common good." The "commonwealth of God" resists every human superpower. Jesus meant it "to be a world in which God's will is done, God's purposes are fulfilled."[3] He saw his work and that of his community as "foreshadowing" that world—by beginning to actualize it here and now.

Creedal Omission

It is not just a recent, Americanized, and increasingly globalized style of evangelism that dishes out a processed Christ. The *basileia*-free, Jesus-less abstraction is encapsulated in the creeds of the classical mainline tradition. The familiar Apostles' Creed has us "believe . . . in Jesus Christ, his only Son, our Lord; who was conceived by the Holy Spirit and born of the Virgin Mary; he suffered under

Pontius Pilate, was crucified, dead and buried; he descended to hell; on the third day he was raised from the dead; he ascended into the heavens, and sits at the right hand of God the Father almighty . . ."

What is wrong with this picture?

Isn't something missing? Like, the *life?* The creeds all emphasize a supernatural origin, then cut right from his birth to his death and resurrection. They lack all mention of his living and speaking and loving, of his preaching, wisdom, healing, and prophecy. Not a whisper. Priest and womanist theologian Kelly Brown Douglas nails it: "His ministry is virtually ignored."[4]

This *lack* became the very stuff of piety—as though we are to concern ourselves only with the "divine part" of him, the supernatural identity: "the Son of God, begotten from the Father; only-begotten—that is from the substance of the Father . . ." elaborates the earlier Nicene version.

The creeds are important historical witnesses to past forms of unifying belief. But they are all frame, no portrait: they discretely overlook the Gospel testimony to that Jewish person, the Afro-Asian, fleshly, talkative one. The one who modeled a new style of com/passion toward the suffering and the vulnerable others. Indeed, who exercised what liberation theologians in a suffering Latin America of the twentieth century would call the "option for the poor." New Testaments during the same period have reconstructed a compelling portrait (not a snapshot) of Jesus as a Galilean from the peasant or, more precisely, artisan class, who preached the unfolding *basileia* of God, who urged people to rethink their lives in that light, and whose message implied criticism of the *basileia* of the Caesars.

My own Christianity would have long since dissolved into a vaguely spiritual relativism without the discovery of that dusty, on-the-ground, and sometimes underground Jesus. Yet I don't want to limit its meaning to "Jesus the Liberator," the prophet of social ethics—which is also a framing device.

For a theology of becoming the identification of Jesus as the Christ does not lose importance; rather, the question of the Christ-identity may be called again into alignment with the priorities of the Gospel Jesus. The frame does not dissolve but cracks open. What comes into focus may not be the historical Jesus but his own ultimate concern: the way of the *basileia* might open. I don't want to lose the inexhaustible radiance of the Christ-symbol.

I *do* want to put the breathing room back in Christology: an interval of *ruach*, right in between "Jesus" and "Christ." Otherwise the meaning of *each* of these terms gets dissipated: one a proper name, the other a symbolic title, a Greek translation of the Hebrew term *messiah*, meaning the "anointed," as were kings in the Davidic line. "Jesus" and "Christ" became inextricably linked a couple thousand years ago for Christians; but neither term can deliver its historical and prophetic significance without the breathing room, the pause. I plead with my students, many of whom are already practicing church-based ministries, to undertake the spiritual discipline of not saying "Jesuschrist" for the semester. When Jesus of Nazareth is not enough, try referring in the ancient style to Jesus *as* the Christ. Just for a while. In that pause a more *spirited* Christology becomes possible.

Revealing or Concealing?

In the interval of the breath, the question of Jesus' *identity* begins to shift—sideways, not up, not down. It shifts into the question of his *priorities.* He shifts it himself, in advance. Sometimes he is so explicit as to the priority, as in the double love commandment, that one wonders how the Christian right could miss it. Or as in the beatitudes. Reflecting on the "attitude of beatitude," the Reverend Bob Edgar, General Secretary of the National Council of Churches, asks simply: "What part of 'Blessed are the peace-makers' don't they understand?"[5] Often, however, Jesus has encoded these priorities—at once hidden and revealed them—in the deceptively simple form of *parables.*

Parables, a style of nonelite wisdom throughout the world, are the Gospels' privileged style of sideways discourse. Parables are shibboleth-resistant micronarratives. They thwart theological abstractions from the start. "Nothing could be more unauthoritative than the parables of Jesus," according to one leading scholar. "Their whole purpose is to enable the listener to discover something . . ."[6] The word *parable* first means "to set or throw to the side," as in making a comparison, an analogy, a metaphoric link between a concrete story and a more elusive meaning: truth told not straight but slant. Scholars concur that Jesus preferred to speak in parables, and that it is in this sidelong form that he was at his most original. So in them we are most likely to hear his voice (in contrast to the interpretations of the parables that were added by scribes, as in "the seed stands for the word of God," and so forth). This does not mean that all the parables were uttered by Jesus, let alone remembered and recorded accurately. Even if they were, the parables are a cagey genre from the start.

Deliberately and simultaneously they conceal what is revealed and reveal what it concealed. "To you it has been given to know the mysteries of the kingdom of heaven," Matthew has Jesus saying to his disciples (13:11). But "the reason I speak to them [the multitudes] in parables is that 'seeing they do not perceive, and hearing they do not listen . . .'" (13:13). Talk about speaking God's wisdom in a mystery! He is alluding to Isaiah, as he often does. Disturbing, really: Why hide the meaning from the masses? Isn't that mystification rather than mysticism? But then in the very same chapter he cites the prophet opening his "mouth to speak in parables" and so to "utter things hidden from the foundation of the world" (13:35). So a parable may pry open the very order of the creation, scooping a bit of meaning from the bubbling depths of the *tehom*. The creative style of parables—Albert Nolan calls them "works of art which reveal or uncover" truth about life—amplifies the creativity of genesis itself.[7]

Seems that this very form of speech sets us on the mystery! It may be the opposite of mystification: perhaps this is Jesus' strategy of demystifying false mysteries and cluing us into real ones. After all—as the title of John Caputo's *What Would Jesus Deconstruct?* signals—Jesus was always deconstructing the operative absolutes, the do's, don'ts, and I believe's. To deconstruct is not to destroy but to expose our constructed presumptions. The sidelong move of a parable—setting the (then, still) mysterious notion of "the kingdom of heaven" next to, say, the mustard seed—creates an interval. The parable produces its own breathing room, its truth-space. Not unlike a Zen koan, a parable is a wisdom story that interrupts presumptions with *an open-ended interaction*. It silences the pious shibboleths and resists translation into new ones.

If ultimate concern gets expressed in direct propositions it may too readily harden into truthiness—*except* for those who already have ears to hear. These would be the ones called "disciples" who have become adept in a new discipline of thinking and living. It is not a new elitism Jesus is advancing. It is a way to communicate with a complex multitude, with all their inevitable prejudices. Parables do not hide the truth but rather protect it from false certainties. They do not close anyone out by their concealment. At the edge of the unknowable, they advance a wayward dis/closure. "Parable," writes one New Testament scholar of parables, "is always a somewhat unnerving experience."[8]

Theology, with its inflated Western blocks of abstraction (mea culpa), has lost the economy of parable. It may have lost its nerve as well. So we are learning again to "speak God's *sophia* in a mystery." For "by teaching in parables," as one commentator puts it, "Jesus assumes Wisdom's roles."[9] Thus Paul interprets Jesus as "Christ the Wisdom of God" (1 Cor 1:24). (Thus Elizabeth Johnson has developed from Paul and the Gospels a Christology of Jesus as the Wisdom of God, or "Jesus Sophia."[10])

The wisdom-parable becomes a parable for the third way we are following in this book. It points waywardly beyond any absolutism of an unquestionable, unquesting truth of revelation. Yet it does not dissolve into a banal concealment concealing nothing, *nihil.*

In Joy: Discerning Priorities

In the light of the understanding of parables internal to the Gospels, it is brilliant that Matthew has placed within the very same chapter 13 a parable that performs this double-gesture of concealing/revealing not just in *form* but in *content.*

Hidden, found, covered up again, and then joyfully claimed; concealed and revealed, re-covered and discovered: what is this hide-and-seek "kingdom," this *basileia*? "Kingdom" suggests the social field organized around a dominant power—that of a *basileus*, a king or emperor, the primary form of governance in the ancient world. Yet the parable at the same time deconstructs any notion of a king-like intervention. What kind of power operates in the parable? The parable scuttles any simple "God did this" sort of logic. The very form of the parable, and the locution of the *basileia*, deflects interest from a divine Person or substance. (Indeed, Matthew's Jesus is too good a Jew to name The Name—hence he prefers *ouranion.*) The parable shifts focus to the metaphoric realm, or better, force field, of the dis/closure.

> Consider that the kingdom of heaven is like treasure hidden in a field: when someone finds it, that person covers it up again, and out of sheer joy goes and sells every last possession and buys that field.
>
> —MATT. 13:44

Let *joy* be your guide? Really? How discerning is joy?

This desire for the treasure is no casual fleeting desire. Does it not suggest the passion, the holy Eros, that we have been considering? If there is a divine power operating in this micro-narrative, would it not be precisely the force of love? As love is its own reward, so this treasure is not for buying other things, but rather is itself the thing most treasured. It is that for which we are willing to *give our all*—not out of a grim spirit of self-denial or self-sacrifice, but, as the parable says, "in sheer joy."

Of course, this joy is riskier than it seems. "And sillier," comments Melanie Johnson DeBaufre, my colleague in New Testament. "I am struck by how foolish the treasure makes the man appear. The parable can be heard as a joke—what does the guy have now? Nothing really. A field with a buried treasure? So what! If the treasure is not uncovered, it makes no difference for him in concrete terms. Thus to those who don't know about the treasure he appears quite the fool."[11]

This foolhardy joy is tough. First of all, we may not really know what we want. Our priorities fall routinely out of focus. And then if we do clarify our priorities, we have choices to make in order to act on them. These choices may cause hurt, not joy. For example, the parable says to me at this moment: give up all you can in order to find enough time to write. In writing I find treasure. But it is a costly joy. It means giving up activities that I also enjoy, activities that nurture my institution, my friendships, my spouse, my family. I don't take it to mean give up the things I *have* to do (since I have to do them). Nor does it ask me to give up things that I *truly want* to do. On the contrary, it seems to be all about discerning what I *really* want, what the mystics call "the heart's desire." Recall the "love-counsel" of Hadewijch—not easy! Impossible choices become possible in the excitement of discovery, of dis/closure, of new-found love.

Some would say, nah, the treasure is Christ, and the choice is a once-and-for-all yes or no. OK. But is it irrelevant that Jesus does not tell parables about *himself* but about the *basileia* of heaven (in Matthew) or of God (in Mark and Luke)? Isn't this parable of the treasure precisely not about the *identity* of Jesus but about his own sense of *priorities*? And therefore about how to discern *our* priorities? How to actualize the lure, the love, they reveal? We can *theologically identify* this priority as Christ, the *logos*, the son or indeed the wisdom of God—or even as "the historical Jesus."[12] But we must take care not to lose Jesus' own priorities in the focus upon—who Jesus *really* is. The identity may again swallow the priority.

Parables unnerve abstract generalizations or point-by-point interpretations. For instance, this joy: Whose is it precisely? How do I tell the difference between *my* desire and the *divine* desire? Does the power of God come down to this attraction—a love-counsel that lures us to give our all? The *basileia* is a profoundly relational notion. Yet this discovery seems intensely, even possessively, personal. Does this person "own" the truth after all? And doesn't the parable seem to sanction private wealth—rather than a *commonwealth*? Yet the *economic priority*, material and spiritual, becomes vivid in other parables.

Overpaid Idlers: Economics of the *Basileia*

Take, for instance, the parable of the laborers:

Not surprisingly, this parable is infrequently cited in U.S. Christianity. Our economic system relies upon excess labor, maintaining a certain level of

The landowner hires workers at dawn to work in his vine-yard. But he returns to the town square a few hours later, he finds more of them hanging about. He hires them. He returns several times. "And about five o'clock he went out and found others standing around; and he said to them, 'Why are you standing here idle all day?' They said to him, 'Because no one has hired us.' He said to them, 'You also go into the vineyard'" (cf. Matt. 20:6-7). As though shocked at the unemployment levels, he gives everyone who is seeking work a job. They are not avoiding work, they just cannot find it. The proprietor then at the end pays everyone for a full day's work—even those who started at five. Understandably this annoys those who worked hard all day in the sun. When they complain, in a precise parallel to the better-known parable of the prodigal son, he points out respectfully that he has paid them the denarius they had agreed to: "'Friend, I am doing you no wrong'" (cf. 20:13). This improper proprietor gently challenges their attitude: "Are you envious because I am generous?" (cf. 20:15b)

un- and under-employment, in order to give managers the bargaining edge. Conveniently the unemployed get branded as lazy. Racial stereotypes reinforce the ease with which the system blames its victims. It is telling that in our statistically very Christian nation, three out of four Americans think that the Bible says, "God helps those who help themselves." Actually it was Ben Franklin. Amazed by the biblical illiteracy of our statistically Christian nation, Bill McKibben remarks that this "über-American idea, a notion at the core of our current individualist politics and culture . . ." is "not only not biblical, it's *counter*-biblical."[13] Indeed, if God or the godly is represented in this parable by the landowner, he is helping folk who cannot help themselves without first *being* helped.

If love for enemies poses a limit-case for agape, love for prodigal sons, daughters, or workers poses a more constant and annoying demand. Com/passion for the latecomers, the underachievers, the undocumented immigrants, the prodigals, the last and the least comes hard for me, if I'm a hard-working, fiscally responsible American. I don't hate them. I just don't want them to be treated like me—this devalues my hard work! If we are "compassionate conservatives," we argue (following the theorist of that phrase, Marvin Olavsky, in *The Tragedy of American Compassion*) that it is bad for them, for their self-esteem and work ethic, to receive more than they earn.

Com/passion in the parable plays no such zero-sum game. Yet the landowner does not enact an alternative economic model. The story belongs to a context of patronage in which a landowner's act of generosity could aptly image the divine Agape. Read anachronistically, however, his choices seem patronizing. What remains radical in the parable for our context, where systemic justice for laborers is at least an ideal, is this: everyone willing to work deserves a living wage. Scripture invites us to "have life, and have it abundantly" (John 10:10). Not surprisingly, abundance of life is often taken to mean literal wealth—thus giving rise to the "prosperity gospel."

Another recent poll showed that 61 percent of U.S. Christians think "God wants people to be financially prosperous."[14] Abundance surely includes having the material you need to celebrate life—and to share that abundance. For a worthy life cannot by definition in New Testament terms build itself upon a hoard of personal wealth. Life cannot be celebrated privately. Even if we disregard such inconvenient and typical texts as "sell your possessions, and give alms" (Luke 12:33), abundance is not zero-sum but an open-ended, embodied interactivity. The abundance at stake in the *basileia*, the "treasure," cannot mean material wealth. But material wealth and other privileges with which we have been blessed may become, through just love, worthy *means* to the basileic abundance.

If the "prosperity" gospel makes a mockery of Jesus' priorities, nonetheless it has mass appeal among both haves and have-nots, on all continents. Social-justice theology bears some responsibility for the distortion. We have too often neglected the affirmation of abundance, preaching a cross of personal self-denial that is more of a turn-off than a lure to the multitude. Thus people think social justice means excessive personal self-sacrifice rather than risking oneself for social change.

We might instead affirm Jesus' priority of love and his option for the poor while acknowledging that the parable does not implicitly condemn landowners for their privilege; what matters is how that privilege gets used.[15] The economics of the *basileia mattered* to Jesus—materially and spiritually. But the abundance is the gift of a generosity that mimics the omni-amorous divinity.

In different moods and media, the Gospel Jesus strained his listeners with this amorous excess, asking them to rehearse this difficult joy, to try it in concrete acts of compassion toward this specific neighbor, this specific opponent. He was reciting the Hebrew rigorous tradition of love of the *ger*, the stranger, the immigrant, and the enemy.

This agape is in its incipience always gift, beyond and before our deserving. And if we receive it we give it in the same spirit. But even within the archaic metaphor of the patron, the gratuitous character of love bears no resemblance to George H. W. Bush's "thousand points of light"-style of charity. How distant are such "points" from the primal flow of agape. *Caritas*, Latin for agape, translated into "charity"—and slowly degraded into private short-cuts through the collective requirements of economic justice.

For what is the commonwealth of heaven if not a metaphor that sets our life—in divine perspective? But that life only *lives* intertwined with all the other lives in our concretely emerging context *now*, within the genesis collective. So Jesus was simply not interested in people's relations to God in abstraction from their relation to others. He didn't care about their souls in abstraction from their material practices and conditions. He touched souls bodily, and bodies soulfully, as sites of spiritual healing and material well-being. Between divine love and human loves: no zero-sum game.

Heaven, Hell, and Here

By the same token Jesus in the Gospels was not interested in his listeners' relationship to *him*—in *abstraction from all their other relations*. It is in the great parable of final judgment that the shift from the Christ-identity to Jesus' priority becomes explicit. This is the story of the "king" who offers to the "sheep" he has separated from the "goats" "the kingdom prepared for you from the foundation of the world" (Matt. 25:34). This is not a parable *about* final judgment, any more than the last one was *about* a literal landowner. It uses the drama of judgment, so familiar to his listeners, as a parable: about how to live now.

The scene is eschatological, addressing all of humanity. There follows a parallel exchange with "the goats," those who think they would have fed, clothed, and otherwise succored "the King" if they had met him. To them the response is devastating: "Truly I tell you, just as you did not do it to one of the least of these, you did not do it to me" (25:45). It isn't just that our agape toward the marginalized

> "'For I was hungry and you gave me food, I was thirsty and you gave me something to drink, I was a stranger and you welcomed me, I was naked and you gave me clothing, I was sick and you took care of me, I was in prison and you visited me.' Then the righteous will answer him, 'Lord, when was it that we saw you hungry and gave you food, or thirsty and gave you something to drink? And when was it that we saw you a stranger and welcomed you, or naked and gave you clothing?' . . . And the king will answer them, 'Truly I tell you, just as you did it to one of the least of these who are members of my family, you did it to me.'"
>
> —MATT. 25:35-38, 40

counts as care for this Lord. But in failing to care for *one* of these—at least one? a particular one? *every* one?—we doom ourselves.

Such unnerving apocalyptic imagery means to slice through the fog of our personal habits and social assumptions. It convenes a truth process, in this case, truly a trial. The point is not at all that there is a literal king up there who is saving and condemning individuals: that scene is the parable. It suggests quite the opposite: that salvation comes in realizing that the ultimate ("last") meaning of my life is from the divine point of view inseparable from those inconspicuous others huddled at the margins of my vision. Again, this is not a parable *about* punishment and reward—they provide the archaic metaphors. It is about the ultimate stakes of agape. That love is demanding. The com/passion was ever passionate, never sentimental. To persist in it might take all the resolution we can muster.

Here Jesus yanks "Christ" right out of the gilded frame. If in the face of the child abused next door, or joining a gang downtown, or starved and terrified in Darfur, we do not notice the Christ—we have missed him. Which is to say, we betray the ultimate meaning, the "final" meaning, of our own lives. Of our *shared creaturely life.* It is not just that *Jesus* is inseparable from the most vulnerable members of our own species: it is that he is teaching that inseparability as our *own* ultimate condition. Dorothee Sölle expresses this truth thus: "there is no salvation apart from the whole." Salvation, from *salvus,* meaning health, well-being, wholeness, cannot take place for one part of a body while the rest is ill. Salvation is a sticky process; we are stuck in our creaturely condition all together, and there is no indication that any eternal life will unstick us.

What about the final separation of sheep and goats? Isn't that, you might argue, a great unsticking?

Indeed, it separates those who have lived in the delusion of separateness from those who embraced their sticky inseparability from "the least." The least are the test-cases of the human: the ones who fall between the cracks of the system. They test what it means to be human. Both for those of us who find ourselves marginalized, and for those of us content to leave the margins as they are, our humanity is at stake. For after all our humanity—and humanity means nothing but a shared life—remains in process and sometimes truly on trial. Our inner "goat" (goats seem to have symbolized to ancient farmers a greedy, competitive aggressor) couldn't care less about those inconsequential others.

Yet many grow from the greedy needy ego into a wider life. Those living from that larger life "in spirit" practice what Paul Tillich called a theonomous self, a God-directed self, in contrast to a delusional, head-butting *autonomy*. But must we call them "sheep"? There's a metaphor that gets lost in translation! In an ancient agricultural context, sheep had connotations not of penned-in, passive, and pretty obedience, but of a roving co-existence in the wilderness. The parable puts a premium on that cooperative, peaceful spirit, countering the culture of competition and predation. We are not called to be sheepish. No one sheepish visits prisoners or works for the homeless or challenges the predatory systems that keep some poor that others may have abundance. We are called to "flock"—to congregate, to gather, to con/spire in the original sense: to collaborate in the spirit of just love.

The parable raises the stakes of that radically relational spirit—to eschatological ultimacy. What is at stake is a place "in the kingdom prepared for you from the foundation of the world." That *basileia* remains grounded, founded, in "the world," that is, *this* creation. Yet for most Christians Jesus is really talking about heaven after death. I don't want to exclude that dimension of ultimacy from the present interpretation. How could I? What seems key to me is Jesus' own priority: not the metaphoric rewards and punishments, but the shock to all those religious folk who worship the Lord properly—and then hear they had misplaced their faith. He didn't want their obeisance. This Lord wanted to be found in all the suffering faces. In all the irreligious, improper places. Now.

Nonetheless, what about that final judgment after life? I think about it like this: if we cannot make the transition into the larger love-life, if we cling grimly to what we have or crave bitterly what we cannot have—we wouldn't want to be in this "heaven" anyway! We would not belong. Wrong club, wrong neighborhood, wrong retirement community. For what images does the Bible have of that kingdom, or of the new creation, or of "heaven"—except intensively *relational* metaphors of feast, embrace, wedding, endless singing and dancing *togetherness*. With those others we ignored, found so spiritually irrelevant, uninteresting, repulsive, or just unreal in our actual existence? Now we should be tangled eternally together with them? In a subtler body that won't shield me (as do my skin, clothing, church) from them? Yuck!

If I do not learn here and now that these chaotic multitudes of suffering and marginal humans are my kin, if I cannot shift into identification with the larger life of the world, then how should I *abide* that largest life? What pleasure would there be in spending eternity with those multitudes of haunting *others* gathered into God? What would there be in it for *me*?

What would be heaven for some will be hell for others. Not because a punitive Lord sends them to a different place—that is just the folksy metaphor. The context-dependent metaphors like kings and sheep will shift, but the divine com/passion remains steadfast. So *we can only abide in God by abiding in the spirit and the truth of that love.* The eschatological metaphors warn passionately that there will be no individual, separate salvation, some eternal retreat for me 'n' my Jesus. The faith that clings to its own salvation may be just another form of greed and need. No matter how tightly some Christians hold on to their Jesus—he has made his own "identity" clear: he *is for us none other than the other.* The historical Jesus lived, testified, and died. After the resurrection, the Christ no longer appears *as* the person Jesus. He is then for us the one we encounter *not* in the person who was "the Lord" but in the persons who are of *the least.*

When Christians focus on Jesus' lovely identity rather than on his love priority, they make the mistake of the goats.

Salvation in Process

No love of God will save us from the God of love. For this edgy care expresses something about who we most fundamentally *are*—"from the foundation" and in the end. Thus in this book we have utilized the categories of process thought to clarify the way we creatures are nothing more and nothing less than open-ended processes of interaction. We don't exist apart from our relations. So we have no self-esteem without esteem for the others who comprise our world. And vice versa. The metaphor of "eternal life" suggests that in some mysterious sense the individual process does not come to an end—unless its *way* gets blocked. Unless it loses touch terminally.

If Jesus the parabler gives voice to the ultimate stakes of our human relationships, those stakes have in our time heightened for our species, almost apocalyptically. The least of these may now appear as the earth itself, which we may also turn into a hot living hell.

No wonder so many turn to an other-worldly, greedy-needy salvation system for themselves; and, at the same time, no wonder so many others just indulge their needs and greeds in the world. For if our salvation depends upon redeeming this whole—we're doomed, aren't we? What kind of love is that? Where is the joy?

Not in trying to save the world! The parables don't actually tell us to redeem anyone or anything. A messiah complex, however virtuous, is a formula for burn-out. It will take us right off the mystery. Redemption—or salvation, or atonement—is a process that infinitely exceeds human capacities. Inasmuch as the love-priority becomes our own, we *take part* in redemption; we *participate* in the new creation, in the renewal that is the *basileia*: it *begins*. Never from nothing. The parables lure us with joy and with urgency to actualize what is *possible*. Within ourselves, within our worlds.

By what we can predict with the apparatus of a calculative certainty, the odds seem poor for our shared future. But we do not know what might be possible. The *basileia* unfolds not amidst the predictable but at the edge of chaos: where what had not been possible, becomes possible. Where possibilities previously closed into impossibility open up: thus the Greek and Gospel word for truth, *aletheia*, literally means the "un-hidden." This truth-process, as we have seen, does not comprise a piece of dictation or information, but an inter-activity. The possibility is the lure for the *basileic becoming*.

In their double gesture of revealing and concealing, the parables express a rhythm of unfolding and enfolding. In this they condense the movement of genesis itself, of the open-ended creation: of God unfolding in the creation, and of the creation enfolded in God. Of a divinity moving in eros and moved in agape: creation and salvation.

Salvation is in process or it is not happening. To the question, "What is *salvation?*" John Wesley answers that it is exactly "not what is frequently understood by that word: the going to heaven, eternal happiness. It is not the soul's going to paradise, termed by our Lord, 'Abraham's bosom' [Luke 16:22]. It is not a blessing which lies on the other side of death; or (as we usually speak) 'in the other world.'"[16] This Wesleyan deconstruction of traditional assumptions opens the space for the salvation he *does* intend: "It is not something at a distance. *It is a present thing* . . ."[17] That blessing, in its present joy and challenge, is neither something that we do on our own, nor something that will be done for us. It is an open-ended inter-activity and a mystery in process: a mystery that we see veiled by the processed Christ but revealed in the living one.

The wisdom we try to speak it with is called Sophia, or Word, or Spirit. Its power, alien to any divine coercion, depicts itself in the delicacy of mustard seeds. Hidden treasure. Birds in a shrub. The sower. Improper and unexpected welcomes, remunerations, parties. But they are images of *the possible.* In their actualization lies salvation. Now or never.

Fermenting Possibility

One more parable: this one delivers a quick, homey image with a transgressive twist. For Jesus' hearers, the yeast was understood to be profane, ritually unclean in comparison to the unleavened bread of Passover. I have only kneaded bread enough to appreciate the skill and strength of those who really do. It feels pretty much impossible at first. But the lump of lifeless flour, massaged through with the force of fingers and permeated by the secret power of a little yeast, arises transformed!

> The kingdom of heaven is like yeast that a woman took and hid in three measures of flour until all of it was leavened.
>
> —MATT. 13:33

The image suggests not effortless magic, but also not mere toil and trouble, but a synergy of effort and grace. The grace-bearer, as ever, seems most unpromising. This small, single-celled fungus that ferments sugars and other carbs is truly one of the least of species. But this little bacterial life that reproduces rapidly by budding lifts the whole doughy lump. This subtle force, in its fermenting, fecundating, foaming fullness, clues us in to the mystery of divine influence. The yeast suggests something modest, a bit threatening. It rises to the apparently insurmountable odds. The impossible becomes possible.

Again we note this Gospel's brilliant play on the hiddenness in both form and content of the parable. It is found in the same chapter of parables, Matthew 13, discussed above, with its utterance of things "hidden" from the foundations. Here the woman "hides" the yeast. And what is revealed is not the yeast itself—it is revealed only to be reviled by the dough—but its majestic and improbable *effect.* Let us not confuse this with any shibboleths of the end-times—as though all will be revealed "in the end." That is not what the parable suggests. The *basileia* is depicted as a process. The bakerwoman's labor signifies the process itself, a process that in style and in content dis/closes the ferment of an alternative power.

The parable invites. It does not compel. It calls and does not coerce. *Grace is not irresistible but amazing.* The lure might be called, in the terms of John Wesley, "initiating grace." That practical theologian of grace put it carefully: "God does not continue to act upon the soul unless the soul re-acts upon God."[18] Not because God withholds grace but because grace is simply not a unilateral force. The influence of the yeast requires the massaging effort of the woman and the interaction with the flour. Or, the treasure must be found and extreme measures taken to acquire it. Or, the soil must actually let the seed germinate. Grace—fishy as it seems to predestinarians—needs our *cooperation*.[19] It is not a power over us, but an empowerment *of* us: "We can do all things in the light and power of that love, through Christ which strengtheneth us."[20] For Wesley another name for that grace is the holy spirit.

There is no hiding from our responsibility for ourselves and for our world. Yet process theology insists that at all times and in all places, the *logos* offers a lure, a possibility, a new chance, for our becoming. It may become ever more inaccessible to us, if we do not learn to discern it. But whatever we do—we are enfolded in the com/passion that "feels with" us. To participate in that agape is to take part in the *basileia*. We have seen that it is depicted in parables of love and judgment because biblical love has an edge, an eschaton. The judgment of our life is—our life. That phrase runs through my mind, from an avant-garde theatre production I saw when I was seventeen. The actors were crawling up and down a ladder at the top of which someone was somehow perched with a megaphone, chanting: "the judgment of your life is your life."

We have this one chance to live this one life of ours, to make our difference: the stakes are high but the grace runs deep. The very same process that dooms us can save us. For it is precisely our interactive life that exposes us to each other so vulnerably—and that collects us sometimes into a great force for good. The church, the commonwealth of God, the new Jerusalem, even the bodily resurrection of all the dead—these are ways, metaphors, parables of what is *possible* for earthlings.

A relational Christology will energize theology through the spirit, in a quite trinitarian sense. Here Jürgen Moltmann's pneumatological Christology is crucial, for the Spirit begins to push free of trinitarian shibboleths while intensifying the radical relationality that is the whole meaning of the Trinity. Very biblically, he incorporates traditional designation of "Holy Spirit" into the wide metaphorical field of "the Spirit of Life."

It is this Spirit of Life that we "get" in Jesus: that we may both receive and conceive. Not a miraculous favor or zap of salvation, not an absolute power to rescue us from the dissolute world—but a *resolute* spirit. In this spirit "which is in Christ" (but by no means limited to Christianity, nor requiring the epithet "Holy" like a first name) we don't give up on the world—or on ourselves. We might shift strategy but we stay on the mystery. We attend to the truth-process: something that was not possible becomes the very yeast of the possible.

> There is no mediation between Christ and the kingdom of God except the present experience of the Spirit, for the Spirit is the Spirit of Christ and the living energy of the new creation of all things.
>
> —JÜRGEN MOLTMANN[21]

The parables' insistence on a subtle, counterapocalyptic scale, is part of the revelation: hidden seeds, bacteria, coins, treasure, and the human "least," on a smallness that suddenly begins to amplify, to magnify. It is like the butterfly effect of chaos mathematics, which got translated into the "tipping point" in sociology. "The extreme sensitivity of initial conditions" that we considered in the doctrine of creation is that principle of a nonlinear process at the edge of chaos. Great effects can come of "the least" of beginnings. Precisely in the interactivity of an open-ended, nonlinear process, extraordinary transformations, "phase transitions," can occur. And it is rather nifty that like the whirlwind of Job, the budding bubbling of yeast is a good scientific instance of nonlinear order unfolding at the edge of chaos. Recall that such nonlinearity funds all complexity and therefore all life in the universe. And it remains unpredictable precisely because of the sensitive interdependence— the subtle togetherness—of its elements. Even of yeast molecules.

Precisely the interdependence that makes us so vulnerable, that indeed seems to condemn us to planetary apocalypse, may be the very means of human redemption. The butterfly effect of the spirit—or call it the yeast effect—suggests the possibility of an unexpected uplift, a tipping point toward the Beloved Community, a spiritual uprising. Or as one comic writer puts it: "a Great Upwising."[22] This is not to indulge a fantasy of omnipotent rescue, but to embrace the risk of spiritual evolution. The love-God of Jesus does not control but does surely unleash the grace of that energizing life. In our very midst. In the very modest circumstances of all our local possibilities.

Recently, a wonderfully engaged congregation in my area hosted an adult-education forum on the parables. Reflecting on the story of the baker-woman, Margaret—a regular—pronounced resolutely: "the leavening is the enlivening!"[23]

The Lure of a Higher Christology

We discussed in the prior two chapters the understanding of divine agency developed in process theology. The enlivening lure, the divine gift of the possible, is shared with a becoming creature as its own "initial aim." Desire ignites desire. This is the invitation, the eros. We also name it the *logos* or the *sophia* of God. Jesus as the Wisdom of God. Christ as the Word signifies that cosmos-embracing wisdom, "The *incarnate* logos is Christ."[24] In other words the *logos* names the universal wisdom—the wisdom of the universe. As incarnate in Jesus, Christians call it Christ. But it seeks incarnation—materialization—not just in Jesus but always and everywhere. The *Logos* of John's prologue, not a concept in the Synoptic Gospels, is a complex Greek term, meaning wisdom, concept, pattern, reason, speech, and revelation.[25] With process theology that *logos* appears as the very content of the lure. Thus the *logos* is always the same and always different, as the possibility for our becoming, here and now.

Within the Christian narrative, the incarnation in Jesus of that divine *Logos*, that world-creative Wisdom, is portrayed as a distinctive event. Indeed, it may be considered unique in this strong sense: only this person, as far as we know, has so *realized* the divine lure as to become "at one" with it. That intimate union or "sonship" is not a metaphysical given but an event of becoming, itself symbolized by Jesus' baptism. But does this make the incarnation an exclusive revelation of God in the final or competitive sense usually meant by identifying Jesus as the "only Son of God"? To the contrary: the whole point of the unique incarnation is to open up a new intimacy with the infinite. The one Gospel that features the incarnation, the "becoming flesh," signifies this open process powerfully: "to all who received him," writes John, "he gave power to become children of God" (John 1:13). In other words, to embrace this *logos is to become a son or a daughter of God.* The standard notion that *only* Jesus is the son of God directly defies the same Johannine text!

When in the same chapter John uses the phrase "like a father's only son" (1:14) is it contradicting itself? No, it is not saying Jesus *is* an only son. The "like" signifies a metaphor or analogy, not a literal identity. In the Gospel of John, the literalists are always wrong. But John uses signs, not parables, to signify Jesus' priorities. And in this first chapter John is signifying how Jesus' unprecedented intimacy with God makes it *possible* for any of us to become a son or daughter of God. This is not about exclusion, this is about a unique new strategy of *inclusion*. Indeed, in the Gospel of John, the language of kinship takes the place of that of the "kingdom." So as a bridge concept we may call upon the "*kingdom of God.*"

In the sticky justice of the *basileia* the fleshly interdependence of all creatures forms the context for the particular revelation of the flesh of God in Christ. But rather quickly classical theology had reveiled the relational process of the revelation, fixating instead on an abstract, immutable Christ-identity, extracted from all the other bodies. It confused the uniqueness of the Christ-event with an exclusive and changeless revelation: and so began to process Christ as some sort of immutable supernatural substance. But the grandeur of this incarnate *logos* lies precisely in its illumination of the word enfleshed in every creature of the creation—and above all in those least.

All the "son o' God" shibboleths threaten to block out the very "light of humanity" that is the life and grace of this Johannine word (1:4). They invariably privilege the gleaming Christ-identity of the Fourth Gospel over the dustier Jesus of the other three, with his parabolic priorities. Yet the "glory" of the word is not like an imperial sunburst wrought of gold. It glows upon the dark faces of those untoward multitudes—human and nonhuman—of the cosmos that "God so loved." "God envelops each and every one of our new births with divine glory," writes theologian Mayra Rivera (gloriously), "transfiguring, without obliterating the marks of their passions."[26] Glory is redistributed along with the incarnation.

The significance of the cosmic Christ extends—from a Christian perspective—infinitely outward, in all directions. It is no more high than it is wide and deep. When the mission that witnesses to its radiation shifts into aggressive exclusivism, the glory itself is blocked. For its glory depends upon embodiment.

In order to hold together the radically relational priority of the Gospel Jesus with the cosmic *logos* of the Christ-identity, a Christology of becoming will mingle the luminosity of the Johannine *logos* with the earthier Jesus of the Synoptics. But does this high Christology not produce yet another processed *Jesuschrist*? Not necessarily—if we make the following theological discernment.

Christ in Process

When we say that Jesus is the Christ, we mean that from our point of view the Jewish expectation of a Messiah was in a certain sense realized. If it was fulfilled in the person of Jesus—it is because he resolutely realized the possibilities tendered him by what he called *abba*. We might say that the initial aim for him moment to moment was to realize the messianic age, or the *basileia*, in the midst of his own limited circumstances. But this is precisely *not* to say that the messianic process was completed or exhausted. On the contrary: the possibility of its actualizaton in our own limited context was given a supportive communal shape and therefore a new imperative.

This present tense of the process lure might seem to lose both the "already" of the incarnation and the "not yet" of the eschaton. Yet the tension between the Christian "has come" and the Jewish "has not" remains profound.

A group of Drew Theological School students went to a service at a synagogue in our New Jersey neighborhood. The rabbi invited their questions afterward. One asked, not unpredictably, "But what about Jesus? He's the real messiah who's coming again. What about Jesus?" "You know I'm a Jew, and Jesus was a Jew," replied the rabbi. "So I think we'll have a lot in common to talk about whenever forever happens. I'll just have to wait. We're all waiting for someone. That's what we have in common. You're waiting. We're waiting. When your messiah comes again, you'll say, "It's wonderful to see you again!" and we'll say, "So, what took you so long?!"[27]

The rabbi was humorously suggesting that we both do and do not share the same Messiah. We share the same Jewish prophetic expectation that formed the Gospels. But if Jesus in no sense fulfilled that expectation for Jews, neither did he fulfill it in any final sense for Christians either. There would of course be no Christian symbolism of the future coming of Christ, of an apocalyptic Messiah or a second coming, if the church had felt that the messianic age had securely arrived and the first coming of the Messiah sufficient. Moltmann names a third way between the mere already and the mere not-yet: "The God of hope is himself the coming God."[28] For a theology of *becoming*, the *coming* is the lure of lures, the lure to our collective becoming. The be/coming of God happens in the endless process of interactivity at the edge of history.

What Moltmann calls "the messianic note of hope," the hope of the new creation, the new heaven and earth, the new Jerusalem—this is all still awaiting actualization, calling for our basileic becoming. As was all too obvious to most Jews, the messianic age had not arrived. Many things got worse in the world. Yet there has also been progress here and there, along the edges of chaos. And some of the worst regressions have come from the attempt to freeze history into some final form—as in the imperial sense that the Church Triumphant had already achieved the best that is possible in this world. The messianic age remains *always* yet to come in history: it is not a literal time-to-come, but an ideal that *resists* every realized eschatology.

This is to say theologically: the messianic expectation was embodied and performed in a distinctive and unsurpassed way in Jesus of Nazareth. In other words, the lure of Christ as the Christian translation of the messianic be/coming is the invitation to self-surpassing communal embodiments. The Christic process does not therefore collapse the tension of already/not yet but gathers it into this moment.

"For this I came into the world, to witness to the truth." That truth was not a mere identity—"himself." But he himself bore it, testified to it, taught and enacted it: he embodied it as fully as a human possibly could, in his living and in his dying. Or to take the confessional rhetoric up a notch: he embodied the truth as *divinely* as a human being could. So that we all who follow might embody and enact its possibilities. As best and as joyously as we can.

How then is *Christ* in process—and not just those who follow Jesus or actualize his *sophia*? The question would be: Is "Christ" alive for us? For nothing is alive if it is not in process—open-ended and interactive. Indeed, if we take seriously Paul's metaphor of "the Body of Christ," we belong to a complex organism that as such must always be unfolding in its metabolic, porous relations. This is not to say it must be *growing*. Church growth is often mistaken for the measure of the life of the institution. Quantitative growth in a mature organism usually signals an eating disorder or a cancer. Growth in wisdom bears only accidental correlation to growth in size. The mystery of life is immeasurable—and yet nonetheless practical.

Jesus died and came alive again in the narrative of the resurrected Christ. The Christ-symbol is alive only to the extent that it is embodied in process. It is in process to the extent that any church is alive. And a church is alive to the extent that it is living—practicing—the amorous justice of the *basileia*.

Becoming Parables

As Jesus' parables revealed what had been concealed and concealed what could not yet be revealed, so he too reveals and conceals—the divinity which was and was not his own. "Christ," Messiah, is not a synonym for God. How then shall we relate the priorities of Jesus to the Christ identity? If we want to say that God was in Jesus, in him indeed in a special way, the way that initiated a new way and a basileic process, but do not want the divinity to eclipse the humanity once again—can we still hold open that pneumatic pause between Jesus and the Christ?

The spirit that breathes between the priority and the identity, between the historical remembrance and the envisioned commonwealth, breathes life into

Christology itself. It keeps it in process and on trial, open to the way of its own future and open to people upon other ways. But when we imagine Jesus as the way itself, what kind of image comes into play?

Colossians praises Jesus as "the icon of the invisible God" (Col. 1:15). This icon (also translated "image") has cosmic dimensionality: "in him all things hold together." So the icon may free us from the flattened idols of a processed Christ. Such a formulation implies no simplistic Jesus = God. It invites us—we who are rendered in the image/icon of the invisible—to our own genesis. But an icon can freeze onto a visual surface, its visible image absolutized. How can we keep the Christ-icon in process and out of stasis?

> The parabler becomes parable. Jesus announced the kingdom of God in parables, but the primitive church announced Jesus as the Christ, the Parable of God.
>
> —JOHN DOMINIC CROSSAN[29]

What if, borrowing Crossan's great clue, we read Jesus as *the parable of God*? Jesus, Crossan writes, "died as parabler and rose as Parable."[30] Not a mirror, not a transparent window. Not a portrait—whatever portrait of Jesus we can recover, it is not then a portrait of the invisible and the infinite. The icon lives only in motion and in relation. A parable in its narrative dynamism captures that movement—as the truth-process of the *basileia* and the surprise of its possibility. Crossan summarizes the connection between "the kingdom of God and the stories of Jesus" in this maxim: "Parables give God room."[31]

The master teller of parables becomes, for those who have ears to hear and eyes to see, the parable of God. That in that space—between us, within us, beyond us—we may also become parables of an infinite becoming. In the becoming-flesh of our possibilities and the breathing room of the spirit, we might also give God some space.

tongues-talk (acts 2:1-35)
jim perkinson

taken-over tongue of spirit-froth
like a fire-head bird beak
shouting syllables of flight over the street-brick
of boot-on-the-back
shouting like never-before-speech
shouting red storms of revelation eyes
singing forever-ness
singing paradise in fives
singing sinai-desert stones on city pride
like a storm on the mind
like rain-rivers of redemption
like riots of word-revolt!

this is the day of broken sky
this is the space of conflagration-breath
speaking border-trespass
this is the feathered swoop of heaven
on the wing of now
the wide open mouth of thick
the tongue of river-bone crying
forking lightning into language
breaking black over white like a baptism
breaking god into prison
breaking the bar of lost-in-the-head-ness
breaking truth from jail!

what is the gift of gospel-funk?
did the twelve hear horns in the ear
like a 120 instrument chorus

did you think this was an orchestra?
is the ghost-groan a gift of incorporation
fixing prices on the scheme of sanctification
like salvation in a k-mart package?
the spirit comes without instructions for assembly

this is
surgeon-general's warning of
"no-way-to-anticipate-it" effect
a break-out of jubilation
on the tongue of mute child
the logic of laughter-belly
the jump of frozen-limb
the shout of deaf-mouth
the vision-explosion of blind eye
the collapse of consternation
the crash of shame
the size of flesh-on-the-rise
against every bullet of can't
the final demise of helpless!

this is the fire-tongued fork of holy-ghost howl
making love on the tongue
like fourth-of-july between the teeth
spitting flames of reconciliation
in the sky of war
making messiah-praise out of the air itself!

this is pentecost in your head
like becoming what you never dared
for the first time and forever.

CHAPTER 8

Open Ending
Spirit in Process

Insoluble Theology

Still. What is the point of a mystery without a solution? I can read mystery novels addictively, and feel cheated anytime an author experimentally breaches the formula: the perpetrator must be revealed and justice done. Theology has its own formulae. To stay on the mystery, we defy those fictive certainties. But say we let go of our received absolutes—even those of a social-justice liberalism that impugns "the tradition" as the perpetrator. Say we resist the casual nihilism that doesn't care anyway. How do we get some closure? At least of this book? What is the pay-off of a theology in perpetual process—for our actual lives, relationships, communities, institutions, churches, worlds?

Even if a solution is not forthcoming, a resolution might be. I have been calling it the resolute. "Becoming what you never dared" takes resolve. And as George Eliot quipped: "It is never too late to become who you might have been." (I bought a magnet inscribed with that *bon mot* as a birthday present, only to realize it would be insulting to anyone I gave it to. Some gifts are only for oneself . . .)

This book has spun us through seven sets of theological tensions. In each case the resolute manifests a positive third way. It appeared in each case differently: as relationality itself, as testimony, as the *creatio ex profundis*, as the omni-amorous power, as the lure that dares us, as the agapic justice, as the basileic process. And in each case, as in a parable, the sense of resolve does not solve but deepens the mystery.

This much may be clear by now: the way of becoming is not about taking control of your life or setting your goals—necessary as those ego-exercises may sometimes be. It is a matter of coordinating your passions and your priorities with larger purposes. Such a process of discernment demands a disciplined spontaneity, retaining always its edge of uncertainty. Its Way, as we have explored it together, hews close to the edge of chaos, the *tehom* within and without, without going over. It remains attentive to the unpredictable. So it can "risk the adventure" that demands of us creative forms of com/passion for *ourselves* as well as for the others. Without some self-respecting agape, our own becoming gets clogged with self-doubts and spurious ambitions.

God-talk can obstruct or foster our becoming, individually and together. I hope I have demonstrated that a theology in process does not happen in abstraction from the breathing, speaking processes that we each *are*. "Speaking God's *sophia* in a mystery" we do not mystify our open-ended interactivities but give them trusty language.

In the particular language of the present work, we have considered a theology of becoming under seven signs, unfolding like seven turns of a spiral. At each turn or fold the spiral recapitulates its trajectory. Under, for example, the sign of *truth* in process, *theology* evades the shrug of the dissolute and the shibboleth of the absolute; but then that truthfulness streams through the fishy *creation*; it flows in the influent *passion* of the possible; it testifies to a resolute *com/passion*, to a *basileia* that reveals a *Christ*-process in parables. And in signs. These seven signs, are *all* truth-processes. They are not synonyms but synchronicities. "In spirit and in truth" they operate in confluence and conspiracy.

I hope it is clear by now that as theological themes, rich in biblical narratives, they perform an unfamiliar style of biblical hermeneutics. Here the Bible has been used to influence and to inspire, not to command assent. Its metaphors, signs, and parables are not stripped of their poetry and indirection. They release spirals within spirals of meaning. This (indubitably) biblical theology deconstructs biblicism as a false authority. Certain ancient and future voices may speak "with authority and not as the scribes do." But that doesn't mean that clergypersons or theologians can co-opt that authority through citation. Quoting others—even biblical authors—as though one thereby takes possession of their truth is precisely to miss the divine call recalled in the text itself. That lure invites an interactive process of interpretation, in which we own up to our perspectives even as we open them up to criticism and influence.

To root our own thinking in theological traditions is to exercise a critical fidelity toward those traditions. So they neither demand assent nor exclude non-Christians and post-Christians from the conversation. Other traditions of faith, wisdom, and ethics unfold worthy ways that we could not explore within the scope of this book. This theology of becoming has meant to support a process of discernment that in turn spirals into your own open-ended interactivity.

The spiral of this book, as I predicted in the beginning, could have unfurled differently. The doctrinal themes chosen to exemplify the present process of theological thinking comprise one *possible* set of markers. Its signs mark a way that never begins from nothing and does not end for long. They form the frame of this perspective. A spiral frame remains open to deconstruction and revision. Yet the themes have not been arbitrarily chosen. They have emerged with a certain insistent force from ongoing interactions of my own—especially with my wildly various, multi-tongued, adventurous students of theology.

To conclude a process that remains by definition open-ended only means to pass it off. To you. To use, criticize, alter, or ignore its theology as you see fit. The project remains necessarily in suspense, the outcomes uncertain. But a certain resolution is nonetheless possible. Under the sign and the process of that spirit sometimes nicknamed the Holy Spirit, we enter a final twist of the spiral. This spirit has permeated the entire theological process, welling up in Samaria, rocking the *tehom*, blowing in the whirlwind. . . . So this eighth sign unfurls as a recapitulation of the first seven and an anticipation of signs beyond an author's control. Though this *spirit in process* bears a brief message of its own, encrypted in mysterious tongues and apocalyptic codes, it comes mainly to allow us to find our end—and keep it open.

Hot Tongues

In the scene in Luke-Acts, the small collective of Jesus' friends bursts into audibility on the Jewish feast of Pentecost. They had, we recall, quietly retreated after the trauma of the crucifixion and the mystery of the resurrection. Their altered state of consciousness—truly a knowing-together!—is festively pictured: "divided tongues, as of fire" dance on each of their heads. They "began to speak in other languages"—other tongues. Curiously, in languages they do not know; and more curious, in the multicultural crowd that gathers in the square, each hear their "own native language": "Parthians, Medes, Elamates, Mesopotamians, Judeans, Cappadocians" (Acts 2:3ff.). And the list continues at length.

This phenomenon of spontaneous translation comprises the New Testament event of empowerment by the holy spirit (1:8). Any Christian pneumatology—doctrine of the spirit (Greek *pneuma*, for wind or spirit, like the familiar *ruach*)—begins here. The spirit is manifest as in "a sound like the rush of a violent wind," and is said to fill them all and to endow them with this ability to speak foreign languages. The artful compression of Luke's narrative is stunning in its own play with language: the words themselves are "divided," like the tongues of fire/mouth/language; the *pneuma* as wind/breath/speech of the spirit. The meanings spiral and multiply, impossible to limit to a pneumatological shibboleth like "the baptism of the Holy Spirit."

These Galileans are so blissed out on hermeneutics that some bystanders sniggeringly accuse them of dissolute behavior: "They are filled with new wine." No, no, replies Peter, in one of the great non sequiturs of the Bible: "these are not drunk, as you suppose, for it is only nine o'clock in the morning" (Acts 2:15).

So here we have the *locus classicus* of the odd phenomenon known as "speaking in tongues" or *glossalalia*. When contemporary charismatics practice it, it loses the real foreign tongues, though not the ecstacy. People report a pleasurable release, a flow not at all chaotic and yet outside of ego-control—or doctrinal correctness. Absolutes of belief dissolve in the experience.

The spirit is all about flow. "I will pour out my Spirit upon all flesh." Thus Peter in Acts—to dispel the aura of a dissolute ecstasy—quotes at length from the prophet Joel, who is quoting God. "And your sons and your daughters shall prophesy, and your young men shall see visions, and your old men shall dream dreams" (2:17). Spirit alters con/sciousness, it alters social and theological constructs together. "*Taken over tongue of spirit-froth,*" chants Jim Perkinson in his spirited poem on this passage, to be read with a hip-hop beat: "*like a storm on the mind / like rain-rivers of redemption / like riots of word-revolt!*"[1]

> The Spirit of God acts in the same way as the rain which, coming down from heaven, enables an entire landscape with the most varied living beings to burst into new life together, full of freshness and vitality.
>
> —MICHAEL WELKER[2]

Spirit pours, it flows, it froths. It pushes toward new ways of knowing-together, of God-talking together. The image of the "pouring-out," writes Welker, suggests that the Spirit of God "brings the unfolding of God's righteousness from the most varied foundations and surroundings."[3] Many of us "daughters" and sons, "old men" and women, who because of sexism or agism or classism or racism or nationalism, would have been inaudible, invisible—come under the influence.

Joel's vision belongs to the apocalyptic edge of the eschatological heritage. They announce "the last days." Quoting it at length centuries later, Peter is thus linking ancient prophecy with existential immediacy. In other words it turns out that *those last days were really first days.* Pentecost is, after all, considered the founding event of the church. But the point is larger than ecclesiology: the message of Pentecost is that the end is really the beginning: the eschaton is an opening end, an end that opens the new beginning. "For the first time and forever."

The birth pangs of the new may be intense, the actualization of truly new possibilities may shake up the most entrenched stabilities, indeed, poetically speaking, "the sun shall be turned to darkness and the moon to blood." Transitions can be fearful, traumatic events, especially for those who resist them—whether individuals or civilizations.

We considered in the last chapters how the coming of the *basileia* confronts us with the unbecoming consequences, indeed the self- and world-destroying consequences, of our own actions. We rightly fear those consequences. The prophetic tradition is one long warning against the consequences of our need and greed systems. When it goes apocalyptic it is intuiting especially dire, totalizing consequences of human power-drives. But the Apocalypse remains part of the prophetic tradition, and it speaks in the tongues of metaphor, of artful oracle, parable, poetry. There is hardly a literalist bone in the whole body of eschatological writings—including its (literally) most extreme case, the Apocalypse attributed to John of Patmos.

> Now in these dread latter days of the old violent beloved U.S.A. and of the Christ-forgetting Christ-haunted death-dealing Western world I came to myself in a grove of young pines and the question came to me: has it happened at last?
>
> —WALKER PERCY[4]

Earlier we deconstructed the absolute beginning encoded in the *creatio ex nihilo*, as an inadequate reading of the first book of the Bible. Now—only briefly, in order to keep the *disclosure* within our closure—let us see if we can open-end the Apocalypse. For we do not want The End clogging our process—personal, textual, or terrestrial. A dispiriting version of the "last days" has too frequently been derived from the Bible's last book.

WMD: Word of Mass Destruction

"Hear, you who have ears to hear, what the Spirit says to the churches." (Rev. 3:22)

Yet Western history has been rent by violent literalizations of apocalyptic rhetoric. From the Crusaders and the Conquistadors forward, demonization of the un-Christian enemy has justified one bloody imperial power drive after the next. The Third Reich (the word for "kingdom," as in *Reich Gottes* or "Kingdom of God") was named in mimicry of a European prophecy of the apocalyptic thousand-year rule of the saints as the "third age."[5] And very recently we heard: "This will be a monumental struggle of good vs. evil, but good will prevail."[6] The apocalyptic absolute takes both secular and religious form—always threatening its enemies, and often the world itself—with dissolution.

Fantasies of the end-times abound. Check out the Rapture Index Web site online. Especially disturbing is the popularity of the *Left Behind* novels, a form of apocalyptic absolutism that millions of readers now confuse with biblical prophecy. When the so-called Jesus touches down, for his so-called Second Coming, just outside of Jerusalem, "men and women, soldiers and horses seemed to explode where they stood. It was as if the very words of the Lord had superheated their blood, causing it to burst through their veins and skin." So the Word of the Lord becomes a weapon of mass destruction.

"I am the Alpha and the Omega," Jesus said, "the First and the Last, the Beginning and the End, the Almighty . . ."
And with those very first words, tens of thousands of Unity Army soldiers fell dead, simply dropping where they stood, their bodies ripped open, blood pooling in great masses. "I am He who lives, and was dead, and behold, I am also forevermore. Amen."[7]

Jesus goes nuclear. This is the sort of omnicidal Christianity that drives ethical people to atheism. Processed from biblical quotes ripped out of context, its literalism—even when couched as "Christian fiction"—kills the spirit of the text. "Jesus will do all the work," announces Chaim, a Jew for Jesus in the novel, glowing with pious anticipation, "and the battles—three more following this one will not really be battles at all, but rather one-sided slaughters."[8]

Thus the old logic of omnipotence translates into a slick new messianic unilateralism. The fiery spirit of Pentecost can only testify *against* the vengeful mythology of such bad-news Christendom. The preprocessed apocalypses obstruct the Christ-process itself.

For the messianic eschatology of the prophets and the Gospels brooks no literal "end of the world." It announces the "last days" of the status quo, it announces a mission to the "*ends* of the earth" (Acts 1), but it does not propose the last days of the creation. Was our intricately wrought universe created over fourteen billion years so that we could waste our beautiful bit of it? And then to call our mass destruction, our care-less, righteous evil, the will of the Lord? Power-driving apocalyptic absolutists end up with the most dissolute view of all: they anticipate, with frissons of righteous excitation, the dissolution of the creation itself.

Whatever horrors *we* as a species may perpetrate against the earth and all its populations, the spirit in process continues to call us toward the "new heaven and earth": the *renewal* of the creation. "End" in Christian eschatology signifies *purpose*, not *termination*. We studied that purpose, depicted as final judgment, in the parable of sheep and the goats in the last chapter. It offers a lure to collective transformation. It calls us urgently to participation in a present and persistent basileic becoming: "*making messiah-praise out of the air itself!*" Here Perkinson suggests the way possibility can seem to materialize from thin air: making a way where there was none.

> We may be a doomed species, destined for a short tenure in this little corner of the universe. Or, having exhausted violence and war, we could embrace our possibilities for peace. We, as a species, have moved out of some of our earlier barbarities.
>
> —DANIEL C. MAGUIRE[9]

The vision of a desirable future remains a *possibility*—a tipping point that we may or may not collectively actualize, a butterfly effect upon the currents of the windy spirit. Against the odds, against the predictable, the end remains open.

We considered the open-ended interactivity of Jesus' parables of the *basileia*. In style and content they *counter* an early form of apocalyptic dualism. With their subtlety of message and minimalism of form, the parables deconstruct the eschatological absolutes. In the alternative eschatology of the mustard seed, the lost coin, the yeast, the treasure—no WMDs concealed here—we can make our difference in the world. That difference will flow not from fear but from the joy of open-ended possibilities.

The kingdom of God, *Reich Gottes* or *basileia tou theou*, is not a Final Solution.

Hope as Counter-Apocalypse

Here, in the poetry of the second Isaiah, occurs the classic instance of "messiah praise":

> The spirit of YHWH God is upon me,
> because YHWH has anointed me;
> [God] has sent me to bring good news to the oppressed,
> to bind up the brokenhearted,
> to proclaim liberty to the captives,
> and release to the prisoners . . . (Isa. 61:1f)

The prophet thus indelibly links the messianic and the pneumatological. The bearer of the spirit "awakens a song of praise instead of a faint spirit," writes Michael Welker.[10] It effects neither a self-sacrificial weakness nor "some sort of charitable good deed toward the weak." This is not a spirit that waits for God or Christ to do our world-work for us. The messianic hope activates a liberating com/passion, not a cowardly passivity. "*Against every bullet of can't / the final demise of helpless!*" raps our more recent poet. We are not helpless to transform our own lives and the life of the world. As Rita Nakashima Brock and Rebecca Parker note in their study of paradise, this prophetic text of Isaiah, echoed in Luke, itself resonates back to Genesis 1 and 2, depicting how life was, is, and will be good and blessed, just and loving, when a spiritually in-spirited humanity lives in the world created for it.[11]

This hope lets us take the next step—*theologia viatorum*. It lets us *realize* the talents we have. In the gifts we are given and the gifts we can give lies the way forward. The way to make a difference for the world as a whole is to actualize our own difference. For Paul the "gifts of the spirit" (including *glossolalia*) express at once our most unique individuality and our utter interdependence within the body of Christ: "*the size of flesh-on-the-rise,*" chants Perkinson. So faith, if it steps forward, steps with an embodied hope, not a totalizing apocalypse. As Moltmann makes clear, Christian eschatology concerns not end things but hope: "In its eyes the world is full of all kinds of possibilities, namely all the possibilities of the God of hope."

Why then do so many Christians surrender—sometimes wholeheartedly, sometimes subliminally—to the apocalyptic absolute? I think they fear that it is the only alternative to the dissolute secularism. And they have good reason to worry. If we cannot put our faith in a linear scientific progress—and how can we, after the technoscientific enabling of the Armageddons of the past century?—what remains for any pure secularism? As a certain Elbert Hubbard put it over a century ago: "just one damn thing after another."

So what would the third way of the spirit signify for our apocalyptically charged moment in history? It was in my book *Apocalypse Now and Then*, in response to the nuclear and environmental threats of a self-fulfilling apocalypse in our time, that I first began to explore the notion of a third way. I called it the "counter-apocalypse." It signifies a resolute alternative to both the literalization of apocalypse and to a reactive secular anti-apocalypticism. A counter-apocalypse retains the original sense of apocalypse as not annihilation but "revelation," literally, unveiling. Jesus' wisdom teaching—in tension even with certain elements of the Gospels—had already unveiled to me and to others an early counter-apocalypse.[13]

If we do not counter the literalization of end-times—putting a wedge in the door of the apocalypse, as it were—the future slams shut in our imaginations. And if we cannot imagine ourselves as a just and sustainable genesis collective, we are not entertaining its possibility. We are neglecting the lure.

> From first to last, and not merely in the epilogue, Christianity is eschatology, is hope, forward looking and forward moving, and therefore also revolutionizing and transforming the present.
>
> —JÜRGEN MOLTMANN[12]

In other words, a deformed eschatology cancels out the very hope that defines it. It obstructs the will of God and so the wisdom of an interactive process. As long as the purposefulness of human life seems to dissolve in a preplanned conflagration, theology indirectly reinforces the culture of nihilism.

The political love required to answer the absolute violence sanctioned by religion, sometimes even by our own, takes *couer*-age; we take heart. In the face of the holy warring horrors of our own civilization, the prophetic tradition spits *"flames of reconcilation / in the sky of war."* No wimpy style of forgiveness, no placating style of reconciliation, this; the solar ferocity of agape outburns the enmity. We answer fire with fire. Hear the *passion* of Perkinson's *"fire-tongued fork of holy-ghost howl."* This nonviolent intensity of protest rages up from the creativity at the heart of the world. It bursts out of a joy deeper than anger, deeper than grief, deeper than judgment.

The heat of transformation burns high. The *logos* lures. Language is charged with multilingual attraction. This heat melts our own hardheartedness, our own resistance. Only if the divine desire ignites our desire. *"Making love on the tongue."* For a theology of the omni-amorous God does not accidentally wax erotic: we heard the Song of Songs speaking a love-tongue. Making love, making truth, making justice: to embody the lure is to actualize the possible.

Double-Edged S/Word

Yet the stern and purposeful edge of the eschaton remains unmistakable amidst the ecstasy. That edge, under too much pressure, too much oppression, morphs into the double-edged sword-tongue of the Messiah in the Apocalypse. It verges on a loveless justice. But we must not therefore ignore the book of Revelation— or so I have been pleading with students and pastors of the mainline traditions, who, like me, went through seminary without ever opening it. But as liberation theologians have also insisted, it is a book passionate for justice. Indeed, in its denunciation of the whore-queen of Babylon (Rome), some reckon it the strongest anti-imperialist document of the ancient world.

To ignore it, at any rate, just abandons it to reactionary deployments.[14] The religious right interprets the text by means of the modern U.S. tradition of dispensationalism, with its garishly abstract, fold-out timeline of descent to the sexy exotic whore-queen, the tribulations, and then the "rapture" and "second coming." Similar to the classical creeds, but with less historical capaciousness, this framework overpowers the gospel priorities. As I hope it is clear by now, everyone reads scripture with a prioritizing perspective. We are involved in an open-ended truth-process willy-nilly. But literalist traditions claim to have the shibboleth "word 'o God" rather than a human perspective.

The religious right reads the *basileia* through the lens of the Apocalypse. I suggest we do precisely the reverse: let us read the Apocalypse through the lens of the *basileia*.

We might test this reversal on a difficult text of Revelation: as when an angel announces that "now is the time . . . for destroying the destroyers of the earth" (11.18). John of Patmos means here the followers of the beast and the imperious whore, who symbolizes the global superpower of the day. Interestingly, the vision recognizes Rome's global hierarchy of power and greed—not God or the messianic warrior—as destroying the earth. A handy proof-text for eco-theology!

Yet surely even the greenest of Christians do not pray for the destruction of, say, the oil company executives. With the gospel and its nonviolent basileic lens, might we read such a verse as a kind of cosmic judo? The destructive power, if it will not accept the call to convert, is turned upon itself. The very force of the divine eros, abused by the dissolute empire, becomes a power of self-dissolution. This turning of evil against itself is symbolically amplified in the (misogynist) text of the beasts turning on the whore: "They will make her desolate and naked; they will devour her flesh . . ." (Rev. 17:16).

Contrary to the sort of Christian indifference to the biosphere noted under the sign of the creation, the earth is not expendable. Even for the Apocalypse, the earth is not acceptable collateral damage for the new creation. Earth is the very stuff of our open-ended becoming. The religious right may police private sexuality rather than corporate destruction of the environment. No doubt they think they thus prepare the way for the Lord's Second Coming. But "all flesh" remains the very site and matter of any messianic coming.

In John's vision, to be sure, a bitter mood prevails. "From his mouth came a sharp, two-edged sword" (Rev. 1:16a). So the word is sword: a tongue turned hard and cold. Indeed, the book of Revelation is itself a double-edged sword. It has been all too traumatically wielded in Christian violence. But if we hold the text accountable to the basileic priority, the double-edged word of the apocalyptic messiah turns against those who wield it in righteous destructiveness. Not to destroy them but to stop their destructiveness. To make a salutary transition from their conflictual context to our own, these ancient New Testament symbols need our ongoing hermeneutical help.

How then might we help the sword-tongue of conflagration morph into the burning tongues of celebration? How might we—in the spirit—translate it into the Pentecost of just and com/passionate life? Perhaps we must reclaim the ill-used words of the same passage of the Apocalypse: "'I am the Alpha and the Omega,' says the Lord God." In other words, the beginning and the end are one. This "I AM" (contrary to fundamentalist rumor) is not Jesus. It is the very I AM of the burning bush, the name-resistant "I am who I will be." The one who *lets be*. This divinity is the fiery mystery in whom the creation and the eschaton are one process. Our beginnings and our endings are not the bookends of a linear history, but the double-edge of time itself. "The beginning is often the end / And to make an end is to make a beginning."[15]

Burning bush and burning tongues: these are spirit-signs of the third way. If the spirit is holy it is the one that *burns through* the deadlocking, dehumanizing polarities of our innocence vs. their absolute evil. The priority of the gospel Jesus remains counter-apocalyptically clear: the love we are to emulate shines and streams on both just and unjust. Similarly, the apocalyptic imagery that appears in Peter's long recitation of Joel is already a *counter*-apocalypse. Hope for that which is *to come* lives in our embodied *becoming* now: "My heart was glad, and my tongue rejoiced; moreover my flesh will live in hope" (Acts 2.26f).

That joyful tongue holds the cure of every apocalyptic absolute. "Pentecost in your head." Not a miracle in past tense, not a supernatural future, not an exotic altered state. But a con/sciousness altered amidst our struggling daily interactivities, differing, speaking, and together.

Cases of Spirit

What does a theology of becoming look like in action? Where concretely—on the ground—does "flesh live in hope?" Let me share two striking, human-scaled examples of the spirit in process.

Case 1: Here is a community that offers incarnational clues for all of us. I share it as reported in a journalistic context, with a certain density of detail that concretizes its realness.

The Georgetown Gospel Chapel is in the heart of one of Seattle's most economically challenged neighborhoods, which abuts an active Superfund site and that contains several toxic "brownfields." Being in this city's most industrial area, the neighborhood also deals with incessant noise pollution from an adjacent Boeing field. Despite this compromised context and its own financial difficulties, the Chapel stands as an abundant oasis.

Twenty years ago, the Chapel faced a decision of whether or not to pay two thousand dollars to repair their lawn's sprinkler system. They decided instead to tear out the sprinkler system and the lawn. They turned the church property into a large garden that could nourish the broader community. Its beautiful produce is free for the taking, supplementing the diets of the economically stressed neighbors. The Chapel's rainwater reclamation system helps to water the garden, saves on the utility bills, and prevents storm water from running into the adjacent, salmon-bearing Duwamish River, carrying chemicals from lawns, industries, and leaked oil from cars.

Among the many ministries provided, Pastor Hedman offers his skills to the community as a certified master gardener and a composter. He and Chapel members help build gardens for neighbors and provide them with seeds and gardening/composting training. They also host a recreation/tutoring/mentoring program for children and youth—one that (in addition to being fun!) also introduces dozens of young people to basic Earth-care principles and activities. The Chapel has "adopted" their street. Not only do they keep it litter-free, but they've also distributed hundreds of tree seedlings to residents there. The trees greatly enhance beauty, air quality, and habitat for other creatures.

Inside, the community is lessening its contribution to global warming. By changing every light in the sanctuary to an energy-efficient compact florescent lightbulb, and investing in better insulation and in energy-efficient appliances over time, it has reduced the amount of energy consumed by 75 percent. Savings each year are estimated at three to five thousand dollars, not to mention the prevention of sixty thousand pounds of CO_2 from entering into the atmosphere. First the Chapel used their savings to reimburse the initial costs of the retrofits. Now it donates the money to help retrofit a local Christian camp and financially strapped members' and neighbors' homes.

The Chapel also serves as the repository for publicly accessible documents related to the cleanup of the Superfund site, empowering neighbors to work with government agencies and local business to help carry out the processes.[16]

The eco-social justice accomplished by this congregation illustrates the relationality of a widening love—an agape that draws multiple cares into just structures of creaturely coordination. It is just one humble, contextual example of the mysterious ripple effect of the spirit in process. If a bit of the commonwealth of God appears, it reveals a complex self-organizing system of com/passion: for the membership, for the neighborhood, for the salmon, for the atmosphere. This is a Christianity for the genesis collective, led by a daring pastor using such unlikely talents as gardening (at least in my seminary we don't teach it!). The community is making truth: *facere veritatem*. Spirit matters.

This pastor and this congregation materialize the theology of open-ended interactivity. They risk the adventure. For they resist the sense of doom that economic and race injustice combined with environmental discreation bring down on us. They practice apocalypse in the original sense of "disclosure." They reopen the process of creation, they do not close it. They do not wait passively for a messiah to come or to come again. In their becoming Christ is in process. They cannot save the world, nor would they imagine they do. But they take part in salvation. Creation is not negated in the *basileia* but humbly recycled, reused, renewed.

Case 2: More personally, I think of Sharon, my teaching assistant for the sort of systematic theology class that might be reading this very book.

In March of the spring semester, Sharon sprained her ankle carrying her daughter down some stairs. The swelling wouldn't stop. Turned out to be a case of the rare necrotizing fasciitis, the new flesh-eating disease that calls to mind the plagues of the Apocalypse. The odds were firmly against her surviving. Within one hundred hours her leg had been amputated. It happened to be her birthday. When I visited her after the surgery, I muttered something about a birthday from hell. O no, she said. She had felt herself hovering close to death. Now she knows she will live: birthday in earnest. She reports experiencing an altered state of consciousness in which she floated for hours on a glacial blue sea that she called the spirit.

Recently, she says, what has been foremost in her memory has been "the surgical suite when I woke to know what was transpiring (immediately before amputation), how the doctors were trying to be faithful with the limited bits of knowledge." The picture of this faithful knowing amidst distressing uncertainty surfaces for her like a parable: "How we were in this huge library from which we held but several limited volumes and yet the womb of the library was compassion."

Sharon's body went on to heal. It will not accept a prosthesis, but she wields a mean crutch.

"The womb of the library was compassion": like a parable, that mysterious image is dense with unexpected meanings. The radical limitation of human knowledge is contained within a universe of wisdom we cannot begin to possess. Yet that limitation does not signify failure or humiliation but compassion. The passion of her doctors facing their limits revealed for her, at the most horrifying limit of her life, the glimpse of a womb of unlimited compassion. Recall that in Hebrew *rechem*, "womb," is the root of "mercy."

She treats her wounded and resilient body with love. Her laughter and her grace did not dry up. In the tehomic spirit of the sea-vision—another womb—

they deepened. She had already outgrown any theology that would have seen the loss as God's will. And so her crisis was not theological. Her faith was a resource, not a liability.

It had been clear to me at the time that her improbable survival had to do with that faith. It was not a faith that God would intervene to rescue her, but that she was held enfolded in the spirit and sustained by a remarkable network, including the medical personnel whose gifts she unfailingly remarked upon and appreciated. Their science was forced out of any reductionist certainty by this barely known disease, leaving them attentive to the mystery of this person and her distinctive process.

Her family, congregation, and friends stuck with her—stickily. She now teaches theology and changes lives in a seminary in Canada. Out of her experience of the spirit and the politics of disability, she has just authored a stunning book.[17] The divinity pictured as a library/womb of compassion will be enriched by yet another volume. Synchronistically, it will come out right along with this one. Her creativity conveys a gift of textual tongues. Indeed, the church launched at Pentecost would find endless inspiration in writing—from the texts of scripture on through millennia of theology.

These stories do not display persons or communities finding a solution to all their problems. Far from it. They beat the odds, but their daring interactivities generate more problems. They go their way with resolution. They do not seek salvation from matter but within it, within our delicate, difficult interactivities: the spirit in flight within and not beyond the world. "*This is the feathered swoop of heaven / On the wing of now.*" Cases of such basileic becoming surround us—if we let them. They offer themselves as parables for our own new beginnings.

Absolution, Dissolution, Resolution

Through these seven twists and turns I have characterized two prevalent, opposing moods as the absolute and the dissolute. In this final fold, the first appears as the absolutely final itself, trumping the Way while trumpeting The End. It reacts in modernity against an empty temporality, homogenous and calculable. These views of time mirror each other in their predictable linearity—even when they polarize as apocalyptic regress vs. secular progress. Yet ultimately their lines circle upon themselves, closed to true novelty.

When, however, the messianic figure announces in the beginning of the vision journey of John of Patmos that "I am the Alpha and the Omega," he does not initiate the termination of a linear timeline. The end of the empire is a time of new beginning. His tongue is a double-edged sword, uttering at the same time doom for a closed system and hope for universal renewal—"for the healing of the nations," for "the new heaven and earth."

The figure of the recapitulatory spiral of this chapter suggests a model for time itself: each moment in process recapitulates its history and yet adds its own fresh becoming, its flow neither linear nor circular but helical. Spirit-time is the time of our shared becoming, unfurling beyond our knowledge. The resolution this book seeks to encourage, and encourages us all to seek, lies in the third way of that complex, multiple unfolding—of ourselves enmeshed with other selves, our societies enmeshed with other societies, our spiritual traditions enmeshed with other spiritual traditions, our species enmeshed with other species. Beyond the polarization of an alpha-beginning and an omega-end; beyond the opposition of pure good and pure evil: the mystery of an open-ended way still emerges. And only if we protect it through critical demystification of all that would mistake its predictions for our futures.

Suddenly, however, the double-edged sword-tongue turns and twists critically toward the very heart of this project.

Have I perhaps generated an apocalyptic polarization after all—between the absolute and the dissolute? I think not. For the resolute identifies with neither of them, and works to break up the binary opposition. That is the point of a third way.

The real danger is worse: What if I have in fact manufactured a double polarization? What if this resolute relationalism occupies a position of apocalyptic virtue vis-à-vis *both* poles? Versus the absolute on the one hand, and the dissolute on the other? Might I have led us down the path of a double demonization? I can cite and recite the agapic nondualism that pours on the righteous and the unrighteous. But is my position innocent of self-righteous dualism? Doesn't the counter-apocalypse borrow the absolutism of the Apocalypse? Does the third way thus produce a *double* either/or, in fact a double polarization? I fear it may, without another twist of the spiral. A reconciling turn.

We may after all need to offer the absolute some com/passion. Given the strong biblical root of a theology of becoming, we will first have to admit that from the scriptures onward, the most redeeming, attractive bits of theology—not just John's Apocalypse—often verge on absoluteness. We may interpretively highlight their swerves away from authoritarianism; we may—in the name of Jesus!—privilege the amorous and the open-ended. But in order to strengthen that swerve, in order to lure the present absolutists back onto the mystery—we will have to *love something in their absolute.*

For starters, we noted the meaning of absolute as a radical transcendence that in fact sometimes argues for a negative theology—and that sense of God as the absolute, the mystery beyond all human beliefs and projections, this project already shares. But what of the conservative Christian absolutism that has been our primary worry?

Even as we dispute the particular contents and strategies it may deploy, might we not bless in the absolute its conservation of rich traditions, its passion for truth, its commitment to the good, and the will to a responsible life? Surely we share worries about cultural dissolution and meaningless self-indulgence, about exploitative and objectifying sexuality, about the evacuation of faith from the public square. Surely we share—or envy—the enjoyment of celebratory worship-communities characteristic of religious conservatism.

And so we recognize our debt and our affinity to them, even as we put the truth back into process. Even when we must testify against the theologies and ideologies of the absolute, we do so in the name and flow of a truth we no more own than they do. Disagreement is not demonization. If only for strategic purposes, we may find in every absolute some *relative* truth. And given the proclivity of religious progressives to mirror the totalizing claims of the right, honesty requires the admission of the relative truth of the absolute—or else we land in the absolute truth of the relative!

We may therefore surely beam respect toward the religious absolutists even if they remain enemies, an agape that is more than a condescending gesture of goodwill. Our self-respect is at stake. For it is the log in our own eye as religious folk that we are trying to remove.

So let us then offer absolution to the absolute.

And what of the secular relativists, not surprisingly a more cluttered cluster, harder to label. How easy it is to share their anger against the religious absolute, with its hypocrisies propelling both imperial aggression and their apocalyptic reaction. How necessarily we partake of the defense of secular pluralism, science, and law against the religious right—even to protect our own *religious* difference. The cutting edge of nihilism is but the shadow of a prophetic critique turned against the tradition of the prophets—a double edge, turned against the tradition's infidelity to itself and to the creation. At the depth of secular protest, nihilism may convert into what Tillich called "the divine abyss"—beyond the mirror play with the *ex nihilo*.

What about the erotically coded dissolute—object of moralist ire? Without blessing the many modalities of loveless sex, we are endebted in our relational becoming to several generations' countercultural explorations of eroticism, recuperating earthly joys repressed by moral absolutism.

What though of the other side of relativism, where value-free secularism blurs conveniently with the earth-consuming values of consumerism? Surely most of us reading this book would have to recognize that we add to the blur. We are largely beneficiaries of the global economic system, even as it poisons our planet. Pilate may shrug, with his imperial relativism, indifferent to the difference embodied before him. But we who are part of today's Rome can hardly protest from a perspective of purity. And if we try—our testimony echoes the apocalyptic absolute.

So the dissolute edge of relativism flickers and dissolves under closer scrutiny—into its own nihilism or into its mimicry of the absolute. And what remains is the relativity we need—the relationality that holds all our perspectives in relation to all others without for a moment flattening their differences. This relatedness is in a certain sense absolute! No living being is exempt from it. So relativity works like a solvent on the hard edges of our own absolutes.

And thus we may offer dissolution to the dissolute.

Is there a last resolution to offer to the resolute?

If there were, it might sound something like this: the way still bends into the unknown. And yet we may knowingly, in a trusty wisdom, take that next step. If we have ears to hear what that spirit is saying—the alpha of beginnings is always now, the omega of our ends is always just before us. It has been imagined long before we were born. It lures us toward a future long past our deaths. Possibility dances like flame along the edges of our finitude. We make true what we can. We become something more than we had been. Yet our vulnerability is heightened by our spirited stretch beyond ourselves. We unfold into that which enfolds us. It—You, YWHW, *Ha Shem*, Sophia, library-womb, even plain old God—escapes our knowing and our names. And yet it accepts all the names— volumes of them—we offer in love. The creative process in which we take part does not end, though each of us doubtless does. In another sense—the sense we call eschatological, and leave on the mystery—it seems that we may always be part of it.

"Becoming what you never dared
for the first time and forever . . ."

ACKNOWLEDGMENTS

Theology is never anything but an open-ended interactivity between many voices, living and dead. As I think of the voices that join in this text, featured as citations or hidden between the lines, the ancient metaphor of the "communion of saints" insists itself upon me. In this case the hidden voices are often the living ones. I cannot surface them all here. More vividly than I have known before, they have permeated the process of this book, from beginning to end. It was born from the experience of teaching an introduction to theology over twenty years at Drew. But the Systematic Theology classes of 2005, 2006, and 2007 valiantly read early drafts and gave me invaluable feedback. I particularly thank Jeff Gamblee, Carol Paterson, and Barbara Snyder for helpful early responses, Susan McRae for her canny support, Nick Stepp for research assistance, and Lisa Green both for her engagement and the chapter-by-chapter test run of the manuscript with her online Interweave chat group. Among colleagues at Drew I must thank especially Melanie Johnson-DeBaufre for lifesaving New Testament interventions, and our theological librarian Ernie Rubinstein for indispensable research more closely related to the older Testament. Teachers of introductory theology courses elsewhere, especially Marion Grau of Church Divinity School of the Pacific, Sharon Betcher of Vancouver School of Theology, and Mayra Rivera of Pacific School of Religion, offered gracious encouragement. Deb Ullman bestowed a late gift of writer's aid. Thanks beyond language to Elliot Wolfson for the cover vision of *Cruciform*. With editorial charm and theological acumen, Michael West of Fortress Press has made a book out of a text. I am grateful also for his contribution of the questions for each chapter. Thanks also to Josh Messner for effective management and David Lott for smart copyediting. Jason Starr, who accompanies me through life and work, prodded this prose toward accessibility. Finally I must announce that for her multidimensional editorial labors through the summer, Dhawn Martin rocks the casbah.

TEACHING RESOURCES

Reading this Book

Some clues as to reading strategies may be helpful to those still new to the theological journey. These chapters unfold a single theology, and they do so in an organically developing sequence. But it would be possible to read whichever chapters appeal to you, in whichever order—with perhaps the help of the index to find missing presuppositions or definitions that will have come before. I have tried to avoid unnecessary technical terminology and to provide definitions when necessary, without descending to the patronizing simplicity of some introductory texts. The reader will quickly notice a preponderance of scriptural citations. These are offered not as prooftexts but as narrative perspectives. They do not require prior buy-in. By returning occasionally to their context, and often by keeping key Hebrew or Greek words such as *tehom* and *basileia*, for instance, I hope something new and fresh leaks through. Similarly I sometimes put slashes into familiar words, like dis/closure or com/passion, to remind us of lost and possible meanings. To further encourage the reader's own theological quest—in classrooms, in book reading groups, or in private—the volume includes questions for the discussion of each chapter. These are to be found after this page, accompanied by short bibliographies with further recommended readings for each chapter as well. The quotes sprinkled in boxes throughout the text pertain directly to the material on the page—and may suggest further reading directions, as will the ample material in the endnotes.

Chapter 1

For Reflection and Discussion

1. What does the author mean by "absolute and dissolute truth"? Can you identify examples from literature or art or philosophy or theology?
2. How does this dichotomy of absolute vs. dissolute play out politically today? Or in popular culture?
3. How does the author propose that theology figure in the inception of and response to this perennial conflict?
4. How does the author propose that the practice and importance of theology relate to human suffering?
5. Keller claims that "Truth, like the manna, cannot be hoarded." How then does she relate truth to God, faith, metaphor, and mystery in her process theological model?
6. How might the model of the third way be related to received church teachings or doctrines?

For Further Reading

Brock, Rita Nakashima, and Rebecca Ann Parker. *Proverbs of Ashes: Violence, Redemptive Suffering, and the Search for What Saves Us.* Boston: Beacon, 2001.

Johnson, Elizabeth A. *She Who Is: The Mystery of God in Feminist Discourse.* New York: Crossroad, 1992.

Jones, Serene, and Paul Lakeland, eds. *Constructive Theology: A Contemporary Approach to Classical Themes.* Minneapolis: Fortress Press, 2005.

Lanzetta, Beverly J. *Radical Wisdom: A Feminist Mystical Theology.* Minneapolis: Fortress Press, 2005.

Wallis, Jim. *God's Politics: Why the Right Gets It Wrong and the Left Doesn't Get It.* San Francisco: HarperSanFrancisco, 2005.

Whitehead, Alfred North. *Science and the Modern World.* New York: Free, 1967.

Chapter 2

For Reflection and Discussion

1. What different notions of truth are at play in John's account of the interrogation and torture of Jesus?
2. Where in your relationships—personal and impersonal—do you encounter that shrug of Pilate?

3. How can "truth as testimony" be worthier of ultimate mystery than the absolute—and helpful in theology?
4. The author proposes elements of testimony, trust, and creative fidelity in her notion of theological truth. How are they exemplified in the story of Job as she interprets it?
5. In this chapter, the Bible is used in specific ways to illumine religious and theological truth. What is the interpretive role of the Bible? Does it embody "absolute truth"?
6. What religious shibboleths worry you?

For Further Reading

Griffin, David Ray, John B. Cobb Jr., Richard A. Falk, Catherine Keller. *The American Empire and the Commonwealth of God: A Political, Economic, Religious Statement.* Louisville: Westminster John Knox, 2006.

Keyes, Ralph. *The Post-Truth Era: Dishonesty and Deception in Contemporary Life.* New York: St. Martin's, 2004.

Moltmann, Jürgen. *The Spirit of Life: A Universal Affirmation.* Minneapolis: Fortress Press, 2001.

Moore, Stephen D. *Empire and Apocalypse: Postcolonialism and the New Testament.* Sheffield: Sheffield Phoenix Press, 2006.

Rieger, Joerg. *Christ & Empire: From Paul to Postcolonial Times.* Minneapolis: Fortress Press, 2007.

Tillich, Paul. *Dynamics of Faith.* New York: Perennial/Harper & Row, 1957/2001.

Chapter 3

For Reflection and Discussion

1. What are the reasons stated for studying Genesis here? Where does it fit in the theological truth-quest? What is at stake in our understanding of Genesis?
2. What insights about the character of creation and of truth can be seen in the Genesis story? In what ways does it reframe your notions of God or of science?
3. How is Genesis presented as supportive of a process approach to theology?
4. In your experience, what elements of darkness, the deep, or chaos can be seen in human life, and how does this reading of Genesis address them?
5. What does the author mean by the "genesis collective," and how does it relate to concepts of evolution, emergence, complexity, and Intelligent Design?

6. Traditional notions of gender roles, sexuality, and dominion over the natural world are often traced to the creation account in Genesis. How does this chapter alter that tendency?

For Further Reading

Baker-Fletcher, Karen. *Sisters of Dust, Sisters of Spirit: Womanist Wordings on God and Creation.* Minneapolis: Fortress Press, 1998.

Barbour, Ian G. *When Science Meets Religion: Enemies, Strangers, or Partners?* San Francisco: HarperSanFrancisco, 2000.

Gribbin, John. *Deep Simplicity: Bringing Order to Chaos and Complexity.* New York: Random House, 2004.

Kearns, Laurel, and Catherine Keller, eds. *Ecospirit: Religions and Philosophies for the Earth.* New York: Fordham University Press, 2007.

Keller, Catherine. *Face of the Deep: A Theology of Becoming.* London: Routledge, 2003.

McDaniel, Jay. *With Roots and Wings: Christianity in an Age of Ecology and Dialogue.* Maryknoll: Orbis, 1995.

McFague, Sallie. *The Body of God: An Ecological Theology.* Minneapolis: Fortress Press, 1993.

Suchocki, Marjorie Hewitt. *The Fall to Violence: Original Sin in Relational Theology.* New York: Continuum, 1994.

Chapter 4

For Reflection and Discussion

1. How would you characterize your idea of God's power? How does it resemble or differ from the traditional notion of divine omnipotence sketched in this chapter?

2. Has the "why me?" question ever hit close to home? Has the tension of God's power and love ever come to a crisis in or close to your own experience?

3. Does God "will" the many tragedies resulting from natural disasters, accident or disease, or human action? How or how not?

4. Compare the respective stances of the Book of Job and theologian John Calvin to the notions of divine omnipotence and divine will. What alternatives are offered by the process notion of divine vulnerability?

5. How might a theology of divine vulnerability understand victimhood in natural disasters? Or in consequence to human evil?

For Further Reading

Bonhoeffer, Dietrich. *Letters and Papers from Prison.* Ed. Eberhard Bethge; tr. Reginald H. Fuller. New York: Macmillan, 1953.

Caputo, John D. *The Weakness of God: A Theology of the Event.* Bloomington: Indiana University Press, 2006.

Griffin, David Ray. *God, Power, and Evil: A Process Theodicy.* Louisville: Westminster John Knox, 2004.

Hartshorne, Charles. *Omnipotence and Other Theological Mistakes.* Albany: State University of New York Press, 1984.

Keller, Catherine. *God and Power: Counter-Apocalyptic Journeys.* Minneapolis: Fortress Press, 2006.

Niebuhr, Reinhold. *The Irony of American History: The Position of America in the World Community in Light of Her History.* New York: Scribner's, 1952.

Suchocki, Marjorie Hewitt. *The Fall to Violence: Original Sin in Relational Theology.* New York: Continuum, 1994.

Chapter 5

For Reflection and Discussion

1. Thinking of the visionary Hadjewich, and of your own experience, relate human and divine love. How do they affect one's idea of divine power?
2. "God is the poet of the world, with tender patience leading . . . ," said Alfred North Whitehead. How does his concept of the divine figure in this statement?
3. Based on the process account in this chapter, how does divine being figure in the concrete unfolding of events in the universe? Why is it termed "divine Eros" and "the divine lure"?
4. In light of this account of divine power, do you think miracles are possible?
5. How does the divine Eros relate to what we normally call "erotic"?

For Further Reading

Brock, Rita Nakashima. *Journeys by Heart: A Christology of Erotic Power.* New York: Crossroad, 1991.

Burrus, Virginia, and Catherine Keller, eds. *Toward a Theology of Eros: Transfiguring Passion at the Limits of Discipline.* Transdisciplinary Theological Colloquia. New York: Fordham University Press, 2006.

Cobb Jr., John B., and David Ray Griffin. *Process Theology: An Introductory Exposition.* Philadelphia: Westminster, 1976.

Irigaray, Luce. *To Be Two.* Tr. Monique M. Rhodes and Marco F. Cocito-Monoc. New York: Routledge, 2001.

Park, Andrew Sung. *The Wounded Heart of God: The Asian Concept of Han and the Christian Doctrine of Sin.* Nashville: Abingdon, 1993.

Walker, Alice. *The Color Purple.* New York: Harcourt Brace Jovanovich, 1982.

Chapter 6

For Reflection and Discussion

1. Contrast the notion of *eros* and *agape* in their traditional framework (articulated by Anders Nygren) with that proposed by a process perspective.
2. How do you practice compassion in your daily living?
3. How does process theology envision the workings of "the creative love of God" in relation to "the responsive love of God"?
4. What are the *ethical* implications of *agape* as presented here? The *political* implications? How does it refine or reframe or redefine *justice*?
5. How, in this account, does personal initiative relate to divine com/passion?
6. How does process theology react to the traditional concept of the Unmoved Mover? In what way can God still be seen as God?

For Further Reading

Kidd, Sue Monk. *The Secret Life of Bees.* New York: Penguin, 2002.

Cone, James H. *Martin & Malcolm & America: A Dream or a Nightmare.* Maryknoll: Orbis, 1991.

Cone, James H. *Risks of Faith: The Emergence of a Black Theology of Liberation, 1968–1998.* Boston: Beacon, 1999.

Gebara, Ivone. *Longing for Running Water: Ecofeminism and Liberation.* Tr. Ann Patrick Ware. Minneapolis: Fortress Press, 1999.

Isasi-Díaz, Ada María. *Justicia: A Reconciliatory Praxis of Care and Tenderness.* Minneapolis: Fortress Press, forthcoming.

Joh, Wonhee Anne. *Heart of the Cross: A Postcolonial Christology.* Louisville: Westminster John Knox, 2006.

Chapter 7

For Reflection and Discussion

1. How do you personally understand or envision the figure of Jesus? How does your picture of him relate to that of the Gospels or of the creeds? Can you identify and explain any problematic aspects of each?
2. What aspects of Jesus' life and teaching does Keller particularly lift up?
3. Which images from the parables discussed feel fresh and joyful to you?
4. Which aspects of Jesus' priorities and of the parable genre are highlighted in the discussion of the parable of the laborers?
5. How does the author's treatment of Jesus' parables lead to an explicit process Christology? How are the person and status and work of Jesus understood in that framework?
6. How do Jesus' traits—as wisdom, logos, parable—relate to other commitments in the process theology vision, as seen in prior chapters?

For Further Reading

Borg, Marcus J. *Meeting Jesus Again for the First Time: The Historical Jesus and the Heart of Contemporary Faith.* San Francisco: HarperSanFrancisco, 1995.

Crossan, John Dominic. *The Dark Interval: Towards a Theology of Story.* Allen: Argus, 1975.

Edgar, Robert. *Middle Church: Reclaiming the Moral Values of the Faithful Majority from the Religious Right.* New York: Simon & Schuster, 2006.

Grau, Marion. *Of Divine Economy: Refinancing Redemption.* New York/London: T&T Clark, 2004.

Griffin, David Ray, John B. Cobb Jr., Richard A. Falk, Catherine Keller. *The American Empire and the Commonwealth of God: A Political, Economic, Religious Statement.* Louisville: Westminster John Knox, 2006.

McElvaine, Robert. *Grand Theft Jesus: The Hijacking of Religion in America.* New York: Crown, forthcoming.

Moltmann, Jürgen. *The Way of Jesus Christ: Christology in Messianic Dimensions.* Tr. Margaret Kohl. Minneapolis: Fortress Press, 1990.

Chapter 8

For Reflection and Discussion

1. Recall your initial associations to "theology." How have they shifted in the course of this journey?
2. How does the End of the World scenario appear in your field of vision—in terms of religion, popular culture, or the state of our world?
3. What is apocalyptic thought? How does the author relate the prophetic biblical tradition to the apocalyptic one?
4. How does the presentation of apocalyptic thought here contrast with end-time scenarios that inform much traditional apocalyptic thinking? What difference does that make to *eschatology?*
5. How do Christian ideas about the kingdom of God and the work of the Spirit of God figure in a process-influenced vision of the human future? What difference might this make to Christian discipleship, Christian community, and Christian presence in the public sphere?
6. How in this model does the end mirror the beginning?
7. In your own theological quest, what questions now feel most urgent?

For Further Reading

Betcher, Sharon V. *Spirit and the Politics of Disablement.* Minneapolis: Fortress Press, 2007.

Brock, Rita Nakashima, and Rebecca Ann Parker. *Saving Paradise: How Christianity Abandoned Love for This World and Turned to the Heresy of Crucifixion and Empire.* Boston: Beacon, 2008.

Keller, Catherine. *Apocalypse Now and Then: A Feminist Guide to the End of the World.* Boston: Beacon, 1996.

Moltmann, Jürgen. *Theology of Hope: On the Ground and the Implications of a Christian Eschatology.* Tr. James W. Leitch. New York: Harper & Row, 1967.

Rossing, Barabra R. *The Rapture Exposed: The Message of Hope in the Book of Revelation.* New York: Basic, 2004.

NOTES

Prologue

1. Pseudo-Dionysius, "The Divine Names," in *The Complete Works* (Mahwah: Paulist, 1987), 109.

2. Jim Wallis, *God's Politics: Why the Right Gets It Wrong and the Left Doesn't Get It* (San Francisco: HarperSanFrancisco, 2005), 7.

3. John B. Cobb Jr. and David Ray Griffin, *Process Theology: An Introductory Exposition* (Louisville: Westminster John Knox, 1976), 9.

4. Elizabeth Johnson, *She Who Is: The Mystery of God in Feminist Theological Discourse* (New York: Crossroad, 1992), 56.

5. Billie Joe Armstrong, "Jesus of Suburbia," recorded by Green Day for their album *American Idiot* (Reprise, 2004), lyrics available at www.lyricsfreak.com/g/green+day/jesus+of+suburbia_10138700.html.

Chapter 1. Come, My Way: Theology as Process

1. George Herbert, *The Complete English Works*, ed. Ann Pasternak Slater (New York: Everyman's Library, 1995), 153. Also set to music by Ralph Vaughan Williams; see, e.g., *UMC Hymnal* 16; miraculously, this began to play from the other room, where my convalescing spouse happened to be watching TV, in a telecast from London of Vaughan Williams's *Five Mystical Songs* just as I wrote this passage.

2. William Butler Yeats, "The Second Coming," in *A Poem a Day*, ed. Karen McCosker and Nicholas Albery (South Royalton: Steerforth, 1996), 458.

3. Sam Harris, *The End of Faith: Religion, Terror, and the Future of Reason* (New York: Norton, 2004), 21.

4. Ibid., 15.

5. Thomas Jefferson, "Notes on the State of Virginia 45-55," in *The Separation of Church and State: Writings on a Fundamental Freedom by America's Founders*, ed. Forrest Church (Boston: Beacon, 2004), 51–52.

6. Harris, *End of Faith*, 52–53. Emphasis mine.

7. Ibid., 226. Emphasis mine.

8. Lakshmi Chaudhry, "The Godless Fundamentalist," *In These Times* 30, no. 12 (Dec. 8, 2006), www.inthesetimes.com/article/2933/the_godless_fundamentalist/.

9. Self-identified "evangelicals," equally professing biblical fundamentals and foundations, have split concerning both policies and theologies of environmental care. For a beginning introduction to the Wise Use movement see Bill Moyer's "Is God Green?" documentary cited in note 11 and www.pbs.org/moyers/moyersonamerica/green/glossary.html; for more information on Creation Care and the Evangelicals for Social Action (ESA) organization visit www.creationcare.org/resources/declaration.php.

10. Cornwall Alliance for the Stewardship of Creation, "Open Letter to the Signers of 'Climate Change: An Evangelical Call to Action' and Others Concerned About Global Warming," 2, www.cornwallalliance.org/docs/Open_Letter.pdf.

11. "Forceful rule" phrase and theory explicated by E. Calvin Beisner, in Bill Moyer's PBS documentary, "Is God Green?," available at www.pbs.org/moyers/moyersonamerica/green/index.html.

12. "We all want to be able to read between the lines of the news reports and hear the truths that are glossed over by the self-serving pronouncements of the individuals who control our businesses, governments, and media (collectively, the corporatocracy)." John Perkins, *The Secret History of the American Empire: Economic Hit Men, Jackals, and the Truth about Global Corruption* (New York: Dutton, 2007), 1.

13. Cornwall Alliance, "Open Letter," 3.

14. Paul is meditating on the problem of unveiling—letting "God's word" shine publicly: "by the open statement of the truth we commend ourselves to the conscience of everyone in the sight of God" (4:2). But he recognizes the danger of ego-inflation in this ministry: "For we do not proclaim ourselves; we proclaim Jesus Christ as Lord and ourselves as your slaves for Jesus' sake" (4:5). But of course this very distinction has fallen prey, in ways that might not surprise Paul, to self-proclamation. At the time of Paul's writing, when Christianity was a lively but highly vulnerable movement, the uses of Christian proclamation to suppress, indeed enslave, others was not imaginable.

15. The Athanasian Creed as translated in *Creeds & Confessions of Faith in the Christian Tradition, Vol. I: Early, Eastern and Medieval*, ed. Jaroslav Pelikan and Valerie Hotchkiss (New Haven: Yale University Press, 2003), 676.

16. For incisive review of the history of the "Formulas of Concord—And of Discord," see Jaroslav Pelikan, *Credo: Historical and Theological Guide to Creeds and Confessions of Faith in the Christian Tradition* (New Haven: Yale University Press, 2003), in particular 186f.

17. The Second Council of Constantinople (553 C.E.) amply illustrates the structure and content of anathemas: "1. If anyone will not confess that the Father, Son, and Holy Spirit have one nature or substance . . . let him be anathema. . . . 2. If anyone will not confess the Word of God has two nativities . . . let him be anathema. 3. If anyone declares that the [Word] of God who works miracles is not identical with the Christ who suffered . . . let him be anathema. . . ." Pelikan, *Creeds & Confessions*, I:201.

18. Delores S. Williams, *Sisters in The Wilderness: The Challenge of Womanist God-Talk* (Maryknoll: Orbis, 1993), 6.

19. Ibid., 193.

20. Karl Barth, *Church Dogmatics* IV, 3 (Edinburgh: T&T Clark, 1962), 938f.

21. Barth, *Church Dogmatics* III, 3 [33], in *Church Dogmatics: A Selection with Introduction by Helmut Gollwitzer* (Louisville: Westminster John Knox, 1994), 82.

22. Priscilla B. Hayner, "Same Species, Different Animal: How South Africa Compares to Truth Commissions Worldwide," in *Looking Back, Reaching Forward: Reflections on the Truth and Reconciliation Commission of South Africa*, ed. Charles Villa-Vicencio and Wilhelm Verwoerd (Cape Town: University of Cape Town Press, 2000), 33, quoted in James L. Gibson, "Truth, Justice, and Reconciliation: Judging the Fairness of Amnesty in South Africa," *American Journal of Political Science* 46, no. 3 (July 2002):541.

23. Truth and reconciliation processes have been followed in several postcolonial situations in the two-thirds world since. Gibson, "Truth, Justice, and Reconciliation."

24. Herbert's poem written with the religiously-fired English civil war in mind.

25. U2, "One," from the album *Achtung Baby* (Island, 1991); lyrics available at www.u2.com/music/lyrics.php?song=81&list=o.

26. Rita Nakashima Brock and Rebecca Ann Parker, *Proverbs of Ashes: Violence, Redemptive Suffering and the Search for What Saves Us* (Boston: Beacon, 2001), 21.

27. Nelle Morton, *The Journey is Home* (Boston: Beacon, 1985), 128.

28. Alfred North Whitehead, *Science and the Modern World* (New York: Macmillan/Free, 1967), 51f.

29. T. S. Eliot, "Burnt Norton," from "Four Quartets," in *Collected Poems 1909–1962* (New York: Harcourt, Brace & World, 1970), V, 180.

30. Meister Eckhart, "Sermon 83: Renovamini spiritu (ep. 4.23)," in *Meister Eckhart: The Essential Sermons, Commentaries, Treatises and Defense*, trans. and with introduction by Edmund Colledge and Bernard McGinn (Mahwah: Paulist, 1981), 207.

31. Subsequent First/Old Testament biblical references in this text tend to maintain use of original Hebrew to name the character of God: YHWH and/or *Elohim*. See *The Five Books of Moses: The Schocken Bible, Vol.1*, trans. Everett Fox (New York: Schocken, 1995).

32. Based on Lev. 24:1. An Orthodox Jewish text explains *Ha Shem* thus: "So that God's name is not used in vain, it is customary to refrain from saying Adonai (the Lord) except in prayer and during the actual recitation of blessings. When reference is made to God in the course of conversation, even when quoting passages, the term HaShem (The Name) is used instead. . . . Other commonly used terms that refer to God are: HaKadosh Baruch Hu (The Holy One, Blessed Be He); Ribbono Shel Olam (Master of the Universe); Avinu She'ba Shamayim (Our Father in Heaven)." Hayim Halevy Donin, *To Be a Jew: A Guide to Jewish Observance in Contemporary Life* (New York: Basic, 1972), 174.

33. Augustine, *Sermon 52*, c. 6, n. 16, quoted in Elizabeth Johnson, *She Who Is: The Mystery of God in Feminist Theological Discourse* (New York: Crossroad, 1992), 105.

34. Eckhart, "Sermon 83," 207.

35. Nicholas of Cusa, "On Learned Ignorance" in *Nicholas of Cusa: Selected Spiritual Writings*, trans. and intro by H. Lawrence Bond (New York: Paulist, 1997), I: 86, 126.

36. Johnson, *She Who Is*, 117.

37. Franz Rosenzweig, *The Star of Redemption*, trans. William W. Hallo (New York: Holt, Rinehart and Winston, 1971), 23.

38. Karl Barth, *Church Dogmatics* II, 1, [38] in *Church Dogmatics: A Selection*, 84.

39. Elliot R. Wolfson, *Language, Eros, Being* (New York: Fordham University Press, 2005), 289. Regarding extralinguistic expressions, please note that this same Wolfson has kindly permitted his painting "Cruciform" to grace the cover of *On the Mystery*.

40. John B. Cobb Jr. and David Ray Griffin, *Process Theology: An Introductory Exposition* (Philadelphia: Westminster, 1976), 29.

41. Laurel Schneider, *Beyond Monotheism: The Multiplicity of God* (London: Routledge, 2007).

42. Cobb and Griffin, *Process Theology*, 21.

43. Ibid., 23.

44. Joseph Bracken, Roland Faber, and I have drawn process theology into the proximity of negative theology.

45. Whitehead, *Science and the Modern World*, 201.

46. Brian Wren, "We Are Not Our Own," in the *New Century Hymnal* (Cleveland: Pilgrim, 1995), #564, written in 1987 for the tenth anniversary of the Liturgical Studies Program at Drew. Lyrics and melody by Wren, arranged by Fred Graham (Drew Theological School alumnus) for the hymnal version, copyright © 1989 Hope Publishing Company.

Chapter 2. Pilate's Shrug: Truth as Process

1. Emily Dickinson, "Tell all the truth but tell it slant," in *The Poems of Emily Dickinson: Reading Edition*, ed. R. W. Franklin (Cambridge: Belknap, 1999), 494.

2. Excerpts from the October 17, 2005 episode of *The Colbert Report*, Stephen Colbert; see the Wikipedia entry at en.wikipedia.org/wiki/Truthiness.

3. Daniel J. Boorstin, *The Image: A Guide to Pseudo-Events in America* (New York: Harper Colophon, 1964), 226, quoted in Ralph Keyes, *The Post Truth Era: Dishonesty and Deception in Contemporary Life* (New York: St. Martin's, 2004), 3.

4 Ralph Keyes, *The Post-Truth Era: Dishonesty and Deception in Contemporary Life* (New York: St. Martin's, 2004), 183. But postmodernity deserves a better rap!

5. Søren Kierkegaard, Journals. *A Kierkegaard Anthology*, edited by Robert Bretall (Princeton: Princeton University Press, 1947), 9.

6. Stephen D. Moore, *Empire and Apocalypse: Postcolonialism and the New Testament* (Sheffield: Sheffield Phoenix, 2006), 52.

7. Ibid.

8. There is an extensive scholarship on the uses of the relation of John's Gospel to (other) Jews, indeed of its apparent blaming of "the Jews" for the crucifixion, a perennial excuse for anti-Semitic violence. A good starting place is Raymond E. Brown, *An Introduction to the Gospel of John* in Anchor Bible, ed. Francis J. Moloney (New York: Doubleday), 2003.

9. The translation debate is well narrated by Moore: "More decisively even than the Markan formulation, however, the Johannine formulation seems to thrust the lash into the prefect's hand: 'Then Pilate took Jesus and scourged him.' (*Tote oun elaben ho Pilates ton lesoun kai emastigosen* [19:1]). Why not simply take the statement at face value . . . ?" It is objected "that the spectacle of Pilate himself scourging the accused would have been beneath his dignity as a Roman official. But perhaps the Johannine author is not unduly concerned with the dignity of Roman officials . . ." Moore, *Empire*, 56–57. The NRSV—upon which the present book depends—is thus concerned, however, and opts for the less literal translation: "Then Pilate took Jesus and had him flogged" (19:1).

10. Ibid., 59.

11. Fernando F. Segovia, "Biblical Criticism and Postcolonial Studies: Toward a Postcolonial Optic," in *The Postcolonial Bible*, ed. R. S. Sugirtharajah (Sheffield: Sheffield Academic, 1998), 57.

12. Jennifer Glancy, "Torture, Truth, and the Fourth Gospel," *Biblical Interpretation* 13 (2005): 118 (*Digest of Justinian*, 48.10.15.41; cf. 48.1928.2), quoted in Moore, *Empire*, 60.

13. "While there are few strong claims to truth in a cultural climate determined by postmodern sensitivities, there are nevertheless commonly accepted truths that support empire and that are never open for discussion or questioning." Thus, concludes Rieger, "in this context we need to uncover not only the hidden truth of empire (its real face) but initiate a search for an alternative truth." Joerg Rieger, *Christ & Empire: From Paul to Postcolonial Times* (Minneapolis: Fortress Press, 2007), 316.

14. John 4:16ff. "Significantly, the reasons for the woman's marital history intrigue commentators but do not seem to concern Jesus. Nor does Jesus pass moral judgment on the woman because of her marital history and status. . . . When interpreters speak of the woman

as a 'five-time loser' or a 'tramp' (as has been the case in recent scholarship), they are reflecting their own prejudices against women, not the views of the text. Gail R. O'Day, "John," in *The Women's Bible Commentary*, ed. Carol A. Newsom and Sharon H. Ringe (London: SPCK, and Louisville: Westminster John Knox, 1992), 296.

15. See my longer reflection on this scene, and its notions of spirit, truth, gift, and reciprocity, in Rosemary Radford Ruether and Marion Grau, eds., *Interpreting the Postmodern: Responses to "Radical Orthodoxy"* (New York: T&T Clark, 2006).

16. Jürgen Moltmann, *The Spirit of Life: A Universal Affirmation* (Minneapolis: Fortress Press, 2001), 43.

17. Heather Murray Elkins, *Worshiping Women: Re-forming God's People for Praise* (Nashville: Abingdon, 1994), 17, 122. See also chap. 5, n.14.

18. Bishop William H. Willimon, "Preaching on the Way of John 14:6," in *Circuit Rider* 31, no. 3 (May-June 2007): 9.

19. Maxie D. Dunham, "The Exclusive Claim of Jesus: The Scandal of Particularity," in *Circuit Rider* 31, no. 3 (May-June 2007):12.

20. Discussion of interreligious dialogue is beyond the scope of this book. I strongly recommend for introductory reading in the Christian theology of world religions: Ariarajah, Marjorie Hewitt Suchocki, *Divinity and Diversity: A Christian Affirmation of Religious Pluralism* (Nashville: Abingdon, 2003); Paul F. Knitter, Introducing Theologies of Religions (Maryknoll: Orbis), 2004; John B. Cobb Jr., *Beyond Dialogue: Toward a Mutual Transformation of Christianity and Buddhism* (Eugene: Wipf and Stock, 1998).

21. In John's Gospel truth is still Jewish, despite Hellenistic influence: it is to be *done* (3:21), borne *witness* to (5:33), to *abide within* (8:44); it *liberates* (8:32); it can indeed be *told*, not in opposition to wrong teaching but to the lie (8:44), calling upon *trust*, "believe me when I tell you" (8:45f)—not true belief. It lacks the abstraction of the absolute: it does not absolve itself from its relations.

22. In the Hebrew Bible there is no distinct word for truth. The word generally used for truth means "constant, reliable, permanent, faithful." God above all is true/real/reliable (Isa. 65:16; Jer. 10:10). People seek God's truth (Ps. 25:5; 51:6; 86:11). People are admonished to judge truly and the lack of truth is lamented (Zech. 8:16; Isa. 59:14-15). Reports and prophecies may be true or false (1 Kgs. 10:6-7). In all these instances, the emphasis is on reliability—that something or someone will stand up under testing. For the Hebrews, truth was moral and relational, not intellectual. Cf. Joanna Dewey, "Truth," in *The HarperCollins Bible Dictionary*, ed. Paul Achtemeier, et al. (San Francisco: HarperSanFrancisco, 1985/1996), 1179–1180.

23. Paul Tillich, *Dynamics of Faith* (New York: Perennial/Harper & Row, 1957/2001), 21.

24. Daniel C. Maguire, *A Moral Creed for All Christians* (Minneapolis: Fortress Press, 2005), 141.

25. John Milton, *Milton: Areopagitica*, ed. John W. Hales (Oxford: Dover, 1921), 90, quoted in ibid., 141.

26. Maguire, *A Moral Creed*, 141.

27. "Thus the texts are 'interactive' in two senses: in the way reading is lively and dialogic; and in the way we get to speak to our companions when we study, debate, and ponder the texts aloud." Barry Holtz, *Introduction to Back to the Sources: Reading the Classic Jewish Texts*, ed. Barry Holtz (New York: Summit, 1984), 18–19.

28. Philip Clayton, "In Whom We Have Our Being: Philosophical Resources for the Doctrine of the Spirit," in *Advents of the Spirit*, ed. Bradford E. Hinze and D. Lyle Dabney (Milwaukee: Marquette University Press, 2001), 201.

29. Sepúlveda was a leading sixteenth-century advocate of "the war against the Indians" and Castilian dominance of the "New World" without regard to native consent. Cited and powerfully contextualized in Luis N. Rivera, *A Violent Evangelism: The Political and Religious Conquest of the Americas.* Foreword by Justo L. González (Louisville: Westminster John Knox, 1992), 220.

30. "Letter to a Non-Commissioned Officer," in *Tolstoy's Writings on Civil Disobedience and Non-Violence* (London: Peter Owen, 1968), 166f.

31. John Caputo and Gianni Vattimo, ed. Jeffrey W. Robbins, *After the Death of God* (New York: Columbia University Press, 2007), 45.

32. Terry Gilliam's *Brazil* from Embassy International Pictures [Brazil Production Company], released in 1985.

33. Luce Irigaray, *To Be Two* (New York: Routledge, 2001), 110.

34. Ibid.

35. Mark Wallace, *Fragments of the Spirit: Nature, Violence, and the Renewal of Creation* (Harrisburg: Trinity International, 2002), 67f.

Chapter 3. Be This Fish: Creation as Process

1. Stuart Kauffman, *Investigations* (Oxford: Oxford University Press, 2000), 139.

2. Peter Cramer, *Baptism and Change in the Early Middle Ages, c. 200–1150* (New York: Cambridge University Press, 1993), 69. Emphasis mine. I thank Rita Nakashima Brock for sharing this story with me.

3. For the full version of the argument of *creatio ex profundis*, including more detailed references, see Catherine Keller, *Face of the Deep: A Theology of Becoming* (London: Routledge, 2003).

4. Ibid., 114.

5. Michel Serres, *Genesis*, trans. Genevieve James and James Nielson (Ann Arbor: University of Michigan Press, 1995), 118.

6. Cf. Brian Green, *Elegant Universe: Superstrings, Hidden Dimensions, and the Quest for the Ultimate Theory* (New York: Norton, 99), 135.

7. Gerhard von Rad, drawing from Deut. 32:11 and Jer. 23:9, identifies "vibrate" as an apt translation of *mrhpht*. *Genesis: A Commentary*, rev. ed. (Philadelphia: Westminster, 1972), 49.

8. Cf. Jason Starr's documentary film, *What the Universe Tells Me: Unraveling the Mysteries of Mahler's Third Symphony* (Video Artists International, Inc., 2004). I happen to be one of its talking heads.

9. Karen Baker-Fletcher, *Sisters of Dust, Sisters of Spirit: Womanist Wordings on God and Creation* (Minneapolis: Fortress Press, 1998), 25.

10. Kauffman, *Investigations*, 119.

11. John Gribbin, *Deep Simplicity: Bringing Order to Chaos and Complexity* (New York: Random House, 2004), 120.

12. I thank Wesleyan theologian Tom Oord for pointing me to his research on the importance of philosophy and science for Wesley in his "Address to Clergy." Thomas Jay Oord, "Types of Wesleyan Philosophy: The General Landscape and Personal Research Agenda," *Wesleyan Theological Journal* 39, no. 1 (Spring 2004):156–57.

13. Julian of Norwich, *Showings*, trans. Edmund Colledge and James Walsh, and preface by Jean Leclercq (New York: Paulist, 1978), Long Text, chap. 5 and chap. 8, 184, 190.

14. John Wesley's third sermon, "Upon Our Lord's Sermon on the Mount," quoted in John B. Cobb Jr., *Grace and Responsibility: A Wesleyan Theology for Today* (Nashville: Abingdon, 1995), 50.

15. For the major development of the metaphor of the universe as God's body, see Sallie McFague, *The Body of God: An Ecological Theology* (Minneapolis: Fortress Press, 1993). See a prior form in Charles Hartshorne, *Omnipotence and Other Theological Mistakes* (Albany: State University of New York, 1984); and a subsequent form in Catherine Keller, "The Flesh of God: A Metaphor in the Wild," in *Theology That Matters: Ecology, Economy, and God*, ed. Darby Kathleen Ray (Minneapolis: Fortress Press, 2006).

16. Bill Moyers, *Is God Green?*, www.pbs.org/moyers/moyersonamerica/green/.

17. Ibid.

18. Charles Wesley, "Hymn to the Holy Spirit," 28 (1976) from *Hymns of Petition and Thanksgiving for the Promise of the Father*. For more detailed information see Michael Lodahl, *God of Nature and of Grace: Reading the World in a Wesleyan Way* (Nashville: Abingdon, 2003), 9f.

19. Karl Barth, *Church Dogmatics* III, 1, 41.2 (Edinburgh: T&T Clark, 1960), 107.

20. Augustine, *On Baptism, vs the Donatists*, in *Nicene and Post-Nicene Fathers*, vol. I, ed. and trans. Philip Schaff and Henry Wace (Grand Rapids: Eerdmans, 1980), XXII.18.

21. Nicholas of Cusa, "On Learned Ignorance," in *Nicholas of Cusa: Selected Spiritual Writings*, trans. and introduction by H. Lawrence Bond (New York: Paulist, 1997), 127.

22. Gregory of Nyssa, *The Life of Moses* (Mahwah: Paulist, 1978), 9.

23. Pseudo-Dionysius, "The Divine Names," in *The Complete Works* (Mahwah: Paulist, 1987), 109.

24. Cusa, "On Learned Ignorance," 125f.

25. For more on the relation of "light supremacism" to race construction see "*Docta Ignorantia*: Darkness on the Face (*pne choshekh*)," in Keller, *Face of the Deep*, chap. 12.

26. *Enuma Elish*, in Alexander Heidel, *The Babylonian Genesis: A Complete Translation of All the Published Cuneiform Tablets of the Various Babylonian Creation Stories* (Chicago: University of Chicago Press, 1951), I.37-43, 19.

27. Bernard Batto, *Slaying the Dragon: Mythmaking in the Biblical Tradition* (Louisville: Westminster John Knox, 1992); Jon D. Levenson, *Creation and the Persistence of Evil: The Jewish Drama of Divine Omnipotence* (Princeton: Princeton University Press, 1988).

28. Robin Morgan, *Monster* (New York: Random House, 1970), as quoted in Catherine Keller, *From a Broken Web: Separation, Sexism, and Self* (Boston: Beacon, 1986), 47.

29. Stephen Mitchell, *Into the Whirlwind: A Translation of the Book of Job* (Garden City: Doubleday, 1979), 83.

30. Annie Dillard, *Pilgrim at Tinker Creek* (New York: HarperPerennial, 1985), 9.

31. Baker-Fletcher, *Sisters*, 25.

32. "In the beginning was the word. The word proselytised the sea with its message, copying itself unceasingly and forever. The word discovered how to rearrange chemicals so as to capture little eddies in the stream of entropy and make them live. The word transformed the land surface of the planet from a dusty hell to a verdant paradise. The word eventually blossomed and became sufficiently ingenious to build a porridgy contraption called a human brain that could discover and be aware of the word itself." Matt Ridley, *Genome: The Autobiography of a Species in 23 Chapters* (New York: HarperCollins, 1999), 11.

33. Genes, continues Ridley, "may direct the construction of the body and brain in the womb, but then they set about dismantling and rebuilding what they have made almost at once—in response to experience. They are both cause and consequence of our actions." *Nature Via Nurture: Genes, Experience, & What Makes Us Human* (New York: HarperCollins, 2003), 6.

34. John the Scot (Joannes Scotus Eriugena), *Periphyseon = On the Division of Nature*, trans. Myra I. Uhlfelder and summaries by Jean A. Potter (Indianapolis: Bobbs-Merrill, 1976), 137.

35. See the Discovery Institute/Center for Science and Culture at www.discovery.org/csc/.

36. Ian G. Barbour, *When Science Meets Religion: Enemies, Strangers, or Partners?* (San Francisco: HarperSanFrancisco, 2000), 164.

37. The concepts of sepative, soluble, and connective selves are introduced in Keller, *From a Broken Web.*

38. Susan Niditch, "Genesis," in *The Women's Bible Commentary*, ed. Carol A. Newsom and Sharon H. Ringe (Louisville: Westminster John Knox, 1992), 13.

39. "The Cornwall Declaration on Environmental Stewardship," www.stewards.net/CornwallDeclaration.htm.

40. Quoted from an Associated Press story, "Southern Baptist resolution says that humans not entirely to blame for global warming," in the *Charleston Daily Mail*, June 14, 2007, www.dailymail.com/story/Life/2007061460/Southern-Baptist-resolution-says-humans-not-entirely-to-blame-for-global-warming/.

41. The resolution stands in contrast to a statement last year signed by eighty-six evangelical leaders that said human-induced climate change is real, and that the consequences of warming temperatures will cause millions of people to die, most of them "our poorest global neighbors." To learn more about the Evangelical Climate Initiative and its endorsed "Call to Action" visit www.christiansandclimate.org/statement.

42. John B. Cobb Jr., during a conversation at the Drew Transdisciplinary Theological Colloquium III, *An American Empire? Globalization, War, and Religion*, 2003.

43. IV.153. *Sag an, wie geht es zu, wenn ein Troepfelein / In mich, das ganze Meer, Gott ganz und gar fleusst ein?* Angelus Silesius, *Cherubinischer Wandersmann* (Einsiedeln: Johannes, 1980), 38; my translation.

44. "The consequent nature of God is his judgment on the world. . . . It is a judgment of a tenderness which loses nothing that can be saved." Alfred North Whitehead, *Process and Reality: An Essay in Cosmology* (New York: Free, 1978 [1929]), 346.

45. Mary C. Grey, *Sacred Longings: The Ecological Spirit and Global Culture* (Minneapolis: Fortress Press, 2004), 97.

46. Karen Baker-Fletcher, "Ha Shem," excerpt from the final verses, from *Ecospirit: Religions and Philosophies for the Earth*, ed. Laurel Kearns and Catherine Keller (New York: Fordham University Press, 2007), 538.

Chapter 4. After Omnipotence: Power as Process

1. Alfred North Whitehead, *Science and the Modern World* (New York: Macmillan/Free, 1967), 192.

2. www.presidentialprayerteam.org.

3. John Lind, interviewed by Terry Gross, *Fresh Air*, NPR, October 19, 2004, www.npr.org/templates/story/story.php?storyId=4116619.

4. "Lord God of power and might" is part of the standard English translation of the Sanctus from the Mass (based on Isaiah 6:3):
Sanctus, Sanctus, Sanctus,
Dominus Deus Sabbaoth;
Pleni sunt caeli et terra gloria Tua.
Hosanna in excelsis.

Translated in the *Book of Common Prayer* (p. 362): "Holy, holy, holy Lord, God of power and might / Heaven and earth are full of your glory / Hosanna in the highest." Interestingly, "*Sabbaoth*," not "power and might" is the description of the God whose glory fills heaven and earth in the Latin. Thanks to Dean Anne Yardley for her help in locating sources.

5. See a helpful elucidation of this logic, according to which "some theologians have so emphasized divine sovereignty as to make God look something like a capricious despot." John Macquarrie, *Principles of Christian Theology* (New York: Scribner's, 1966), 189.

6. Elie Wiesel, *Ani Ma'amin: A Song Lost and Found Again*, trans. Marion Wiesel (New York: Random House, 1973), 105.

7. "And if we look back at all the blessings in which Shaddai is over and over invoked, they are about fruitfulness and fertility. God is seen as Infinite Mother, pouring forth blessings from the Breasts Above and the Womb Below, from the heavens that pour forth nourishing rain, from the ocean deeps that birth new life" (cf. Gen. 28.1). Rabbi Arthur Waskow, "The Breasted God: A Word of Torah for the Portion 'Vayechi,'" www.shalomctr.org, 3 Jan 2007. Of course, tremendous indecision surrounds translation of *El Shaddai* as address to God/ YHWH. Etymologically related to breast, mountain, spirit, to name a few, the semantic possibilities invite living and open-ended interpretation. See Ludwig Koehler and Walter Baumgartner, *The Hebrew and Aramaic Lexicon of the Old Testament IV*, trans. and ed. M. E. J. Richardson (Leiden: Brill, 1999), 1416–422.

8. See J. William Whedbee, *The Bible and the Comic Vision* (Cambridge: Cambridge University Press, 1998), and *Comedy in the Bible*, cited in Catherine Keller, *Face of the Deep: A Theology of Becoming* (New York: Routledge, 2003).

9. Herman Melville, *Moby-Dick*, Norton Critical Edition, ed. Harrison Hayford and Hershel Parker (New York: Norton, 1967), 378.

10. I thank my editorial assistant Dhawn Martin for the trope *world-wind* and many other creative additions.

11. Thus Calvin cites Eliphaz as though it is revelation: "How much more abominable and unprofitable is man, who drinks iniquity like water?" (Job 15:15-16). John Calvin, *Institutes of the Christian Religion* I, xii.1, ed. J. T. McNeill, trans. F. L. Battles (Philadelphia: Westminster, 1960), 755.

12. Ibid., I, xvi.2,198–99.

13. Ibid., I, xvi.3, 200. Emphasis mine.

14. Ibid., I, xvi.1, 197–98.

15. Ibid., I, xvi.8, 207.

16. Ibid., I, xvi.5, 204. Emphasis mine.

17. Ibid., I, xviii.1, 229.

18. Macquarrie, *Principles*, 224.

19. Marjorie Hewitt Suchocki, *The Fall to Violence: Original Sin in Relational Theology* (New York: Continuum, 1994), 45, 162.

20. Ibid., 16.

21. See Serene Jones, *Feminist Theory and Christian Theology: Cartographies of Grace*, Guides to Theological Inquiry (Minneapolis: Fortress Press, 2000).

22. See David Ray Griffin, *God, Power, and Evil: A Process Theodicy* (Louisville: Westminster John Knox, 2004), chap. 10, "Calvin: Omnipotence without Obfuscation," 116–30, for the classic exposition of the problem of omnipotence, and for a superb analysis of Calvin.

23. Reinhold Niebuhr, *The Irony of American History: The Position of America in the World Community in Light of Her History* (New York: Scribner's, 1952), 50–51.

24. Ibid.

25. John D. Caputo, *The Weakness of God: A Theology of the Event* (Bloomington: Indiana University Press, 2006), 43.

26. Ibid., 46.

27. Elizabeth A. Johnson, *She Who Is: The Mystery of God in Feminist Theological Discourse* (New York: Crossroad, 1992), 253.

28. Dietrich Bonhoeffer, *Letters and Papers from Prison* (New York: SCM, 1971), 164.

29. James H. Cone, in *Martin & Malcolm & America: A Dream or a Nightmare* (Maryknoll: Orbis, 1991), warns us not to separate Martin and Malcolm, or else the King example becomes an invitation to weakness rather than strength. But this is not because of King's ideals but because of the pressure of the false dichotomy of violent power vs. meek powerlessness on social movements.

30. Johnson, *She Who Is,* 270.

31. Major challenges to the tradition of an atoning, substitutionary sacrifice, in which Jesus suffers as a surrogate for us, come from Rita Nakashima Brock, *Journeys by Heart: A Christology of Erotic Power* (New York: Crossroad, 1991); and Delores Williams, *Sisters in the Wilderness: The Challenge of Womanist God-Talk* (Maryknoll: Orbis, 1995).

32. Alfred North Whitehead, *Process and Reality: An Essay in Cosmology* (New York: Free, 1978 [1929]), 342. There you have pretty much the origin of what is called process theology, whose leading exponents still fan the flames of that flickering Galilean humility. Its God, who works by "lure" rather than domination, cannot therefore legitimate projects of dominance. David Ray Griffin has called this a shift from the power of coercion to the power of persuasion—the democratic art par excellence.

33. Kathryn Rickerts, currently completing her dissertation at the GTU, personal correspondence July 2002.

34. Macquarrie, *Principles,* 103.

35. Ibid., 235.

Chapter 5. Risk the Adventure: Passion in Process

1. "The Noble Valiant Heart," in *Hadewijch: The Complete Works*, trans. and intro. Mother Columba Hart, Classics of Western Spirituality (Mahwah: Paulist, 1980), 185.

2. Ibid., 175.

3. Hadewijch is arguably the most important exponent of the love mysticism that sprang up during the second half of the twelfth century, in the area roughly corresponding to present-day Belgium. It is a preeminently female phenomenon. As the term "love" (*minne*) suggests, it envisions that "union with God is lived here on earth as a love relationship: God lets himself be experinced as Love (*Minne*) by the person who goes out to meet him with love (*minne*)," ibid., xiii.

4. "Daring the Wilderness." Ibid., 231. Emphasis mine.

5. "Defense of Love." Ibid., 178.

6. Dante Alighieri, *Divine Comedy: Paradise,* in *Dante Alighieri's Divine Comedy, Vol. 5, Paradise,* trans. Mark Musa (Bloomington: Indiana University Press, 2004), canto XXXIII, 145.

7. "Old in Love," *Hadewijch,* 202. Emphasis mine.

8. James Baldwin, *No Name in the Street* (New York: Dell, 1972), 194.

9. *Hadewijch,* 202.

10. Mel Gibson, *The Passion of the Christ* (New Market Films, 2004). *Glorious Appearing* by Tim LaHaye and Jerry B. Jenkins is the twelfth book in their Left Behind series (Wheaton: Tyndale, 1995).

11. Andrew Sang Park, *The Wounded Heart of God: The Asian Concept of Han and the Christian Doctrine of Sin* (Nashville: Abingdon, 1993).

12. *Hadewijch,* 185.

13. John B. Cobb Jr. and David Ray Griffin, *Process Theology: An Introductory Exposition* (Louisville: Westminster John Knox, 1977).

14. "The worship forms we value have a lively, growing nature. They are relational, but they are not to be arbitrarily imposed or universally inherited. Authority with, *not over*, is the critical principle . . ." Heather Murray Elkins, *Worshiping Women: Re-Forming God's People for Praise* (Nashville: Abingdon, 1994), 122. See chap. 2, n.15.

15. Athanasius, *Christology of the Later Fathers*, Library of Christian Classics, vol. III, ed. E. R. Hardy (Philadelphia: Westminster, 1954), 71.

16. Alfred North Whitehead, *Process and Reality: An Essay in Cosmology* (New York: Free, 1978 [1929]), 346.

17. Luce Irigaray, *To Be Two* (New York: Routledge, 2001), 42.

18. Ibid., 42.

19. St. John of the Cross, *Assent to Mount Carmel*, 1.2.1, 74–75 in *The Collected Works of St. John of the Cross*, trans. Kieran Kavanaugh and Otilio Rodriquez (Washington, D.C.: Institute of Carmelite Studies, 1979). For an accessible discussion of St. John and other mystics of the dark night of the soul, cf. Beverly J. Lanzetta, *Radical Wisdom: A Feminist Mystical Theology* (Minneapolis: Fortress Press, 2005), 120.

20. Richard Kearney, "The Shulammite's Song: Divine Eros, Ascending and Descending," in *Toward a Theology of Eros: Transfiguring Passion at the Limits of Discipline* (Transdisciplinary Theological Colloquia), ed. Virginia Burrus and Catherine Keller (New York: Fordham University Press, 2006), 309.

21. Tod Linafelt, "Lyrical Theology: The Song of Songs and the Advantage of Poetry," in Burrus and Keller, *Toward a Theology of Eros*, 303.

22. Kearney, "Shulammite's Song," 339. Emphasis mine.

23. Saint Augustine, "Wisdom Itself," vol. 11, chap. 9, *The Confessions of St. Augustine*, trans. John K. Ryan (Garden City: Image, 1960), 284.

24. Alice Walker, *The Color Purple* (New York: Harcourt Brace Jovanovich, 1982), 167.

25. T. S. Eliot, "Little Gidding," from "Four Quartets," in *Collected Poems 1909–1962* (New York: Harcourt, Brace & World, 1970), V, 208.

26. Michael Welker, *God the Spirit*, trans. John Hoffmeyer (Minneapolis: Fortress Press, 1994), 124.

27. See the discussion in chapter 2.

28. "I am about to do a new thing; now it springs forth, do you not perceive it? I will make a way in the wilderness and rivers in the desert" (Isa. 43:19); ". . . Praise the Lord with the lyre; make melody to him with the harp of ten strings. Sing to him a new song . . ." (Ps. 33:2-3); "O sing to the Lord a new song; sing to the Lord all the earth" (Ps. 96:1); "O sing to the Lord a new song, for he has done marvelous things . . ." (Ps. 98:1).

29. John B. Cobb Jr., *Grace and Responsibility: A Wesleyan Theology for Today* (Nashville: Abingdon, 1995), 437.

30. Walker, *The Color Purple*, 167.

31. Alfred North Whitehead, *Science and the Modern World* (New York: Macmillan/Free, 1967), 192.

32. See chapter 3, "God as Creative-Responsive Love," in Cobb and Griffin, *Process Theology*.

33. Ibid., 105.

34. Whitehead, *Process and Reality*, 351.

35 Irigaray, *To Be Two*, 42.

36. My use of "omni-amorous" is akin to the "polyamorous" divinity of Marcella Althaus-Reid, *The Queer God* (London and New York: Routledge, 2003), 55.

37. *Hadewijch*, 213.

Chapter 6. Sticky Justice: Com/Passion in Process

1. Sue Monk Kidd, *The Secret Life of Bees* (New York: Penguin, 2002), 288–89.

2. Ibid., 110.

3. For a powerful feminist theological rereading of Mary, cf. Elizabeth Johnson, *Truly Our Sister: A Theology of Mary in the Communion of Saints* (New York: Continuum, 2003).

4. The love teaching, and especially love of the enemy, comprises the strongest distinguishing mark of the gospel. Yet it roots in the "love your neighbor as yourself" of Lev. 19:18, which "is a summary of commandments in 19:9-17, which requires leaving food in the field for the poor, not stealing, not oppressing one's neighbor or cheating one's servant, and so on. The person who acts in these ways 'loves' the neighbor." E. P. Sanders and Margaret Davies, *Studying the Synoptic Gospels* (Philadelphia: Trinity International, 1989), 319.

5. Anders Nygren, *Agape and Eros*, trans. Philip S. Watson (Philadelphia: Westminster, 1953), 31. For a critical engagement of Nygren, see Virginia Burrus, "Introduction: Theology and Eros after Nygren," in *Toward a Theology of Eros: Transfiguring Passion at the Limits of Discipline* (Transdisciplinary Theological Colloquia), ed. Virginia Burrus and Catherine Keller (New York: Fordham University Press, 2006), xiv.

6. Nygren argued in *Eros and Agape* that eros characterizes human striving and as such all willful human efforts at self-salvation—a very Lutheran sense of sin. Agape, on the other hand, is divine, and impossible to humans, except through grace. His influential polemic against eros was at the same time a Protestant critique of medieval mystical traditions of desire for God (such as, for instance, would be exemplified in the poetry of Hadewijch in the last chapter).

7. Cf. Rita Nakashima Brock's classic feminist work, *Journeys by Heart: A Christology of Erotic Power* (New York: Crossroad, 1991). See also Rita Nakashima Brock and Rebecca Ann Parker, *Proverbs of Ashes: Violence, Redemptive Suffering, and the Search for What Saves Us* (Boston: Beacon, 2001).

8. Reinhold Niebuhr, *Love and Justice: Selections from the Shorter Writings of Reinhold Niebuhr*, ed. D. B. Robertson (Louisville: Westminster John Knox, 1957), 25.

9. Ibid.

10. Martin Luther King Jr., "Letter from Birmingham City Jail," in *A Testament of Hope: The Essential Writings and Speeches of Martin Luther King, Jr.*, ed. James M. Washington (San Francisco: Harper & Row, 1986), 290.

11. "The American Dream," Ibid., 210.

12. Cf Martin Luther King's doctoral dissertation, "A Comparison of the Conceptions of God in the Thinking of Paul Tillich and Henry Nelson Wieman." Boston University. Differently from them, like Whiteheadian process theology and under the influence of his Boston Personalism, he insisted upon a personal deity mediating infinite creative process. See Gary Dorrien, *The Making of American Liberal Theology: Crisis, Irony and Postmodernity, 1950-2005* (Louisville: Westminster John Knox, 2006), 152f.

13. King, "Letter," in *A Testament of Hope*, 290.

14. Ibid.

15. James H. Cone, *Risk of Faith: The Emergence of a Black Theology of Liberation, 1968–1998* (Boston: Beacon, 1999), 107. See also *Martin & Malcolm & America: A Dream or a Nightmare* (Maryknoll: Orbis, 1991).

16. Ada María Isasi-Díaz, *Justicia: A Reconciliatory Praxis of Care and Tenderness*.

17. Ivone Gebara, *Longing for Running Water: Ecofeminism and Liberation* (Minneapolis: Fortress Press, 1999), 215.

18. Kwok Pui-lan, *Postcolonial Imagination & Feminist Theology* (Louisville: Westminster John Knox, 2005).

19. Gebara, *Longing*, 213.

20. Michael Hardt and Antonio Negri, *Multitude: War and Democracy in the Age of Empire* (New York: Penguin, 2004), 351.

21. Martin Luther King Jr., "Love, Law, and Civil Disobedience," in *Testament of Hope*, 46-47.

22. Hardt and Negri, *Multitude*, 351

23. Ibid., 352f.

24. Elizabeth A. Johnson, *She Who Is: The Mystery of God in Feminist Theological Discourse* (New York: Crossroad, 1992), 272.

25. "Humankind is, then, redeemed through Jesus' *ministerial* vision of life and not through his death. . . . As Christians, black women cannot forget the cross, but neither can they glorify it. To do so is to glorify suffering and to render their exploitation sacred." Delores Williams, *Sisters in the Wilderness: The Challenge of Womanist God-Talk* (Maryknoll: Orbis, 1995), 167.

26. Josiah Royce, *The Problem of Christianity*, with an introduction by John E. Smith and foreword by Frank M. Oppenheim (Washington, D.C.: The Catholic University of America Press, 2001), 200.

27. John B. Cobb Jr. and David Ray Griffin, *Process Theology: An Introductory Exposition* (Philadelphia: Westminster John Knox, 1976), 10.

28. I thank Angela Ryan, for whom God's love is life-saving, for making the insightful connection between Gen. 6:6 and process theology in her Systematic Theology term paper, Spring 2007.

29. Anselm, *Proslogium* VI, VII, quoted and interpreted in Cobb and Griffin, *Process Theology*, 44f.

30. Aquinas, *Summa Theologica*, quoted in Cobb and Griffin, *Process Theology*, 45.

31. Abraham Heschel, Jürgen Moltmann, Dorothee Sölle, and Elizabeth Johnson, in addition to all process theologians, are the main conduits of the twentieth-century idea of the suffering of God. For a discussion of the traditional antipathy toward a suffering/changing God, see Joseph Hallman's *The Descent of God: Divine Suffering in History and Theology*, which shows how the incarnation created such a problem for the patristic writers and led to two very different levels in their writing: a theoretical God who doesn't change, and a devotional God who does.

32. Cobb and Griffin, *Process Theology*, 41ff.

33. Ibid., 48.

34. Kathryn Tanner, *Jesus, Humanity, and the Trinity: A Brief Systematic Theology* (Minneapolis: Fortress Press, 2001), 13.

35. Alfred North Whitehead, *Process and Reality: An Essay in Cosmology* (New York: Free, 1978 [1929]), 346.

36. Ibid.

37. Ibid.

38. See Paul Tillich, *The Courage to Be* (New Haven: Yale University Press, 1952), in particular chap. 6: "Courage and Transcendence (The Courage to Accept Acceptance)."

39. Anne Wonhee Joh, *Heart of the Cross: A Postcolonial Christology* (Louisville: Westminster John Knox, 2006), 121. "The 'backbone' of *jeong* is relationality of the self with

the other" (18). She does not essentialize *jeong* as feminine, but analyzes its complex possibilities: "Even as *jeong* is acknowledged as a powerful way by which Koreans understand their relationship with one another, often it has been feminized, domesticated, spirtualized, trivialized, or psychologized and viewed as the 'sticky' element of relationality not fit for the 'rational' thinking *man*" (xxii). Joh develops a stunning feminist theology of the cross: "Jesus as the Christ allowed for the full embodiment of *jeong* not only in his ministry, as indicated by his relationships to those who were powerless, but also in his relationships to those who were seemingly powerful, feared, and loathed" (76).

40. Kidd, *Bees*, 277.

41. Whitehead, *Process and Reality*, 346–47.

Chapter 7. Jesus the Parable: Christ as Process

1. Matthew 13:35 in *The Complete Gospels: Annotated Scholars Version*, ed. Robert J. Miller and foreword by Robert W. Funk (San Francisco: HarperSanFrancisco, 1994), 82.

2. Robert McElvaine, *Grand Theft Jesus: The Hijacking of Religion in America* (New York: Crown, forthcoming).

3. John B. Cobb Jr. "Commonwealth and Empire," in David Ray Griffin, John B. Cobb Jr., Richard A. Falk, Catherine Keller. *The American Empire and the Commonwealth of God: A Political, Economic, Religious Statement* (Louisville: Westminster John Knox, 2006), 144.

4. Kelly Brown Douglas, *The Black Christ* (Maryknoll: Orbis, 1994), 112.

5. Bob Edgar, *Middle Church: Reclaiming the Moral Values of the Faithful Majority from the Religious Right* (New York: Simon & Schuster, 2006), 63.

6. Albert Nolan, *Jesus Before Christianity* (Maryknoll: Orbis, 1978), 122.

7. Ibid.

8. John Dominic Crossan, *The Dark Interval: Towards a Theology of Story* (Allen: Argus, 1975), 56.

9. Amy-Jill Levine, "Matthew," in *The Women's Bible Commentary*, ed. Carol A. Newsom and Sharon H. Ringe (Louisville: Westminster John Knox, 1992), 257.

10. Elizabeth A. Johnson, *She Who Is: The Mystery of God in Feminist Theological Discourse* (New York: Crossroad, 1992), 165ff.

11. Melanie Johnson-DeBaufre, e-mail message to author, July 14, 2007.

12. "Rather than deploy genealogical arguments about the *basileia* of God in order to enter the debate about Jesus' identity, I *presuppose* that this expression invokes a complex symbolic vision of an alternative 'order of things' that stands in contrast to and contests with the dehumanizing and oppressive orders of the Roman imperial context. The *basileia* is communal or corporate imagery that draws on the socio-political realities of human life and imagines/projects the world and its power arrangements as if God rather than Caesar were in charge. The imagery of kinship with God, both as the children of Abraham (Q 3:7) and the children of *Sophia* (Q 7:35), carries a similar collective flavor. . . . In both places, it is God not the King or the Lord (*kyrios*) who authorizes and judges proper human relationships and interactions. Throughout this study, we will explore how attention to the unique identity of Jesus can divert our attention from the *basileia* of God and other communal imagery in Q." Melanie Johnson-DeBaufre, *Jesus Among Her Children: Q, Eschatology, and the Construction of Christian Origins* (Cambridge: Harvard University Press, 2005), 24.

13. Bill McKibben, "The People of the (Unread) Book," in *Getting on Message: Challenging the Christian Right from the Heart of the Gospel*, ed. Rev. Peter Laarman (Boston: Beacon, 2006), 13.

14. David Van Biema and Jeff Chu, "Does God Want You to be Rich?, *Time Magazine*, 18 September 2006, no. 12, 48ff. The cover displays a photo of a Rolls Royce sporting a gold cross as its hood ornament.

15. Ada María Isasi-Díaz tells of a grass-roots woman who pointed out that we who have privilege of class, color, culture cannot lose that privilege even if we try. What matters is that we use it for liberation of the underprivileged. Homily at Drew University Chapel, Spring, 2005.

16. John Wesley, "The Scripture Way of Salvation," in *John Wesley, A Library of Protestant Thought*, ed. Albert C. Outler (New York: Oxford University Press, 1964), 273.

17. Ibid. Emphasis mine.

18. Cf. *Farther Appeal to Men of Reason and Religion*, Pt. I, 3, *The Works of John Wesley*, ed. Albert C. Outler (Nashville: Abingdon, 1986), 11:106; and Sermon 91, "On Charity," III:12, *Works* 3:306.

19. This was Wesley's argument with the Calvinist predestinarians. See John B. Cobb Jr., *Grace and Responsibility: A Wesleyan Theology for Today* (Nashville: Abingdon, 1995) for an indispensable exposition of the tension between Wesley's emphasis on free cooperation with grace in the process of sanctification and the classical Reformation emphasis upon justification.

20. John Wesley, "The Witness of Our Own Spirit," Sermon 12 in *The Works of John Wesley*, Vol. I: Sermons I, 1–33, ed. Albert C. Outler (Nashville: Abingdon, 1984), 309.

21. Jürgen Moltmann, *The Spirit of Life: A Universal Affirmation* (Minneapolis: Fortress Press, 1992), 69.

22. Swami Beyondananda, www.wakeuplaughing.com.

23. Margaret Calloway's enlightening and en-leavened response emerged in conversation at the UMC Demarest under the leadership of Rev. Stu Dangler.

24. John B. Cobb Jr. and David Ray Griffin, *Process Theology: An Introductory Exposition* (Louisville: Westminster John Knox, 1977), 98.

25. Miller, *The Complete Gospels*, 200.

26. Mayra Rivera, *The Touch of Transcendence: A Postcolonial Theology of God* (Louisville: Westminster John Knox, 2007), 140. "It is a transfiguration that never bypasses the body in its complex historicity, but transubstantiates matter into divine flesh."

27. Thanks to my colleague Heather Elkins for this and many priceless narratives.

28. Jürgen Moltmann, *The Coming of God: Christian Eschatology*, trans. Margaret Kohl (Minneapolis: Fortress Press, 1996), 24.

29. Crossan, *Dark Interval*, 124.

30. Ibid., 126.

31. Ibid., 121.

Chapter 8. Open Ending: Spirit in Process

1. Jim Perkinson is a theologian, poet, and most recently author of *White Theology: Outing Supremacy in Modernity* (New York: Palgrave Macmillan, 2004).

2. Michael Welker, *God the Spirit*, trans. John Hoffmeyer (Minneapolis: Fortress Press, 1994), 126.

3. Ibid., 127.

4. Walker Percy, *Love in the Ruins: The Adventures of a Bad Catholic at a Time Near the End of the World* (New York: Farrar, Straus & Giroux, 1971), 3.

5. For a more expansive version of the core argument of this chapter, cf. Catherine Keller, *Apocalypse Now and Then: A Feminist Guide to the End of the World* (Boston: Beacon, 1996), chap. 3: "Time: Temporizing Tales." The expectation of the "third status" or aeon is attributed to the prophetic visions of Joachim of Fiore a millennium ago.

6. "We are in a conflict between good and evil, and America will call evil by its name," and then a little later, "By confronting evil and lawless regimes, we do note create a problem, we reveal a problem. And we will lead the world in solving it." "Remarks by the President at 2002 Graduation Exercise of the United States Military Academy, West Point, New York," Office of the Press Secretary, June 1, 2002.

7. Tim LaHaye and Jerry B. Jenkins, *Glorious Appearing: The End of Days* (Wheaton: Tyndale, 2004), 225, 204.

8. Ibid., 217.

9. Daniel C. Maguire, *The Horrors We Bless: Rethinking the Just-War Legacy* (Minneapolis: Fortress Press, 2007), 89.

10. Welker, *God the Spirit*, 117.

11. Rita Nakashima Brock and Rebecca Ann Parker, *Saving Paradise: How Christianity Abandoned Love for This World and Turned to the Heresy of Crucifixion and Empire* (Boston: Beacon, 2008), chap. 1.

12. Jürgen Moltmann, *Theology of Hope: On the Ground and Implications of a Christian Eschatology,* trans. James V. Leitch (Minneapolis: Fortress Press, 1993 [1967]), 15, 16.

13. The "counter-apocalypse" is developed historically and constructively in Keller, *Apocalypse*; and updated for a post-millennium scene in Catherine Keller, *God and Power: Counter-Apocalyptic Journeys* (Minneapolis: Fortress Press, 2005).

14. For a particularly reader-friendly exposé of the popular misuse of the Apocalypse and proposal for a positive reading, see Barabra R. Rossing, *The Rapture Exposed: The Message of Hope in the Book of Revelation* (New York: Basic, 2004).

15. T. S. Eliot, "Little Gidding," from "Four Quartets" in *Collected Poems 1909–1962* (New York: Harcourt, Brace & World, 1970), V, 207.

16. From, with minor adaptation, "A Small Congregation Does A Lot—Georgetown Gospel Chapel," as reported in the *Stories from Congregations* section of the Earth Ministry: Caring For All Creation Web site: www.earthministry.org/Congregations/stories/Georgetown/.

17. Sharon V. Betcher, e-mail message to author, July 5, 2007. Cf. her book *Spirit and the Politics of Disablement* (Minneapolis: Fortress Press, 2007).

INDEX

CPSIA information can be obtained
at www.ICGtesting.com
Printed in the USA
FFOW01n1028180418
46265383-47700FF